'Pye's galloping and flavourso... ...lustrous gem of a book. Studded with racy anecdotes ... Pye unrolls a sparkling string of stories ... In this swarming fresco, which merits a place near Simon Schama's *The Embarrassment of Riches* or Robert Hughes' homage to Barcelona, Pye not only rescues Antwerp's lost "world of liberty", he leads entranced readers through its grubby, glittering streets'
Boyd Tonkin, *Financial Times*

'A wonderfully lively and fact-rich history ... he makes tangible every aspect of life and death in Antwerp'
Michael Prodger, *New Statesman*

'A master class on how to tell the story of a city. Fascinating and gloriously good fun'
Gerard DeGroot

'This was where, before the Dutch unsuccessfully rebelled against Habsburg rule, Bruegel painted 'The Tower of Babel', Tyndale issued copies of his Bible in English, Erasmus and Thomas More thought world-changing thoughts. Antwerp became a refuge for Jews fleeing a Portuguese pogrom; it was a model for what we call globalism'
Simon Heffer, *Daily Telegraph*, Books of the Year

'In a highly readable new book, Michael Pye argues that, during Europe's ages of discovery, it became one of the earliest genuinely global cities too ... If we understood more about Antwerp, though, we might understand more about ourselves and our long umbilical links to Europe'
Guardian

'Entertaining. An impressionistic portrait of its institutions and great men (Bruegel, Erasmus, et al.), emphasizing the lives of now-obscure traders, bankers, entrepreneurs, officials, printers, and booksellers, including a surprising number of successful women and Jews. A vivid look at a great Renaissance city'
Kirkus Reviews

ABOUT THE AUTHOR

Michael Pye's twelve previous books have been translated into fifteen languages; three have been *New York Times* 'Notable Books of the Year', two were British bestsellers and one became a Hollywood movie. He won various prizes in Modern History at Oxford, and went on to be journalist, broadcaster and columnist in London and New York. He lives in Amsterdam.

MICHAEL PYE

Antwerp

The Glory Years

PENGUIN BOOKS

PENGUIN BOOKS

UK | USA | Canada | Ireland | Australia
India | New Zealand | South Africa

Penguin Books is part of the Penguin Random House group of companies
whose addresses can be found at global.penguinrandomhouse.com.

First published in Great Britain by Allen Lane 2021
First published in Penguin Books 2022
002

Printed and bound in Great Britain by Clays Ltd, Elcograf S.p.A.

The authorized representative in the EEA is Penguin Random House Ireland,
Morrison Chambers, 32 Nassau Street, Dublin D02 YH68

A CIP catalogue record for this book is available from the British Library

ISBN: 978-0141-98246-5

www.greenpenguin.co.uk

MIX
Paper from
responsible sources
FSC   FSC® C018179
www.fsc.org

Penguin Random House is committed to a
sustainable future for our business, our readers
and our planet. This book is made from Forest
Stewardship Council® certified paper.

For the memory of John Holm
in gentil cuore

Contents

List of Illustrations

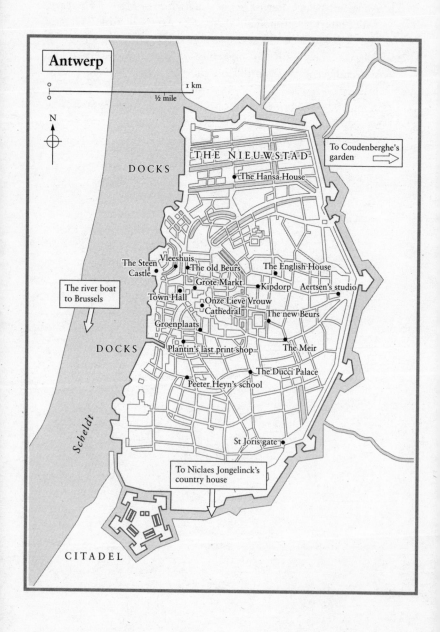

Antwerp

0   1 km
0   ½ mile

N

DOCKS

THE NIEUWSTAD

To Coudenberghe's garden

The Hansa-House

Vleeshuis

The Steen Castle

The old Beurs

Grote Markt

The English House

Kipdorp

Aertsen's studio

The river boat to Brussels

Town Hall

Onze Lieve Vrouw Cathedral

The new Beurs

Groenplaats

DOCKS

Plantin's last print shop

The Meir

The Ducci Palace

Peeter Heyn's school

Scheldt

St Joris gate

To Niclaes Jongelinck's country house

CITADEL

Spanish Netherlands, 1555

0   50   100   150   200 km
0   100 miles

N

North Sea

GRONINGEN 1536

FRIESLAND 1524

DRENTHE 1528

Zwolle

OVERIJSSEL 1528

Deventer

Amsterdam

UTRECHT 1543

Rotterdam

GELDERLAND 1543

Veere
Middelburg

Bergen op Zoom

Antwerp

HOLY ROMAN EMPIRE

Bruges

Ghent

Mechelen

Leuven

Rhine

FLANDERS

Brussels

BRABANT

Meuse

CHURCH LANDS

Binche

Scheldt

Somme

Moselle

LUXEMBURG

KINGDOM OF FRANCE

Lands seized by Charles V

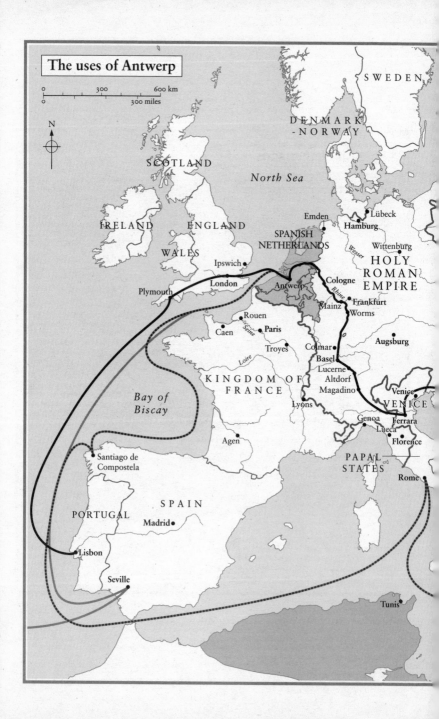

The uses of Antwerp

0 — 300 — 600 km
0 — 300 miles

N

SWEDEN

DENMARK
-NORWAY

North Sea

Lübeck
Emden
Hamburg
Wittenburg

SPANISH
NETHERLANDS

HOLY
ROMAN
EMPIRE

Ipswich

London

Antwerp
Cologne
Rhine
Frankfurt
Mainz
Worms

Plymouth

Rouen
Seine
Paris
Caen

Augsburg

Troyes
Colmar
Basel
Lucerne
Altdorf
Magadino

KINGDOM OF
FRANCE

Loire

Bay of
Biscay

Lyons

Venice
VENICE

Genoa

Ferrara

Lucca

Agen

Florence

Santiago de
Compostela

PAPAL
STATES

PORTUGAL

SPAIN

Madrid

Rome

Lisbon

Seville

Tunis

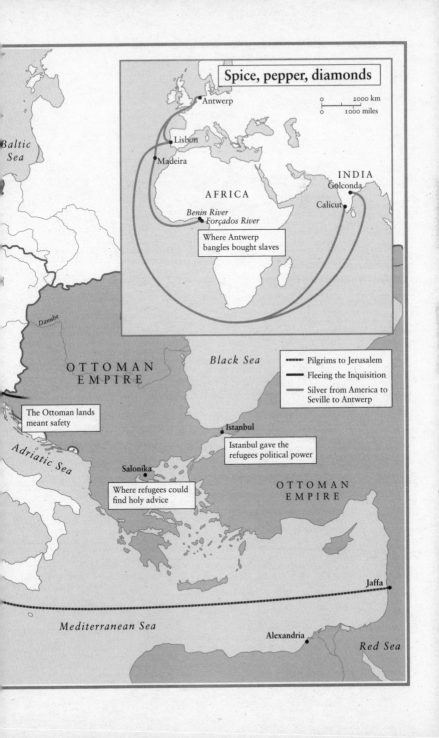

Spice, pepper, diamonds

0   2000 km
0   1000 miles

Baltic Sea

Antwerp

Lisbon

Madeira

AFRICA

INDIA

Golconda

Calicut

Benin River
Forçados River

Where Antwerp
bangles bought slaves

Danube

OTTOMAN
EMPIRE

Black Sea

- - - - - Pilgrims to Jerusalem
———— Fleeing the Inquisition
———— Silver from America to
        Seville to Antwerp

The Ottoman lands
meant safety

Adriatic Sea

Istanbul

Istanbul gave the
refugees political power

Salonika

Where refugees could
find holy advice

OTTOMAN
EMPIRE

Jaffa

Mediterranean Sea

Alexandria

Red Sea

The Exception

Giovanni Zoncha sold cloth in Venice between San Marco and the Rialto, close to the heart of the merchant world around the Mediterranean. He was restless in 1563 and twenty years old. He felt the need to travel, to go north to the heart of the other merchant world that was opening across the oceans: to Antwerp in the Spanish Netherlands.

He stayed for four years, writing home about what he found. He liked the less confining rules: no need to give up butter, eggs and cheese for Lent, and he could walk in the streets at any time with whatever weapons he liked, 'so if you carried a cannon nobody would say anything'. He listened to the Protestant talk but worried that the Inquisition might come soon. Most of all, he liked the girls, even the daughters of the grandees, the *primi della terra*, and their wonderfully open ways. You sat at dinner between two girls who sometimes kissed you, and when you'd eaten you went to sit on the ground in your girl's arms. You talked about anything at all without a language in common, and went walking without anyone to watch you. The girls even knocked the boys' hats into the river just like equals.[1]

Zoncha thought he'd found a world of liberty, very different from courtly, formal Venice but in a city which was at least its equal. Antwerp seemed to be inventing a new way to be rich, cultured and easy at the hub of the ever-expanding world that Europe knew.

The very idea had worried Venetians all century. They had reason for concern, because their life and business were still organized around the Mediterranean and the trade routes that fed into it through the Red Sea. Antwerp was already dealing with India across the oceanic route that rounded the Cape of Good Hope, and with Brazil and

America across the Atlantic by way of Seville and Lisbon. It belonged to a new world and a new system.

One by one the Venetian ambassadors reported home. By 1506, Antwerp was doing more business than its neighbour towns, and the explanation was the open trade fairs twice a year when the city was crammed with traders.[2] By 1525 the Ambassador Gasparo Contarini saw that the great rival Bruges had lost its business to Antwerp. True, most of the business in the rising city was done by foreigners but the locals, Contarini reported, were making money anyway by renting out their houses.

He noticed how the tide came up from the sea and turned back the river waters so that the biggest ships – the caravels and galleys – could easily dock by the walls of Antwerp.[3] Some of them had battled round from Venice itself. The city lay upstream on a deep river with a sheltered anchorage, so the caravels could come in from India or Africa or America to the River Scheldt and their cargo could go out by the branches of the Rhine to the Alps and Northern Italy and beyond, or else by the North Sea and the Baltic Sea. The goods were paid for with the silver and metals that came from the mines in south Germany by water. Rivers and sea were easier than taking the rough roads in heavy Hessian carts, especially in winter and worse yet in wet winters, with 'ways . . . so foul that a double number of beasts could hardly draw half a carriage weight', with ropes rotten from 'long lying in the fields' and horses weak from a diet of stubble. The river at Antwerp might sometimes clog with ice, but at least the sea was as open as storms and the ever-present pirates would allow.[4]

At mid-century, the Venetian Ambassador Navagero wrote home that 'there is in Antwerp the trade of the whole world.'[5]

His successor Marino Cavalli explained all the cities of Flanders and Brabant to the Venetian Senate in 1551 by finding equivalents in Italy, so Leuven was learnèd just like Padua, Ghent as big as Verona and Brussels as well positioned as Brescia. In all this 'huge equivalence' it was Antwerp that corresponded to Venice 'very well in terms of trade'. Cavalli was staggered at the number of businesses dealing in money and every other kind of merchandise, amazed at how there seemed to be some deep well of deals. There was no man 'however lowly, however lazy, who can't be rich in his place and make deals in the markets of Antwerp'. Flashier young men who spent all they could and even more could go to the merchants who, 'looked after anyone for 12 per cent per year'.[6]

Money was a business in its own right, Federico Badoero reported in 1557.[7] The Duke of Alba, he noticed, came marching into the Netherlands to stamp out heresy and pacify the Dutch rebels with 14,000 scudi to his name. He left with 40,000 'through money invested in Antwerp'. Badoero found it 'hard to believe the scale of the business – maybe more than 40 million in gold each year, which is in constant motion'. The cost of money was high, even for the Spanish King Philip II, but not the highest in all his lands; in Antwerp he might pay 24 per cent, which seemed shocking against the 14 per cent rates in Spain, but almost painless compared to the 40 per cent he had to pay in Naples just to get his hands on tax money before it was collected.

What's more, this machine for making riches was also the inescapable hub of all kinds of trade. Paolo Tiepolo, even though he was being ambassadorial in Flanders in 1563 only because Philip II was there with a war to fight, saw clearly that 'All the merchandise, from abroad as well as from their own country, comes through Antwerp where there's a crowd of merchants which makes that city more celebrated, more famous than any other, the market almost all Europe has in common.' Tiepolo reckoned the city was enough to explain how the Emperor could – usually – pay for his wars.[8]

And now comes the paradox, if you came from Venice: Antwerp was rich but refused to make a fuss about it. Badoero saw all the dealing, all the schemes to corner goods in the market. He watched the 'variety and quantity of essential, useful, decent and comfortable goods that come and go by land and sea' and he named Antwerp 'the largest marketplace of the world'. Yet the city itself did not seem a superlative. 'Everyone has a house well equipped with everything necessary, but paying more attention to saving money than spending it on showy things.' The one thing he did notice about the houses was their scrupulous cleanliness. Other people, not coming from a city of *palazzi*, were more impressed. In 1520 the great Albrecht Dürer was taken to see the burgomaster's new house, 'large beyond measure . . . extraordinarily beautiful large rooms . . . a very large garden; in short such a noble house as I have never seen in all German lands'.[9]

The real difference was that Antwerp was short on self-consciousness about courtly manners, holy rules or even what came to table. Badoero noticed that women's clothes were 'very modest', although in other ways modesty had its limits; he was surprised that men talked to other men's wives, and even 'told immodest jokes in front of unmarried girls'. Giovanni Zoncha could have told him that things went even further if you were twenty.

As for the food, 'they cook once a week, food so cheap it would be hard to live more poorly . . .' As Badoero said: 'They don't overdo eating very much'; he added, but 'when it comes to drink they get drunk every day and the women in many places not much less than the men.' This was not a perfectly general rule. 'The men are so drunk,' Badoero wrote a bit later, 'that running businesses is left to the women.'[10]

Until the late fifteenth century, Antwerp had been just one more river port. It had a trade fair twice a year but no royal court to justify its standing, no national government, no army and no navy for trade or war, not even a bishop. It was no city state with a famous dynasty like Milan or Florence; it was a Spanish possession.

And yet the Serene Republic of Venice, a power unto itself, watched Antwerp as an equal. Antwerp became a world city, a centre of stories published across Europe, a sensation like nineteenth-century Paris or twentieth-century New York, one of the first cities where anything could happen or at least be believed. Other cities up and down the North Sea coast showed the power of kings or dukes or emperors, but Antwerp showed only itself: a place of trade, where people wanted or needed to be, or couldn't afford not to be. It was famous on its own terms.

It hardly fitted into the vast Hapsburg idea of a special destiny to become Daniel's Fifth Empire, the very last world order in history, stretching from the Americas to the boundaries of Ottoman territory. It did business with the Portuguese, who had much the same ambition but moving south to Africa and east to India and China and Japan. Philip of Spain liked to be depicted in the chariot of the sun, bringing true faith to the whole world. The Portuguese planned to do the same but with different metaphors.[11] The business of those empires was holy as well as commercial, dynastic as well as practical. Antwerp was quite different. It was not at all secular but it managed a pragmatic kind of tolerance. Its business depended on foreign traders so it had no interest in abolishing the heresies to which so many of those traders were attached. It was a city but it tried to pursue its own interests.

This makes Antwerp a kind of pioneer. As the French scholar Henri Lefebvre wrote: 'In the 16th century, in western Europe "something" of a decisive importance happened.' It was 'not an event you can date, nor a change in institutions, not even a process that can be measured in economic terms like the growth of such and such production, the opening of such and such a market. The West tipped over: the town overtook the countryside in practical and economic terms and in social importance.'

It was a huge and abstract shift, but it was the everyday business of Antwerp, in dinnertime talk and in practical policy. Its citizens were trying to work out what it meant to be part of this most unusual city and also how to survive the unfriendly armies down the road. Music, pictures, language and schooling became commodities, not dependent on patrons but on finding a market: becoming portable, in other words, a matter of exchange. A single broker more or less kept the imperial regime afloat even though he had been banned from the Exchange for cornering the city's cash and threatening to stop trade dead. A single dealer in property planned and reshaped the city as he wanted and the city had no political will to control him.

Lefebvre saw exactly what was happening; as he wrote: 'Money rules the world . . .'[12]

There is an Antwerp nowadays in the same place, a port that is vast and essential and a city of lovely baroque monuments and the memory of the great Rubens. This city has nothing much to do with this book. Cities don't move much and they're not built to hide, and even when they fall you can still make out the pattern of the roads that aim for them like targets. But cities are not just physical facts. Cities are what happened there, the idea and the uses of the place, and how citizens and outsiders saw and understood it, which has as much to do with a particular time as a particular map reference.

This book is about Antwerp in very exceptional years, what used to be called a 'golden age'. There is a tiny industry in arguing about which years, and the argument will never end, because it is entirely artificial. The glory time may have started with a fourteenth-century revolt, or the docking of the first Portuguese spice ship around 1501, and perhaps it ended with the startling iconoclasm in 1566 when the altars were pulled down, or when Calvinists took power in 1577 and Antwerp joined the hot war against the Spanish, or in 1585 when they lost the war and the city's river was blockaded.[13] It all depends on what you mean by glory.

My book begins with the coming of the Portuguese spice ships and ends with the iconoclasm and its long aftermath. Glory to me is the time when the city could be particular and individual, not just another place marker on one of the maps that the Emperor Charles V loved to make to show where he ruled.

Sometimes historians try to define an age by economics, sometimes by institutional change, but really it is a question of legend: what people know, what people talk about and what they remember. You can't ask the people who were there, because golden ages are over and finished by definition; we talk about them to show how human life has been on a dizzying chute of decline ever since. When the poet Hesiod started the metaphor more than two millennia ago he was living, he said, in an age of iron, which came long after gold, silver, bronze, and proper heroes. A thousand years later the philosopher Boethius knew his golden Arcadia had long ago shut down, and the only places with the same ways, where man and animals lived together peaceably, were the edges of Scotland and Ireland. Boethius was much republished in Antwerp during the glory years.

There was also nostalgia for the old Germanic tribes in the forests, simple forefathers being woodsy and bloody. In 1596 the Antwerp geographer Ortelius produced his *aurei saeculi imago*, or picture of a golden age, which is not at all like the golden age we imagine from museum shows and coffee-table books. Ortelius shows corpses hanging in the woods, men trapped face down in mud to drown, the brutish kind of justice of old tribes; he shows families in tents without walls alongside covered wagons, women watching men learning war, funeral fires burning horses alongside men, and an elastic kind of marriage where a man usually had only one wife unless he really needed more.

The golden age in the minds of Antwerp's citizens was almost the exact opposite of the civilized golden age we imagine they were living in. 'Golden' is our word for any period that produced things we still value – pictures, buildings, books, music, riches – but Ortelius saw civilization as where we end up when the golden times are long gone.[14]

The name of Antwerp was familiar all along the trade routes that came together in the queue of ships at its docks: it was city as celebrity. Its stories went out with the English wool on its way to Hungary and the Levant, with traders taking German copper and silver to Africa to exchange for gold and slaves, with the ships sailing back to Asia after dropping their cargoes of pepper, diamonds and spices. They carried the idea of the city and everything that moved through its streets: prices, rates, arrangements, knowledge and medicine and theology, all seen and reported across the trading world. Everything could be read. The deals were watched for clues to politics and war, who was buying guns and armour, who was raising what kind of money to pay troops and where. Naturally, there were spies.

In Italy, in Pavia, the mathematician Girolamo Cardano wrote how Antwerp exceeded all the towns around in size and riches and crowds, was the most famous emporium of Europe and 'an incredible gathering of men and merchants from England, Spain, France, Germany, Italy'.[15] In France, in Agen, the bishop Matteo Bandello considered Antwerp 'the market for all the Christians of Europe and beyond'.[16] In Colmar, in Alsace, the clerk Georg Wickram wrote a novel in which young Lazarus is assembling his qualifications to get married, and he's told to travel and learn French, which means Antwerp, where 'you can find schools that teach any language'. He has to ship out to Brabant to become a 'noble and skilful man'. He is given the regulation warnings against brazen women and getting into fights, and wicked young men in taverns. And then his ship docks and Lazarus sees the city for the first time and he finds it splendid, buildings unlike anything he had ever seen.[17]

Antwerp mattered to English Protestants who needed English Bibles, just as its ships and smugglers would later take Jesuit books to the Catholic English. It was the essential turntable for Portuguese Jews making the exhausting trek from Portugal to some kind of freedom in

Ferrara or Salonika or Istanbul; along the way they almost rebuilt Israel on a Mediterranean island. The word Antwerp was on the prints shipped to the Americas that guided local painters covering the walls of the new Christian churches.[18] It was where a man turned if he had the ill luck to catch syphilis, because many people knew about the famous China root but only Antwerp doctors knew how to use it.[19]

The city was a story that took its substance from what people heard and knew about it, and it was famous for dealing in every kind of information, not just the books produced there in prodigious numbers. The alchemist Paracelsus came to Antwerp in 1519, and reckoned he learned 'more at the marketplace than in any German or foreign schools'. The magus John Dee made a note in the margin of a book in his library that Antwerp was the '*emporium totius Europae*'[20] – a great shop of a city, where all Europe came to do business in secrets as well as spices and wool and silver. He was there in 1562 and 'already I have purchased a book for which a thousand crowns have been by others offered and yet could not be obtained.'[21]

The new world of knowledge depended on the city's trade routes – for exotic specimens and unfamiliar stories, but also to raise the money to buy enough paper to print books and to distribute them. The new world of trade by ocean routes was unthinkable without Antwerp, as much for providing the currency of the slave trade as for bringing Europe the cloves, ginger, cinnamon and pepper that people craved. When the brilliance died down and the city lost its uniqueness, when it was once more just another useful port within the territory of the Hapsburgs, its ideas stayed alive even as they moved north: dealers who sold art, music printed for the people, a new kind of city deliberately built around canals, the idea of taking shares in an enterprise, thinking about the world and its relationships in abstract and financial terms.

Antwerp was trying to invent itself and the future at the same time.

Walk off the Vrijdagmarkt square, go round the corner into Holy Ghost Street: there's a bar with good chips at one end and a knicker shop at the other. There are plain black metal gates with a letterbox that almost lets you see what lies beyond. If you're invited, you go through the gates and right out of the world of cars and streetlights.

You stand for a moment in a wide arcade which runs along one side of a courtyard. There's a carriage door onto the high street which once let in the business of the house. The arches of the arcade look onto the carriageway that runs by the roses and mulberry trees, past the chapel off to the left. Ahead is a merchant house with the obligatory high tower which marks the home of a man who had ships to watch on the river.

In the glory years this used to be the home and the headquarters of a German banker. The shell is still there, adjusted a little, worn and restored, but the same in its essentials. At first that seems natural enough: it is a house full of pride, standing in a city which has been a great port for five hundred years, which has a famous monumental past. You can't miss the unfinished cathedral which came to its present magnificence by 1521. The line of the old streets still opens wide where a market used to be and narrows into lanes, the high street is where it always was between the great market and the old wharves. There are lovely stone and brick façades surviving, the guild houses on the Grote Markt, the very occasional tower from a city that was once famous for towers, squares which have been in use for centuries even if the square for hiring your fancy clothes is now used mostly for parking.

The evidence of the city's greatest years is reduced to islands, clues or accidental survivals. The time when Antwerp defied its rulers, or tried to ignore them as much as possible, has been screened off by another story: the power of the Hapsburg machine, finally and successfully imposed from Madrid. Lovely baroque and very Catholic churches replace an assortment of heresies. The city which valued heretics is gone with the coming of an Inquisition, then a Calvinist regime, then the Spanish insistence on clearing out dissidents. What we can visit now and admire came later, with a bureaucracy fit for purpose, a religious culture which tried to be homogeneous, a city behaving itself inside an empire. It is a magnificent city, but not a world city any more.

It is not like Amsterdam, where the lights at night are so artfully low along the canals that you could almost imagine that tomorrow there will again be barges bringing goods to the merchants' houses. It is more like Rome, where Mussolini edited the most famous parts of its past, temples and the forum, and smashed down the more complicated parts in the interests of a usable story. It is very like Paris, but that is not obvious at first. The boulevards that Baron Haussmann planned in the nineteenth century deliberately abolished the swampy, edgy, wretched remains of the mediaeval city, the streets so narrow carts could barely pass, the citizens inclined to tear up paving stones in times of riot. Each boulevard is a statement: Paris is under control.

Antwerp, too, was interrupted.

Adriaan Hertsen's mother did her best for him: she married well and she married often.

She was born into the power networks of sixteenth-century Antwerp, sister to Aart Schoyte, who was alderman and sometime burgomaster *intra muros*, which means the city's ambassador in the outside world and manager of the legal calendar at home. She married Jacob Hertsen, who was burgomaster in his turn, and Adriaan was their child. When Jacob was gone, she married into the Van der Dilft clan, and when she'd buried that husband she married into the Van de Werve clan, who were lords of a dozen towns. The boy Adriaan had all the friends he needed to be a great man.

He worked at it, of course. He trained to be a lawyer in Orléans, which had famously taught popes before him. He was pious, a member of the Table of the Holy Ghost, which cared for the poor. He was a responsible citizen, ready to defend the city walls as head of the Militia of the Old Longbow. For three years he was burgomaster *intra muros* just like his uncle, and like his uncle he was also an alderman, almost every year from 1512 to 1530.

Adriaan had a house to match his importance. When he died in January 1532 every room had to be counted and catalogued, even the back rooms, and his two country houses as well. Chase the pages of the inventory through the law ledgers of Antwerp and we can wander again through those rooms, see the cupboards, beds, chairs and folding tables, the toys and dolls for his children, the diamonds, glass when it was still almost a luxury, and tapestry on his bedroom door when tapestry was art often finer and usually more expensive than paintings.

Adriaan had gold and he had silver, more than sixty-eight kilos of silver. There were paintings above fireplaces, but also in trunks. There were portraits, which is understandable when a man's connections are so important. There was a set of bellows in his bedroom decorated with a naked Venus. There were a good many holy pictures to show his devotion, and pictures of power or at least of the Emperor Charles V, whose coronation was kept in the chapel alongside a head of St John mounted on a crown, his peace with the French in a room behind the chapel and his triumphant entry into Bologna in a chest alongside various church paraphernalia. The inventory, page by page, is a picture of a man serious and comfortable with family, with power and with his particular God.

It shows his substance, too. His townhouse had bathhouses, a bakery, several kitchens, a warren of cellars and even a room to piss in, a *pis kamerken*; and he had two country houses near the city, a small stone cottage and a house with eight rooms which was not as splashily ornate as the townhouse but still decently comfortable. He had official positions and a fine estate.[22]

And yet he hardly has a story, because of what's missing. He held power in a city famous through the world that Europeans knew, but he left only one exact inventory with all the life missed out. There are sparse mentions in the records of the aldermen, so we do know some of the property he bought after 1514. We have clues to the kinds of objects that delighted him, because he owned them. We have no last will and testament, so no clues to which possessions he valued most, what they meant to him, what sort of person he thought should take them on. He had books, but the only one we can identify is the Bible, so we don't know what he read or what he thought, or why he owned coats of arms for Bavaria and Cleves.

We know nothing for certain about the house itself. Probably, but only probably, it had three floors, long wings and outhouses and a garden or a courtyard. We don't know its name in a city where great houses had names, or the street or even the quarter where it stood, although we can guess at the first quarter, which was the richest district. We can be sure of only one thing: the house is gone. Most things still standing along the streets of Antwerp come from a later and less exceptional time. They are lovely, but they tell, quite literally, another story.

Documents do go astray after five hundred years. What's remarkable about Antwerp is that the brilliant years of the city are much like Adriaan Hertsen's house: sometimes inventoried, obviously dazzling but with such gaps it is hard to make a proper account. Notaries did not have to lodge their records with the city, so those records are scattered, if they survive at all. Antwerp had a history of violent spasms which were not good for archives. Worst of all, mutinous Spanish soldiers in 1576 ran the citizens to the walls, filled the streets with dead bodies and set fire to the new town hall. Whole stacks of the city's records went up in smoke, enough to make the ordinary methods of civic history very difficult.

What survives is often not enough to make secure statements about basic issues like names, crimes, taxes, events, disputes, how to find company for the night, exactly who sold what and where. It would help to have the facts about who joined guilds, what went through the docks, how elections worked, how the city was financed and what it spent. Some remarkable scholarship has tried and still tries to answer those questions, but it can't repair all the damage. Instead, we have to make a mosaic out of songs, paintings, doodles on civic documents, books to teach languages and books to teach manners, laws that tell us about what happened so often it had to be banned; out of how diplomats and foreigners saw the city and how it was used. We need novels written at the time in Alsace and by the River Garonne on the other side of France, we need the archives of Seville, Lisbon, Florence, Venice, London, Zurich as well as Antwerp.

Then we can begin to see the boisterous life of the city that the Duke of Alba once denounced as 'a confusion and a receptacle of all sects indifferently': Babylon itself.[23]

I

1507

Shadows on the walls. The crowd jostles to get closer to the light. They have orders to stand back from the fire and on no account to pitch stones into the hot metal, but there is fascination in the red from embers in the rough furnace by the wall, and the gold and white of hot metal as it pours into the ground and settles in the pit. There is light in all the wrong places.

It is dusk on an April evening in 1507, just after vespers, in the yard of the great Church of Our Lady that will become the cathedral of Antwerp.

This night is not quite a firework show, although it is a show; you don't make so many rules for onlookers if you don't expect any. It is not exactly a ritual, because all the official blessings come later, and it is not part of some calendar, because nothing quite like this has happened for more than seventy years. If you want to be literal, it is one stage in a process of manufacturing. People have come out to watch and celebrate in any case. Twenty-eight men are competing to work the bellows, to see who can force the most wind into the fire.

Tonight the city is casting a new great bell: Carolus, named for the future Charles V who will rule the Netherlands, the Duchy of Brabant and so the city of Antwerp.

The bell will sound out the official history of the city, event by event. It will ring for the birth of princes, the election of popes and the arrival of cardinals, for the sight of fire in the narrow streets, for the safe return of ships that have made the pilgrimage to the Holy Land, and for the executions which put an end to killer bankers or indiscreet sodomites. In 1542, when Maarten van Rossum arrives to lay siege to Antwerp for his French allies, Carolus will ring to tell citizens to grab arms and get to the walls to resist him, on pain of being left out on a scaffold in the square of the Grote Markt. It will ring when unpaid and mutinous Spanish troops turn on the city in 1576, burn the archives in the town hall, go looting and breaking and herd the citizens into the water; and when in 1583 the French inflict one more fury. But when the fireships come up the river in 1585, and the Spanish take back the city and end its part in the revolt of the Netherlands against Madrid, there will be no bells, no celebration for the end of the Calvinist Republic of Antwerp, not even bonfires unless a few Italians light them. History will be back under the control of an empire.

For the moment, the bell belongs to the city. Days before it is cast, carts rattle through the streets to collect donations of tin sheets, metal pots, old candlesticks, even bits of old bells. A few people insist on giving silver but that is sold off separately because the bell is to be bronze, which requires only copper and tin. The bellmaker Guillaume de Moer comes with his brother and two workers, and finds it necessary to inspect the metal very carefully indeed, which means the city is obliged to stand him a great deal more food and drink than they expected.

It takes nine days to dig the great pit. De Moer and his helpers assemble iron to reinforce the mould that will fill it. They use hundreds of eggs to grease the mould along with hemp smeared thickly with lard. Then they build the furnace under the walls of the church. There is a mass of ash for the floor of the oven, cartloads of good clay to form it. They light and nurse the fire and they set the metal to melt.

The workers get cheese, bread and beer during all their work; the two main assistants get two meals each day; but naturally the magistrates of the city have a banquet with wine. The smith who has worked on the bell says he has lost money and demands a tip.

Two men are left in the dark churchyard. They watch the pit as the metal cools.[1]

There were great bells in Antwerp before Carolus. There was Orrida from 1316, whose name means rough, ghastly, likely to make a man tremble. It was the voice of local authority in one of the inland ports in Brabant, not as grand as Bruges, not royal, not holy. The city grew, and the announcements had to carry wider and wider, so Orrida was replaced in 1439 by a greater bell, called Gabriel, named for the messenger angel. It was almost five thousand kilos of bronze. It took three strong men just to start it swinging.

By 1507 Gabriel was not enough. The city was growing denser and more crowded year by year: more and more people coming from other towns, from the countryside and from other nations. It would soon have a population less than Paris but more than London, with everything a capital city has except the seat of power. The English were there selling wool and cloth, buying armour and jewels and taking loans to keep their government working. The Portuguese moved there from Bruges when Bruges lost the favour of the Emperor. Their ships first came up from Lisbon with spices and pepper in 1501. They also brought diamonds from Golconda, pearls from around India, gold from Africa to buy silver and copper from the south of Germany for use in the African trade to buy human slaves. Antwerp was becoming a hub, a marketplace, a crossroads. The Italians came from Genoa and Florence and Lucca, the Spanish were everywhere, the Germans came in two varieties: from the northern trading towns in the Hanseatic League and also from Augsburg and the other mining towns. There had long been two great fairs each year in the city, but now trade filled the whole year.

Such a city needed an even larger bell, six and a half tonnes of metal that would take sixteen men to put it in motion: Carolus. It was a presence, a matter of intense pride. When the Emperor Charles was at the gates of the city in 1549, about to present his son Philip to the city, the town clerk Cornelius Grapheus claimed that it would be hard to find another bell like it for size or density or sweet resonance, that it 'filled the whole city with grand, sweet melody'.[2]

It carried Charles' name because the King undoubtedly commanded enough troops to control Antwerp when he could spare them from his various wars and when he could pay them; but he couldn't pay them without loans from the merchants of Antwerp. He hated heresy, but needed the tax income from a fine assortment of heretic traders from all round Europe: Lutherans in particular, and the new Christians from Portugal still suspected of being Jews, and later Calvinists who went out to the fields to hear sermons and ended with control of the city. When he offered Antwerp's magistrates a bishop in 1563 they filed petition after petition to convince him that they really did not need one; a bishop would bring the Inquisition, upset the foreign merchants and ruin everything.[3]

'Antwerp has as her lord and prince the Duke of Brabant, margrave of the Holy Roman Empire,' as the Florentine merchant Lodovico Guicciardini wrote, 'but with so many and great privileges, obtained from antiquity onwards, that she governs and rules herself almost in the way of a free city and republic.'[4] Over the years those privileges had been demanded, withdrawn, made conditional; they were a means of manipulation. The city insisted on them, but on occasion the Emperor took back permission to print a simple history of Flanders if the privileges were even mentioned.[5]

Whatever the order of the city, bells sounded it out. Unofficial bells were not allowed. Every day the morning bell announced the opening of the gates. Bells said when workers should be at work and when workshops should shut down at night. The fancy trades, the printers, the goldsmiths, the dyers and finishers of fine cloth all had to pay attention. When the new Exchange, the Beurs, was ready in 1531, bells in its two bell towers opened business in the morning and closed it in the evening. A man had to be present when the bell sounded or people would think his credit was suspect, might even decide he was bankrupt.

Bells were more than order, they were also music on the streets among all the other songs and racket. It was usual since 1480 to play tunes on the bells in joyful moments, with the bell-ringer using his hands and feet to pull cords that ran directly to the clapper and avoided the inexact rhythm of making the clapper swing inside the bell. It was something new, something 'learned from a fool'. 'Andreas Franciscanus', most likely secretary to a diplomatic mission from Venice, wrote in 1497 that in Antwerp 'everyone goes in for music, and they are so expert at it that they even play handbells so harmoniously and with such full tone that the handbells themselves seem to sing ... any tune they wish.'[6] When the Netherlands divided on religious lines and the Calvinists came to rule, Jacques Rieulin, the man who played the city bells, was told to play only hymns and psalms.[7]

At night the *diefclocke*, the thief bell, shut the gates and closed down the streets with the shouts of bugles for emphasis. The city got dark, and the darkness was insecure.

The city's reality never quite matched its great name and its ambitions. Pigs rooted round the grandest houses, along with geese, ducks and stray dogs; we know they were always there because the city tried again and again to ban them. New rules in 1582 still allowed the use of alleyways between houses for horses, oxen and other beasts; but if you were moving animals, you had to be told to go directly to the nearest field with the least damage possible. In 1557 there were special orders that nobody was to interfere with the dog catchers when they were out killing.[8]

The city paid three kinds of night worker: 'mud-minders', who collected what houses and workshops threw out, 'dust-masters', who picked up the dry debris from crumbling buildings so the city could use it again, and 'tenants of the cesspit', who checked the city's pools and pits of sewage and emptied them when the levels were too high.[9] Those buildings leaning into the street might fall, and the stench of shit was everywhere. In times of plague, which were common, the city tried to clean up streets that were 'very filthy'. People had to be told not to throw out skins and entrails from domestic animals, the barber surgeons were not to throw blood on the roadways, there was a polite suggestion that the gutters by houses could in fact be cleaned, that dung from the constant rush of horses and carts could be cleared away. There was a hopeful rule banishing any animal with a 'nauseating smell'.[10]

The old city had streets almost too tight and bent to hold all the business of the new city as it grew. They were lined with doors down to the cellars and vaults which undermined the roads; a wife could pop up suddenly at your feet. They were overgrown with canopies, galleries and jetties that jutted out one above another, so people 'with wagons and horses could pass only with difficulty', as the city complained in 1532. Some people built benches on the street itself along with small huts and sheds. The canals that threaded through the city were also overbuilt with galleries and with loos that stank the water. The ships that moored there were regularly flooded by water from the guttering on the buildings above.

Shops spilled onto the same streets, their goods stored in the dark inside but sold outside in the light, shown in cupboards on the walls, on shutters, on trestles; you have to be able to see goods, after all, which was hard inside because glass was too thick and rough to let in enough daylight and the more usual glazing was oiled cloth. Besides, a deal seems more public in the company of the streets, and passing witnesses were supposed to keep a dealer honest.[11]

Shops were for more expensive goods, for gloves or shoes, for gold or pewter; visitors had to know where to find what they wanted. For daily stuff – food, drink, and fuel such as straw and wood – there were markets, sometimes along streets or canals, sometimes a jumble of stalls in a square. The goods were laid out on a trestle or on a sheet on the ground. Once a week there was a 'free' market when growers and makers from outside the city could come and sell directly, and naturally they sold close to the city gates or else door-to-door along the poorer side streets.[12] There was a rush of business alongside the grander trades.

Cobblestones wore down under the heavy Hessian carts carrying goods from the docks and there was never quite enough money to replace them. The people of busy Arenbergstraat complained that 'the street is not paved, so that when it rains and especially in the winter people can barely leave the house.' On dry days they said the passers-by stirred up a lot of dust.[13]

In the city's richest years, the town hall was a stone Gothic pile among the houses on Grote Markt with spiked bars over its windows, a flock of stone birds on its pinnacle, niches for holy statues which were not all full, and with its own wooden gallery among other wooden buildings. It was so unimpressive that a new wooden town hall had to be built in 1549 to greet Philip II properly, a political kind of stage set. The only open spaces with a chance at seeming grand were markets like the Meir, with wood canopies over the shops and elaborate paintings of flowers and people and extra curlicues on some of the façades.

To be exceptional, the city was going to need exceptional uses, and the people who could imagine them.

A SHIP TO JERUSALEM

Dierick Paesschen dreamed of owning a ship, and he came to Antwerp to find one. He left a small German town to find a place where things were possible, even improbable things, and Antwerp had that reputation. When he arrived in the first years of the sixteenth century, Antwerp had no actual marine of its own, no galleys like Venice or caravels like Portugal; its ships were chartered from ports to the north, Middelburg or Amsterdam. Dierick Paesschen still saw the city's uses. He knew it might not have ships, but it had all the necessary conditions for them: money, passengers, insurance and optimism.

He needed a special vessel made for passengers and not for bales and crates. His ship had to be grand enough and heavily enough armed to take pilgrims on the fashionable journey to Jerusalem, to get past the Barbary pirates at the west end of the Mediterranean and the Ottoman war fleets in the east and convince the passengers that, most likely, they would survive.[14]

Paesschen worked his way. He began with marriage to a woman rich enough to need a formal marriage agreement to protect her property. When he sailed out for the first time she went with him, and so did his father-in-law; this was family money, after all. To get his ship, he sold first a mansion called *Wyngaert* in Antwerp and then the house at the back called *Egypten*. The price of houses in Antwerp was always going up.

He put out flyers in German, Latin and French promising a cruise which would stop devoutly at Santiago de Compostela on the way down to the Mediterranean, then at Rome and finally at Jaffa. He made a contract that no stop would be longer than promised; he wouldn't wait for goods, because his business was passengers. He guaranteed wine, food and a space on the ship seven feet by seven uncluttered by goods. Fares were payable when the ship came back to Antwerp. He told the barber Antoine Robyns that any passenger who did not come back would pay only half-fare.

He was all ready by the start of 1511, but the river was not. The Scheldt was iced shut and it held tight his whole future, the ship called the *Salvator*, until 11 February. All he could do was wait while his money ran short and shorter. It took four more days for the ice to loosen enough so that on 15 February he could make a grand show of a banquet on the *Salvator*, a civic celebration. Keen city dignitaries came to celebrate a new enterprise, even the Margrave himself, the local lord and the frontier representative of the Holy Roman Empire. The ship was alive with fluttering flags. Eleven days later Paesschen got round to issuing a receipt for the impressive catalogue of guns he was borrowing from the city, of which the least were two dozen muzzle-loaded arquebuses. Once that was official, the ship could finally weigh anchor for Jerusalem.

The voyage went well. Some of the pilgrims were back in November by the land route from Rome. The ship itself made a glorious return on 24 March, to a shouting crowd and the sound of gun and cannon fire. Paesschen led the pilgrims to the Church of Our Lady and handed over an official present from the Knights of Malta: two great iron balls that hung for years in the high vault.

The city adopted him and he needed the way it worked. He'd paid for his ship on the back of the notion that property could be an investment to sell as well as hold. He depended on customers rich enough and pious enough to give up their time to go far away from home, and distance sold better in a place where people were already used to distant, profitable connections. It helped that money was available in Antwerp, that the city council was a lender. Antwerp bought an annuity in 1493 from Arnold van Berchem, for which he mortgaged three farms, and made a note that he wanted the money so his oldest son could make the journey to Jerusalem.[15]

Within a year Paesschen had a rival, Wilhelm van der Geest, who was building his own great ship for the Palestine run. Paesschen's money situation was fragile; his wife had died, perhaps through sheer exhaustion from the first voyage, and he was losing a battle with his father-in-law over her estate. He did manage a second voyage in 1515, but by 1516, things were even more difficult. He sold one house, mortgaged another and managed to get his *Salvator* out of port in April. Within days it had run aground on a sandbank off the English coast. All the passengers were safe, most of the cargo was salvaged and he even managed to fish some of the cannon out of the water.

Again he was saved by Antwerp, which had no ships but did have a business insuring ships. Evidently that business paid out for Paesschen. He tried everything all over again. He married again, although this time his wife was not as rich. By 1518 he had financed and built one more ship, 'the largest ever seen at Antwerp', and he loaded it with passengers for the Holy Land. Again, he sailed past the obvious obstacles and landed at Jaffa so the pilgrims could make their way overland to Jerusalem. As they stepped ashore, Ottoman guards arrested them, treated them like spies, since they came from the rival Hapsburg empire, and spelled out how much it would cost them to see home again. There was no choice, so the passengers paid. They came back by way of Venice, which had friendlier connections with the Turks. The ship followed safely but the voyage no longer seemed secure for paying pilgrims.

It took three more years to sink Paesschen entirely. His ship was commandeered to lead a war fleet meant to protect the herring ships, and soon after edging out of harbour, the weather turned foul and the fleet broke up. Paesschen's ship went down off Yarmouth. Nothing could be salvaged and many of the crew were lost. Paesschen's fortunes also went down. He turns up in the archives selling off another house, then going back to sea, but not on his own account. His second wife, left onshore, ran out of money and resources, and he died back in Antwerp in 1526.

He imagined how to use the city. He saw houses as a source of money. He saw how the insurance business put away the damage of shipwreck and disaster so his risk could be calculated. His private schemes produced civic pride, the invention of the Antwerp merchant marine with two large ships, and for this he was properly honoured in a city which always needed new businesses. More, he did all this on a fragile financial base, proof of the optimism all around him, the hopeful idea of investment.

That optimism was likely to be tested, again and again.

FIRESTORM

One night in 1534, the Church of Our Lady caught fire. There had been days of rain without a break, the fields around the city were under mud and water, and still all the magnificence of the Church of

Our Lady went up in flames. It was the 'most famous tower in Europe', holy music echoing from its high roof, full of 'gifts of enormous opulence' from gold to marble; it had a secure place in the routine of the city, being the site of the labour market where men went to find work each morning, and the place where guilds went to worship and to show off all the gold and the music that proved their virtue and success. And yet suddenly it was, as Cornelius Grapheus wrote in his eye-witness poem:[16] 'a horrid mass of smoke that made the night darker, that blocked out the light of a full moon'.

There was the rustle of fire, then the urgent clanging of bells, then flames burst through the roof of the church. The doors were flung open to let in people with ladders and grappling hooks to salvage the paintings, the images, the silver and the gold that had seemed so sure and permanent. The altars were on fire, and the vestments. Grapheus remembered that 'The birds in the high towers were driven out in a hideous rain of feathers and bodies.'

After a while he could no longer make out flames, because they were masked by all the houses around the cathedral, the bankers' mansions on Groenplaats, the guild houses on the Grote Markt as well as the muddle of lanes: it was as though fire inhabited the city and put everything solid at risk. Grapheus saw for himself scenes that artists 'might imagine', fires like the ones that obsessed Hieronymus Bosch and light the background to his most fantastic creatures; so fire went deep into the mind. 'The sky was on fire,' he wrote. The scene was like the volcano of Mount Etna in her fury, which is his memory of Virgil in the *Aeneid* who writes not just about the spectacle of Etna erupting but also the fiery forges the Roman god Vulcan maintains in the caves underneath. Fire, to a civic grandee like Grapheus, was a permanent resident.[17]

The city tried to defend itself with rules and regulations, and as usual their effect was limited. There were wooden buildings with thatched roofs despite an ordinance of 1503 that banned thatch, another in December 1513 that insisted on hard roofs, another of 1520 that encouraged the breaking down of wooden balconies and jetties by promising their stone or brick replacements could have the same area. In 1541 the city tried to take the flammable pitch and grease off the galleries that overhung the waterways, to make sure they were sealed with slate, lead or something 'hard'. Nothing much changed. In September 1546 the timber houses on Sint Katelijnevest went up in flames, close to the fine new Beurs, and within two months another row of houses even closer to the Beurs was reduced to ash and rubble: twenty-two houses in all. Nine days later, the city banned wooden outer walls altogether and wrote a rule that nobody could finish or repair any wooden roofs or walls; they had to 'remain in the state in which they are now until they perish of their own accord'.[18] In 1582 they published the order one more time in exactly the same words. Somehow at the very end of the nineteenth century Antwerp still had dozens of houses with wooden façades in a good state of repair.

This wasn't simple lawlessness; it was a habit of mind. Nobody could tell anyone else what to build, although neighbours had the right to complain; but a seemingly reasonable complaint about light could easily fail if there was no clear court order or written covenant. There was a whole body of case law based on settling neighbours' disputes, but the constant nagging letters of Charles V to the Antwerp authorities could not produce a clear account of what this common law said, and how it worked. Cities didn't like telling the Emperor about customs, because they rightly expected the Emperor would want to change, codify or disturb them.

Meanwhile, anyone could build more or less anything but not any-where. That principle was put into writing in 1546, in 1570 and in 1582, so the city's power to shape its own fabric was strictly limited. Only when the Calvinists had control in 1582, and streets were being forced through the grounds of convents and monasteries, did the city talk in terms of general rules and general principles, of making streets straight 'since curved streets were not good for the city's beauty, peace or security', of concepts like elegance, proportion and usefulness instead of a series of sometimes brilliant expedients which reshaped the city without actually giving it a shape.[19]

THE WALLS

The flags belong to France and Denmark, the army comes from Gelderland in the north of the Netherlands and the leader is Maarten van Rossum, a man so ferocious people tell silly stories about him and then shudder. He's supposed to be so fierce that his moustaches stand on end in battle. News of his advance had already reached the city from farmers who had been burned out of their homes. Others had seen for themselves his wrecking and pillaging of the town of 's-Hertogenbosch. Now his army is at the walls of Antwerp because they are enemies of the Hapsburgs and therefore enemies of Antwerp. The grand politics of the European world, separate dynasties and nations, are demanding attention from a town that had rather consider contracts and profits.

It is 1542. Antwerp has done well from the Hapsburg strategy of keeping their war with the French Valois a whole sea and some mountains away in Italy. Unfortunately when the Valois did send their violent proxies, when van Rossum came raiding just as the Danish king Christian was threatening to land troops in Holland and the French were being troublesome on the frontier, the armies of the empire were somewhere else and otherwise engaged. Mary of Hungary, Governor of the Hapsburg Netherlands, told her brother Emperor Charles V that 'we are under attack on so many fronts that I do not know which one I should deal with first. The worst of it is that our enemies are prepared and we are not; they have taken us entirely by surprise.'

The city was left to panic alone, to silence its bells, keep its streets lit through the night, think of flooding the pasture land all around and meanwhile clear out the little people's houses just outside the wall which might give the enemy cover. There were rumours that van Rossum was in the city already, talking in the horse market, checking on his spies. Maybe a thousand or so men originally from Gelderland thought this was a good time to give up their citizenship and get out of town before anyone blamed them for van Rossum.

There were no church bells, not even clocks chiming, in case the enemy could use the time as a signal. The only bell in a city of bells would be the great Carolus, and if it sounded the streets had to be cleared of stalls, all men had to get to their posts and all women had to get off the streets. The prospect of van Rossum had stopped the city dead: no trade, nothing on the streets, none of the usual communal responses to the constant threat of fire, because only named people were allowed to respond if there was a fire alarm. The women were packed away at home even though they had been invaluable moving the earth to reinforce the walls and tearing up paving stones to use as ammunition.

The walls were a problem in their own right. Bandits were coming from all sides against a city whose mediaeval defences were weak and especially uncertain between the Red and Kipdorp gates.

The city called for help from Breda but van Rossum ambushed and bottled up the troops that came; that was on 24 July. His troops were all around the city so that on 26 July the power of privilege broke for a moment and some of the grand houses on the wall, and a convent, and even the holy women in the beguinage were burned out. Then an army of tall men from Flanders – 'giants' from the city's legends about its own past, come back to save it now – crossed the Scheldt even as van Rossum was surrounding the walls.

The enemy demanded surrender, but were startled to find the foreign merchants getting ready to fight alongside citizens. They expected the soft, luxurious response of a trading town and not a common interest in defending what Antwerp had become – not just the fabric, but the idea. Van Rossum's army, meanwhile, considered their chances of finding a decent meal in the countryside they'd already burned. They decided that retreat would be no shame. Three weeks later, the city was enough at ease to stage its regular procession of Our Lady through the streets.[20]

The rich and the powerful crammed into a city which had seemed so very vulnerable. The merchant Guicciardini says the walls helped, and the ditches that fortified them and could be flooded 'with engines that they have'. After the siege the walls were rebuilt so the city was now 'free from all danger and thought impregnable. By means whereof, a great multitude of Noblemen and Gentlemen come to dwell in the towne.' It helped that the wealthy, tasteful suburbs with their gardens and trees were burned down in the war and nobody was allowed any more to build within 3,500 feet of the town wall; 'a great number of wealthy men that before dwelt without the towne have been since and are daily constrained to build and dwell within the town.' The result was that 'houses are dearer let in Andwerp[sic] than in anie other place in Christendom, Lisbonne in Portugal excepted.'[21]

There always seemed to be a building boom, new rooms for the workers coming into the city, grand new palaces for the growing class of rich and ostentatious merchants. Nobody was quite in control of it all. Even the bricks were a little suspect; as early as 1512 the city had to tell the brickmakers of Boom not to hollow them out or 'mutilate them by hand'.

Around the narrow streets of the mediaeval core there were patches of coincidental open space: convent grounds, shooting galleries, the courtyards and gardens of fine houses, the gaps inside the squares of built-up streets. Because there was this open space, and because new people were always crowding in for work and needed a roof, there was a war over where new streets might go. In 1513, the issue was paving the streets, so nobody was supposed to build except on the line of the streets. In 1520, the problem was that just laying down the threshold of a new building meant marking the line of a street, so there could be no new construction without official papers. In 1582 all the rules had to be stated one more time: no streets could be opened through private land or anywhere else without the consent of the magistrates or the controller. You could 'reach an agreement' which really meant 'decide a price'.[22]

The fabric of the city was not the whole story. The new arrivals also took refuge in the idea of the city, an idea as much under construction as the walls.

2

The City as Idea

Niclaes Jongelinck has all the best trades. Every ship in the Scheldt, every cart crossing Brabant, every barrel of wine has to pay him as tax collector. He promotes lotteries for the hopeful, with a sideline in insuring ships for the cautious. His family runs the mint that manufactures money. He has a townhouse on the Kipdorp, but to see the man in his glory you have to leave the city by the square mass and narrow door of the St Joris gate, then follow the causeway over the moat into a suburbia that looks as though it was laid out with a set square. Everything is green like the countryside, contained like the town, but with none of their disorder. The trees are twenty feet apart, exactly.

The villas all have gardens, orchards, grand gates, and the courtyards which are now a great luxury inside the walls, a ration of space and air. Jongelinck has one of the larger plots, number 12, and a house put in verses by Lamponius, although the most effusive line is 'built at unusual expense'. His neighbours are the banker brothers Schetz, so he's in good company.

Such a man claims status that comes from spending and dealing and a bit of bureaucratic money gouging, not land and title and an ancient castle, nothing to do with the old feudal rules of the countryside. So he stages a show of urban taste, good paintings everywhere, fine furniture, bronzes of assorted gods and goddesses. He collects Frans Floris and also Pieter Bruegel, he owns one picture by Albrecht Dürer, art already of such agreed value that it can stand as collateral when he guarantees a friend's debts.

He thinks about the countryside, though. He owns Bruegel's glorious paintings of *The Months*, hunters crossing green-white snow for winter, a bend of rushing cattle for the autumn, the cutting of willows and mending of walls for spring, the haymakers brisking about for early summer and the harvesters stretched out in the half-cut fields with their bread and bowls of porridge for late summer; and he hangs those pictures, a whole country year, where gentlemen did, in the dining room.[1] Dinner is a time to talk and paintings could start the conversation. He also owns Bruegel's first version of *The Tower of Babel*, and that will give his dinner guests their own city to discuss because *Babel* is its portrait.

The citizens have a choice of fantasy: Antwerp as Babylon for all its many languages and faiths or Antwerp as Rome for its self-conscious dignity and importance. They need a fantasy to learn how to be themselves.

With men like Niclaes Jongelinck, the talk keeps coming back perversely to the city's opposite: the countryside. They have an appetite for life outside the walls: a mansion, farms, seigneurial rights and a title, the game of looking like the old kind of lord which is a status with a history, unlike their new kind of position. What used to be power is now their play. The old lords have a convenient habit of pledging their land to get money but not paying their debts, which hands swathes of the countryside to the new men in town. Social position does not come with the land. Peasants are almost obsolete, working now for larger farms rather than digging a subsistence out of their own land. Villages usually make things to sell as well as growing them. There are middle men who make their living between the landowners and the rest; the feudal connection has worn away.[2]

At table with the merchants, you'd expect a sense of triumph. Instead, being urban and above all not being rustic requires effort. You can tell they think about it. The stoneware jugs on grand tables are free of gods and landscapes; instead, they are decorated with peasants prancing to the bagpipes, based on Sebald Beham's unflattering prints. Bruegel made paintings for the richest walls of peasants feasting, dancing, and sometimes in a small upper corner in a kind of attic, fucking. The same gentry, and Pieter Bruegel as well, liked to slip out of town discreetly to the dance and the booze and the wedding riots of the villages. If one of the gentry was painted at some rural event, as the geographer Ortelius was, he'll be prettily starched and formal with a proper ruff and a black suit, making sure you know he doesn't belong. Ortelius out walking on the foreign slopes at Tivoli, drawn for the margins of a map, is capable of being just a sixteenth-century hiker.[3]

If your host approves of *tafelspelen*, plays for dinnertime entertainment, then the point will be even more direct. A remarkable number of the surviving scripts are about peasants. Paid players would come into the dining room and start making jokes against themselves and against the audience. There might be one who thinks he's in the dark insides of a cow, and likes being in the shit, and can't wait to tell the onlookers that they're also full of shit. He then tries different tactics to sell the eggs he's brought, each one more idiotic than the one before, all in highfalutin language because he's trying and failing to be citified. There might be two who play the parts of jobbing actors as hungry and poor as they really are, who've been brushed out of the countryside where they belong and who prove just how different they are by mistrusting the 'intolerant' city people who are paying them. Their turn is itself a joke against the countryside.[4]

The great change that Henri Lefebvre noticed, countryside giving way to the town, is on the minds of citizens. Towns have a new kind of wealth. Landowners' rights and authority are a commodity for new men, not the foundation of a social order. The town is in control, but still trying to make something new from the bits and pieces of manors, duchies, empires. Not being rustic is a good start, but they also have to imagine what a city might be.

Towns became places to work out the compromises needed to make something new from the fragments of the old order: merchants taking power to organize other people's lives, necessary alliances which had to bring together wage workers, craftsmen, oligarchs and traders to replace the remains of a feudal system. Trade involved remaking the city's space, which also means the relationships between people. Cities had to find what it meant to be a city on their own terms. This may or may not be the story of the sixteenth century in Europe, but it is a very useful way to read the story of sixteenth-century Antwerp.

The countryside is the easier part to understand. The town had to keep control because the country was the source of its workers, its food, its fuel and its building materials. It was also becoming an asset, with a property boom just like the city, sometimes in polder land which needed draining, sometimes in established farms. This constant investment explains the remarkable fact that in 1569 the lists for the 100th penny tax show that more than three-quarters of the merchant city's wealth was in property. You might make your money from something as volatile and mobile as trade, but with land you were more than rich. You quite literally had position, at least on a map.

It helps that with land you could always get something to eat. The patrician Aart Schoyte, uncle to Adriaan Hertsen, let out a farm a few miles from the city in 1532 for 20 Carolus guilders, quantities of butter, firewood, rye and also one fat lamb a year. A patrician did not eat rye bread, so the grains would be turned into cash income, but the butter and the lamb fed his household. Other farms paid in wheat, barley, peas, flax and beans, sometimes a calf. And city landlords had one economic advantage over the country kind: their horses covered less distance so they required much less oats.[5]

A STORY OF ABSENCES

Citizens could be sure of not being country people. Now they needed clues to what it meant to belong to a city, and for that they needed some kind of history, or at least legends about how the city had made its own riches and fame. Antwerp had a story of absences, things that the city was spared, and success by default, so the facts simply would not do.

There was a Roman fort on the Scheldt, and some kind of settlement, but all we know is that it was burned in 836 by raiding Vikings. The city decided to have a Roman hero, even so: a soldier called Brabo who was said to have cut off the hand of a giant called Druon Antigon. The monster demanded tolls from the riverbank and cut off the hand of anyone who refused, a fanciful root for the city's name since throwing is *werpen* and hand is *hand*. Antwerp's fictional hero took his stand against taxes and obstacles to trade. That seems more exact than the painters and governors who called it Babylon, or the tablet in the new Beurs that honoured the S.P.Q.A., just like the S.P.Q.R., the people and senate of Rome.

There were two missionary saints, St Eloy and St Amand, which means there were souls to save in a *vicus*, which implies a trading place. There was a curious semicircular castle built around 980 by the German Emperor Otto II, so it was worth defending. But Antwerp had no court, no bishop, no very famous lord to help define its past, only a Margrave on the fringe of the Holy Roman Empire. Even the old-established trade routes did not explain much, because what made Antwerp rich was the change in trade routes: ships going by ocean to Asia and America. Antwerp was waiting for other histories to catch up, and meanwhile it honoured its legend Brabo.[6]

Reality is more mundane. All the ports in Flanders and Brabant were vying for the attention of foreign merchants and selling ease of access to Northern Europe for the trade and goods of the world. In our story that mostly means Bruges in Flanders and Antwerp across the border in Brabant. At the start, Bruges won easily: a rather glamorous town where the Medici would buy pictures and keep an office to trade money. Antwerp's advantage was more prosaic: the old alliance with England that brought wool and cloth to Brabant. All the Flanders towns had their own thoroughly organized industries weaving, dyeing and finishing cloth and wanted no rivals from across the North Sea, but Brabant had a much smaller stake in that industry so the English were welcome in Antwerp. It was made official in 1338 when a convoy of wool ships sailed out of Ipswich for Antwerp with a letter announcing that the English king 'decided to fix the staple for his wool': to name only one town where he would do business.

The city's English connection meant a basic profitable trade, but also a whole network of contacts to bring in what the English wanted, and a chance to lend them money at a good rate. English goods were shipped on from Antwerp to the German states by Hanseatic boat and cart, and then to Turkey beyond; or to Italy in the belly of galleys that would otherwise be plying empty back to Venice. Antwerp was the hub. What Brabant sold the English, aside from its own fine cloth, was Rhine wine, oats, furs, turbot, quantities of grapes, the wood for making bows, hats, empty barrels, live falcons and good wax, among many other things. The town functioned rather like a department store for the wool traders.[7]

It could do much more than that since its guilds and corporations were weaker than in Bruges, with far fewer local industries to protect, so the city did not have all the rules about the quality of goods and the pay of artisans, issues that were settled through local pressures. Antwerp could have designed itself for the merchants of Europe doing business with Asia, America and Africa, back and forth: no local barriers when goods were passing through. When merchants landed, they were not even required to unpack their goods in the city, let alone offer them for sale on the local market as in other ports.

There were safe conducts for the English wool merchants in Antwerp, who could not be arrested for claims that had nothing to do with business done in the town, who paid no tax on goods they imported and had the right to use English law when suing each other. In 1315 Brabant gave the same privileges to all foreign merchants. Still, the Italian Francesco Balducci Pegolotti, who lived in Antwerp in the 1310s, said, 'Bruges is the place where most merchants stay to trade and change money.'[8]

Then came the idea which was to make Antwerp a true exception, the hub of the world that Europe knew. Between 1317 and 1324, Brabant invented a quite brilliant strategy: it would have two fairs a year in Antwerp at Whitsun and around St Bavo's Day on 1 October, and two more at Bergen op Zoom, twenty miles north. Free trade was guaranteed, and now it had a fixed time and place. That brought even the merchants from Bruges, the men from the Hanseatic League and assorted other foreigners with their intricate new techniques of finance. They needed some way to settle their accounts, which meant making a kind of temporary branch office in Antwerp for the great clearing house of Bruges.[9] The fairs worked so well that in the 1430s Bruges was struggling to forbid their local foreigners from going there. By mid-century Italian merchants were complaining that foreigners simply left Bruges during the fairs, and trade was stoppered.

The policy could still be spoiled by events. The Count of Flanders seized Antwerp in 1356, a moment in the contests over the Burgundian succession, and for a while Bruges again had a momentum that could not be matched. Sugar from Madeira came there with the Portuguese, along with spice from the Indies, yew wood for making bows, olive oil and salt. The Spanish sent colours, merino wool, dried figs and raisins. The Italians brought alum to fix the colours when dyeing wool, spice from Africa, gold and silk. The financial hub in Bruges was all-important; after all, the van der Beurse tribe, the people 'of the purse', named the square in that city which gave the word Beurs or Bourse to the exchanges.

Politics had one more spoiling action, and it concerned the titles of Archduke Maximilian of Austria. He wanted to be Count of Flanders in his own right, not just as head of the regency council the local citizens had appointed, and he took an army to Bruges in 1484 to insist that the town agreed. The town was unhelpful so he took the best revenge: he ordered all foreign merchants to leave for Antwerp. When the merchants saw Maximilian's army at the gates a year later they started to move. In 1488, when the Archduke had become King of the Romans and was expecting to be Emperor very soon, he came back to Bruges. He was allowed to enter, but his army stayed outside. He found himself shut up in the grand Huis Craenenburg with a view onto the market square. Where other royals had watched tournaments and celebrations, Maximilian watched the execution of his associates.

He was a prisoner all through the spring, three and a half long months. He had to sign a promise to respect all the privileges of Flanders to get his freedom but, unsurprisingly for a man sure he was about to be Emperor, he did not mean to do anything of the sort. He was no longer in favour of bothersome Flanders and he had had more than enough of rebellious Bruges. One more time he ordered the foreign merchants to move to Antwerp and this time they had every reason to obey. All around Bruges war had ruined the land, there was plague and the price of grain kept rising; the town was short on its old glamour. There were even more immediate and practical issues. Bruges had never been directly on the water and the Zwin, the closest tidal channel to the North Sea, was silting up. Antwerp might be further inland but it was better connected, with a deep river and convenient tides to sweep ocean-going ships to its docks.

War between Maximilian and Bruges blocked the merchants' way even if they wanted to get back there. Antwerp could sit aside and win by default. It first took the trade in alum, the potash that came up from Italy; it made sense to ship to Antwerp rather than drag the stuff overland. The 1496 treaty between England and the rulers of Burgundy set up the Merchant Adventurers guild out of London, with a promise to sell wool only in Antwerp and Bergen op Zoom. The Portuguese moved their *feitoria*, their headquarters, dormitory and warehouse, to Antwerp, bringing all its trades, especially spice and even more especially pepper. Trade followed trade, as it does. The merchants from Cologne, who liked the light wool cloth from England, came to town and paid in the metals that came from southern Germany; and when the Portuguese arrived to sell spice, they also came to buy the German copper and silver they needed in the African trade. They bought fustian (a mix of flax and cotton) from Germany, but now they bought it in Antwerp, because it was more convenient.

Antwerp didn't want an empire and took its time even to build its own ships instead of hiring them from the northern Netherlands. Antwerp was hardly even a polity, which was its secret advantage in keeping its autonomy because it never seemed an obvious, old-fashioned threat to imperial authority. So Antwerp had to use its imagination.

The city said it was Rome on the Beurs, the new Exchange, and on the new town hall when finally it was built in the 1560s. When Cornelius Grapheus published a view of the interim town hall, the wooden bluff thrown up in a month when Philip of Spain came visiting, he captioned it in large letters: 'The length of an Antwerp foot matches the ancient Roman foot.'[10] Grapheus was very insistent on measurements, and the measure of Antwerp was Rome.

The fact that 'Antwerp today has grown to the very greatest size and dignity' required a Greek poem with a Latin foreword to show its antiquity; George Schroegel provided one.[11] A new Rome rising on the Scheldt, the English diplomat Daniel Rogers wrote when he arrived in 1565 and, in the best humanist manner, produced an ode in the style of Sappho almost as soon as he landed. He enthused about marble monuments, about a city that people said 'breathed the splendour of Rome'; 'the whole world bustles in this small world'. He found the circus and amphitheatre of Caesar's time in the Beurs at eleven each morning.[12]

This classical stuff was a performance. For all the talk of Rome, the fashion was moving to the local, the immediate: the Netherlandish. History, especially the history of local things, no longer seemed to need a classical advertisement. Adrianus Barlandus produced editions of what was variously known as either the chronicle of Brabant or the history of what the Dukes of Brabant did. The 1526 edition had a Latin title, and a preface full of Roman references; Pliny assured the readers that 'history is always a delight' and Cicero told them that they were children if they knew nothing of what happened before their birth. In the 1555 edition the language was Netherlandish, newly respectable and no longer reserved for technical subjects like herbals and botany; it was about to need its own weighty dictionaries. The Latin names, and the quotes, had disappeared.[13]

You could now be wise in the vernacular. History in general was in question, at least in the books published in Antwerp. In the 1530s, Cornelius Agrippa von Nettesheim wrote that history was not useful and not truthful, that historians wrote only to please their readers. Their books were packed with lies and 'countless fictions'. Juan Luis Vives took their sources apart, said often their only evidence was rumour, or letters from a friend telling a friend things he has heard.

The city was ready for myth, local myth. Jan van Gorp, a doctor who retired to Antwerp to give his life to dictionaries and languages, tried putting the city into its place in the world in a single book which otherwise goes right back to Noah and the question of whether he was a giant, how the Amazons taught the Greeks to ride, the flooding of Egypt, when the Venetians went to Troy, when the Trojans went to Egypt, why swallows do not nest in Daulis, and the curious fact that in the Alps 'only men climb the Swiss peaks that are close to the clouds ...' Van Gorp covers the Ganges, and also Greenland. In all this encyclopedia of stuff, Antwerp has its place at the centre.

He does deal in fact: he reports the last Viking raid on Antwerp, which did happen. He puts down legend: he wonders if the bones of giants might not be simply the bones of elephants, and he remembers the elephant that came to Antwerp 'that conformed very well to Aristotle's description, although the genitals were hidden under the huge body'. He is against those who tell the story of the tyrant giant Druon Antigon who was killed, and whose hand was thrown into the river. He thinks the name of Antwerp has to do with the name of a county called Antwerf, 'on the wharf'.

He reasons his way through all his history and his knowledge of languages, and he decides in the end that all the peoples of Europe were propagated from the same family stem. He takes the origins of Antwerp back to the Crimea, to the Cimmerians, who had been off the historical record for almost two millennia but who were much in demand again as the lost fathers of Frankish kings, the forgotten ancestors of assorted Germans, the Welsh and the inhabitants of Cappadocia. Van Gorp chooses a capacious origin story. He starts with languages, and in comparing the origins of words he comes to think that all peoples once had the same language. He sets out to find what language Adam and Eve spoke, thinking to identify it among living languages by finding the one with the simplest, shortest words. It turns out, which is not entirely surprising, that all mankind once spoke like the people of Brabant. Antwerp is no longer just Rome; it is the town that talks like Paradise.[14]

Or perhaps Antwerp came to seem like Babel, star of a biblical morality play, the tower built by human arrogance so overwhelming that God had to punish the builders. It was a natural fear for a city still being built ambitiously.

Bruegel painted two versions of the tower of Babel in 1563, one in Antwerp which hung on the walls of Niclaes Jongelinck's house and one after he moved to royal and official Brussels. He left town for work, but also because he was newly married and his new wife, and more particularly his new mother-in-law, wanted him a decent distance from his usual mistress. The move clearly changed his point of view.

The Antwerp version, the first, is disconcerting. The tower is not collapsed as it was in some images, so the story is not over; nor is it solid. It is under construction, a strange heap of grey rock and pink brick, a kind of masonry cake, being frantically built on all sides and then clad in grey stone to mask all its oddities. There are huts and rough sheds, washing out on the line, there are cranes and ladders everywhere, there is a detailed catalogue of building techniques all being worked up and down the tower, which is like Bruegel's other catalogues in other paintings – of children's games in one, folk sayings in another. The plan of the tower is roughly a rising spiral but if you look closely there are inside sections as abrupt as chutes going down floor after floor; nothing could easily stand there. Furious, muddled energy is building a heap which will have the look of a city.

If pride is the infection in the Babel story, mankind too sure of ourselves, then this is its site: a monumental lesion bursting out of a pale, blue-green landscape. The more you look at that landscape around the tower, the more you almost recognize Antwerp: built low but with church spires, towers, gables, mills and waterways, all surrounded by defensive walls beyond which lies a river curling off into a flatland with windmills. There is a wharf below the tower which is busy with great ships and there are sails on the water beyond, which shows this Babel is not exactly quoting Genesis, which puts the town on a 'plain in the land of Shinar', very far from harbours.

There is a king, the legendary tyrant Nimrod, standing in the foreground while stonemasons prostrate themselves, rather overdoing deference. There is already a town around the tower. Nimrod seems curiously irrelevant to the great tower that dwarfs him, hardly noticing it, rather as the Emperor could hardly begin to control the furious activity in Antwerp. The second version, made once Bruegel was in Brussels, is far more orderly, nicely connected to the wharf below, and the tyrant Nimrod has gone home. Babel is not alive any more, it's simply monumental.

Neither picture is propaganda, neither has some single meaning; even the biblical sources are ambiguous. There is the question of pride, as in Genesis 11, where men set out to 'build us a city and a tower, whose top may reach unto heaven; and let us make a name ...' The Lord took notice of the fact that they all shared the same language and was troubled that 'nothing will be restrained from them, which they have imagined to do.' His reaction to such enormous possibility was 'to confound their language that they may not understand one another's speech' and then scatter them 'upon the face of all the earth'. Success bred such terrors.

Nimrod the tyrant is not in Genesis; his arrogant defiance of God, his insistence he could build a tower so tall that it would stand above the waters if God sent another flood, is in the first-century AD Jewish historian Flavius Josephus[15] along with the fact that Babylon gets its name from Babel, the Hebrew for 'confusion'. Nimrod 'gradually changed the government into tyranny, seeing no other way of turning men from the fear of God', according to the *Antiquitatem Juduicarum*. In a Netherlands newly subject to the Inquisition, that was an immediate issue and the text was familiar: apart from the Basel editions of the 1550s in which Erasmus was involved, a Dutch version of Josephus was published in Antwerp by Symon Cock in 1553. Nimrod did not have to be explained.

But Babylon is also (according to the Book of Revelation 18) simply a trading city in ruins 'and the merchants of the earth shall weep and mourn over her; for no man buyeth their merchandise any more'. They had 'waxed rich through the abundance of her delicacies', the silver, gold and precious stones, the spice and cloth; but 'all things which were dainty and goodly are departed from thee, and thou shalt find them no more at all.' The great city where all were made rich, 'all that had ships in the sea', was finished and made desolate. Any moment when Antwerp seemed fragile because of a siege, a war, some godly dissension or simply the violent, broken state of the streets, Babylon was remembered.

The *griffiers*, town clerks, had bound books for writing out court decisions. The *vonnisboeken* had blank flyleaves, empty covers which were the perfect place to check the ink on their quills and practise their more ambitious calligraphy. Naturally, they doodled. Their scuffed marks are an oblique view of what was on the unoccupied minds of the most senior civil servants: there's a chubby bare bottom ascending into heaven, the outline of a foot soldier who's said to be poor and loyal, skulls among the heads with feathered hats, women and wine and dice and persons with beards. They are clues to the anxieties of the city, which is something officials almost never like to put on record.

We can't name which of the *griffiers* doodled where, but we do at least have dates. So someone senior and important was worrying in the first decade of the sixteenth century about the traps that might upset a man's life and he draws them from a Latin proverb: three dice, a pitcher of wine and a woman. He's not moralizing so much as worrying about the way such things can take away a man's money: 'Once I was a rich man, but these things have stripped me naked.' There is a moral, though: 'Rule yourself, not other people.'

Come the second decade, and along come the fools. Good humanists were reading Erasmus' *In Praise of Folly* after 1511, sometimes drawing in the margins, as Holbein did, images mostly of fools, fools' caps and the sticks that fools carry. Someone makes a note that some things are numberless and probably he means fools. Alongside the jester's stick with a carved head on it someone writes in Latin: 'However many men the richest of lands can hold, that's how many of these "sceptres" they deserve to hold in their hands.'

A quote from Horace: 'Citizens, citizens, your priority is hunting money. Virtue comes after cash ...' The town, by 1520, doesn't seem a matter of individuals keeping up their defences against booze and gambling and women; it has become a community dedicated to money, and the trade that provides it.

Nobody looked after doodles as they did the serious town records around them, at least not until the invention of art history, and the records of Antwerp were culled by fire in 1576. There are long gaps when there is nothing to be decoded. But we can see the pens move again in 1544. The city has been put under a shaky kind of siege by van Rossum and was shocked to discover how imperfect were its defences. The foreign merchants rallied to the walls, a sign that they were serious about belonging, but the walls had to be rebuilt at great expense so the merchants would be happy to stay. Now the *griffier* scratched in Latin: 'O citizens, citizens living in the shade of the high walls of Antwerp ...' The walls, not the docks, define the city.

Nothing seems quite certain, not the position of the old city families in the face of the merchants from abroad, not the politics of the great powers and what war might do to the city. The fine houses and estates from a feudal past were up for sale to the new men with money, who bought themselves titles. They used cash, not pedigrees. Lines from Juvenal came to mind, about the uselessness of having a long pedigree and distinguished ancestors ('*stemmata quid faciunt ...*') and about the Emperor Aemilianus, 'standing in his triumphal car', who won a famous victory, became emperor with the backing of his army but lasted only three months before another general with a bigger army displaced him and he was killed by his own men. He boasted of a good lineage. Nobody cared.

The uncertainty went deeper. Here's a *griffier* who remembers his

Ovid in 1554: 'All that a man has is hanging by a fine thread, and the most secure things can collapse quite suddenly.' The line haunted the books; it turns up again in 1559 on a front cover. It could be a reasonable reaction from anyone who has watched law courts as closely as the clerks were obliged to do, seen the fragility of business or life itself when it came to the attention of the law, but the doodlers return to themes of chance and doubt. 'Think what's involved in playing dice: your death, and what you own and what will become of you.' And if you want certainty in a town of markets, then think of 'our Dominicus' who 'thinks himself blessed when his coffers are full; he's right to think that and he's not deceiving himself'.[16]

They're just doodles, a moment's thought, but they're suggestive: the echoes of doubts about what's happening to the old social order, the morals of money, the shallowness of city pleasures and the chase for cash instead of virtue.

There was a quite different city in the unofficial stories people told each other, wrote down for their amusement and sometimes printed. Antwerp had sex and killers, wild women and doubtful money, a sense of scandal.

This real city slides into accounts of Luilekkerland, the land of Cockaigne; the lazy, lovely fantasy of a place and a time where everybody always eats meat and also sweetmeats. There is a prose version of the story which was printed in Antwerp in 1600, maybe making sharp moral points about the past since the story goes back much further to 'the year written as one thousand sugar cakes, five hundred custard tartlets and forty-six roast chickens', which sounds like 1546, and there are title pages all the way through the volume to show it collects many earlier editions. It is a snapshot of the city's reputation over at least half a century.

In town you get paid for lying, for sneering at respectable people, a bonus for a really good fart. Money grows on trees. Luilekkerland describes an information city where 'true tidings' of the world are printed and sold on the street, where the spice trade is so well settled that the edible palaces have nutmegs for nails, where it snows sugar; and where debt and credit are everything although your debts will vanish if you just go away for a year and quietly eat roast chicken.

Money and reality are living apart. All the success of the town is mocked. All the schemes and operations of finance seem like farce alongside the truly respected professionals of the town, who are the whores, and 'the more wanton and frolicsome they are' the more they got respect. They were not cheap, but then we're told that everything in Antwerp was for sale.[17]

3

Knowing Things

In 1515 Thomas More ran out of money in the Netherlands and had to ask Cardinal Wolsey for help: 'Master More at this time, as being at a low ebb, desires by your grace to be set on float again.' He'd been away on diplomatic business which had dragged on far too long. He would have been glad to be back in England since 'at that time I had been more than four months away from them, my native country, my wife and my children.'[1] The Flemish negotiators had just gone off to Brussels for new and maybe different instructions, and More went off to Antwerp as a kind of consolation.

Erasmus had already written to the town clerk Peter Gillis to tell him to expect 'the two most learnèd men in England', More and his diplomat colleague Cuthbert Tunstall. More was already a friend of the city. He had lawyered and interpreted on Antwerp's behalf when it was trying to bring the English Merchant Adventurers' cloth staple back from Bruges and now he was trying to stop Bruges again becoming the great port for English trade. As his colleague Richard Sampson said, the decline of Bruges was what made Antwerp 'one of the flowers of the world'.

He was welcome as lawyer, but also welcome as a humanist, the same mixture that made Antwerp famous: trade and knowledge, the logic of the docks and market and exchange but also the information and the thinking that came with all the connections in town. Antwerp had no great and famous school to keep printers occupied, not like Zwolle or Deventer further north, but by the end of the fifteenth century it had the greatest share of the book trade in the southern Netherlands. Printers needed a booming town to find the money to buy paper while waiting for their books to sell, and they needed a powerful trading network to send books and ideas around the world. Antwerp had both. When Christopher Columbus' letter about the islands he found on the other side of the Atlantic was put into the international language of Latin, the text was rushed out in Rome in 1493, then within a year in the famous print centres of Basel and Paris and also in Antwerp. The printer Dirk Martens lifted the text of the Roman edition for his own and passed it on to people who wanted to know.

The mix of trade and connections and scholarly ambition made Antwerp a place to find things out and understand them. So More starts his famous story of another newly explored island, *Utopia*, in the Grote Markt, which is where a man might hope to hear stories of the world newly opening up to Europe. As he tells it, he goes to Mass in the high loveliness of the Church of Our Lady – it was a parish church then, not yet a cathedral – and meets a great friend in the doorway as he comes out. This is Gillis, the town clerk, who is entirely welcoming. He was famous for his 'agreeable company and delightful talk', a scholar of classics as well as the man who ran the city. He will be the bridge from the real city to the imagined, philosophic island of Utopia.

Gillis is talking to some bearded, sunburned seaman in a loose cloak. The seaman is not as plain as he looks; he is more of a philosopher, enquiring after strange peoples and strange lands. He says he once sailed south with Amerigo Vespucci and found a world beyond the burning heat of the Equator. Now he has a story to tell of a distant island empire which shares its mobs of sheep and its moral issues with England, but is also a philosophic ideal, a commonwealth which works on Christian principles.

More says he is in Antwerp to learn about such things. He goes back to Gillis' garden to hear what the man has to say.

His story was an oddity, a learnèd book from England. It was published first in Leuven, then Paris, then Basel; always in Latin. Nobody put it into English until 1551. Nobody put it into Netherlandish, either, until Hans de Laet's edition of 1553, which was also the first from Antwerp; so the setting More chose was not a sop to local publishers.[2]

It was, however, the place to launch the book. More's friend Gillis wrote around for blurbs from famous names to make it credible. Erasmus was already convinced, said he had always thought very highly of More's work, but had doubted his own judgement because of 'the very close friendship between us'. The great Guillaume Budé, the man Erasmus called the 'marvel of France', liked the book so much he let himself be distracted from running his country house; 'what nonsense, I thought, is all this bustle over maintaining a household, this whole business of constantly accumulating more and more.' He took so long writing his preface to the Basel edition that the Paris version appeared first, but the wait was worth it since he was founder of what would become the Collège de France and he brought the very highest approval. Gillis himself added to the book: four lines of verse about how Utopia had not always been an island, written in the Utopian alphabet, which looks oddly like some shorthand codes of the day.

Erasmus could tell More that a burgomaster at Antwerp was so pleased with *Utopia* that 'he knows it all by heart.'[3] More himself was also launched, and to prove it Erasmus and Gillis sent him presents. They commissioned portraits of themselves to be painted by Quentin Matsys, perhaps the most distinguished Antwerp painter of the time. It was not a rapid job – Erasmus took a purge on his doctor's advice and it changed his appearance so much that work had to be suspended for a while – but when it was done the painted Erasmus sat there writing his own name, and the painted Gillis held a letter addressed to him, and both were hanging in More's own house. Nobody could miss the point: More belonged in their network now.[4]

He was an easy fit with the scholars he knew in Antwerp as diplomat, lawyer, philosopher and storyteller; but there was a difference. Often those scholars were also the merchants who needed the city and its flood of information to make money and make deals. Antwerp was one single system for humanists, Latinists, wool traders and spice dealers. Outsiders like the English humanist Roger Ascham noticed this. He came through the Low Countries in 1550 and wrote home in a quite unfriendly fashion about this 'low' Germany that many may think is 'the pits'. His solid Protestant principles allowed him to find the whole territory 'weak' and 'abandoned'. But that was 'apart from the noble gatherings of merchants'. He admired their literacy, their scholarship, their attachment to their idea of Rome and the ancient. He was more at home with them than with the magistrates.[5]

That tradition lasted almost a century. Consider the mapmaker Ortelius, Abraham Wortels, whose spectacular *Theatrum Orbis Terrarum* brought maps out of a curious category of privileged information and put them into bookshops for anyone to buy. He 'burned with love for study' but his father died when he was only twelve and left him to make his own way just like the sons of merchants who were expected to learn on the job. Ortelius became dealer and scholar both, very unlike More, who had two formal years at Oxford before becoming a lawyer.[6] He was close to Johannes Radermacher, a man who lost his father when he was sixteen, was blocked from university and obliged to sign indentures with a substantial local merchant called Aegidius Hooftman. Radermacher knew Emannuel van Meteren, himself cousin to Ortelius, whose father had bolted to England for safety after publishing Coverdale's Bible in English. Van Meteren shared Radermacher's fascination with history and also felt he had been kept away from study by 'the drudgery of business'. They formed a circle to complain and study together.

GOD'S SMUGGLERS

Woollen cloth was what the English sold abroad, and nine-tenths of all of it went through Antwerp: landed, traded there. The connection went back to the time when Brabant was an independent duchy, to old political alliances which left this one serious trace. The English goods were shipped on from Antwerp, especially the finer cloth, the lighter kind of kerseys, to the Maghreb and throughout the Levant. The war of 1542 blocked the overland route to Cologne and brought the trade almost to a halt, because it was the Germans who were shipping the cloth on into Hungary and beyond. The prospect of a truce with Turkey which meant open seas could send their prices up quite dramatically. What's more, the agents of the wool trade in Antwerp bought almost anything they could and anywhere they could, carrying out other people's orders and buying from suppliers or merchants in London or Venice. Their consignments went in all directions, in all shapes and sizes, from bales of coarse ribbed cloth to turquoises and mohair and silk. The bales and barrels and bundles had to be labelled and sealed. The best English wool already had brand marks like the Broom or the Two Keys.[7]

Goods of every kind, with private marks to show what they were and where they were going that not everybody understood. Smugglers could use a network like that.

There was another trade between Antwerp and the English ports. The printing presses of Antwerp, at least sixty of them, gave the English most of their books for many years: grammars for the schoolroom, handsome psalters, hymnals and missals with music printed in red and black, holy calendars with moral lessons for each day of the week, books on the value of silver and gold, books about commodity prices and rates of exchange, even a travel book about the world's 'new lands' by King Manoel of Portugal which included real unicorns and a sensational account of the English hero Robin Hood. There were almanacs, predictions, a book on needlework and one on hygiene: the Bishop of Aarhus in Denmark suggested praising God and also fumigating.

All these were shipped in quantity. The print was often more meticulous than English presses could manage, with a special feature of intricate woodcut borders on the pages. The books were sold at fairs, in shops, by pedlars in the streets. The holy books were often the first books that members of a congregation had ever handled. At a time when the work of other foreign craftsmen was controlled or banned in England, the law said 'any Books, written or printed' could be freely imported. Printers from the Netherlands found it worthwhile to set up agencies in London, to suss out the market.

Antwerp printers like Christoffel van Ruremund and Johannes Hillenius printed almost all their books in English. English printers complained of unfair competition, and the law eventually agreed that 'a marvellous number of printed books had and still do come in ... whereby many of the King's subjects be destitute of work.' Antwerp's answer was often to change a single line of type on the title page so the books at least claimed to be printed in England.

English governments were also terrified of sedition, holy or ordinary. Catholic kings were edgy about Lutheran texts, the Bible in

English alarmed them, every kind of monarch was disturbed by slander and direct attack, and Protestant kings and queens were nervous about Catholic texts, especially knowing the famous talent of Jesuit arrivals for bluff and masquerade. Robert Parsons SJ claimed when he landed in England with a cache of banned books that he was a mercenary returning from the fight in Flanders, and nobody doubted him in time.

Books became contraband. Seamen smuggled, of course, but so did printers, dealers and true believers. They stowed the flat printed sheets inside bales of cloth, they sank watertight boxes into barrels of wine, they buried books in salt casks and hid them in flour sacks, they made a point of not being unnecessarily exact in describing any cargo. When Thomas More was interrogating the Bible smuggler George Constantine, trying to find out the sources of money for printing and shipping the New Testament in English, he found the man seemingly penitent 'and utterly minded to forsake such heresies and heretics forever. In proof whereof he not only detected, as I said, his own deeds and his fellows', but also studied and devised how those devilish books which himself and others of his fellows had brought and shipped might come to the bishop's hands to be burned. And therefore he showed me the shipman's name that had them, and the marks of the fardels [bundles] by which I have since his escape received them.'[8]

Secret marks and colours were only the start. The books landed at various ports to confuse the issue. Richard Bayfield, who was once a monk, collected them at Colchester, at St Katherine's Dock in London and some harbours in Norfolk, and moved them to London in a mail coach. George Constantine 'passed and repassed the seas upon the same errand', counting on the forgiveness of the English authorities. Then the books were delivered – often to Mr Fyshe in Whitefriars, who otherwise got his quota from an Englishman 'being beyond see [sea]'. A whole network sold to the countryside, to other cities, and sometimes, to make things even more complicated, a smuggler like Robert Necton would buy from Mr Fyshe to sell on. It was godly, but a godly kind of business.[9]

All this depended on Antwerp with its presses, its docks, its constant tide of ships sailing out to ports up and down the English coast and most particularly to London.[10] The priest William Tyndale put himself at that centre because nowhere else would do. Antwerp made possible his work of turning the Greek and Hebrew of the Bible into a glorious, singing English, and shipped and sold it where it was needed. Antwerp was not taking sides; on occasion it also made public bonfires of his work.

Tyndale knew the printing trade and he knew the wool trade; his brothers made and graded cloth in the Cotswolds, spent their lives in an area almost as famous for Lollards and the first signals of Reformation as for sheep.[11]

He was a precise man who worked to find the exact meaning of the words in the Greek he knew and the Hebrew he was learning. To the clergy he was often correcting, this made him a dangerous pedant. To royal officers obsessed with Church authority, he was plain subversive. To anyone who wanted direct contact with Scripture in English, Protestant or not, he was their hero.

He had tried to start work in England. It was still illegal to own a Bible in English, but the Greek texts of the New Testament were in print and freely available, written English was stable enough to be widely understood, and printing meant the world could have access to any new translation. Always hopeful, Tyndale zigzagged his way to see Cuthbert Tunstall, the scholarly Bishop of London who had once been Thomas More's companion in Antwerp: a letter here, a contact there, a friend talking to a friend. But Tunstall was appalled by the very idea of an English Bible, sure the awful disorder of Lutheran Germany would certainly follow.

Tyndale knew that not only 'was there no room in my Lord of London's palace to translate the New Testament but also that there was no place to do it in all England'. So he sailed. He went to Cologne, but the authorities discovered what his presses were printing and shut them down. He fled up the Rhine to Worms carrying half the print run, but he needed somewhere with protection, somewhere closer to England since the Bibles were for England.

He came back to Antwerp not for certain protection, but for everything that was ambiguous, the true strength of the place. Almost every year between 1526 and 1539 there were more and more English-language editions of the New Testament printed there. The first full

Bible in English may have been printed in Antwerp in 1535. Sometimes things went well. There was a new law in 1525 which made the penalties for handling or publishing the wrong books much more stringent, but the Antwerp magistrates hated to lose business and they made it clear they would follow the Emperor's orders only if compelled. Madrid wanted book crimes to carry the death penalty but the worst Antwerp threatened was ten years more or less theoretical banishment and loss of citizenship, which mattered less than it sounds.

Tyndale's New Testament translation was reprinted at Antwerp in 1526 as he arrived. He could have been in the watching crowds, less than a year later, when the whole of the same print run was burned.

The printer of Tyndale's New Testament was Christoffel van Ruremund, whose more admissible line was orthodox books: he printed missals. He also had a taste for the Lutheran, the vernacular and the forbidden. Usually, the Antwerp authorities were not too worried by books made entirely for the export trade, but when the New Testament in English appeared the English ambassador, Sir John Hackett, was told to take the book to law. Bibles in English had been burned in England, so he argued that they ought to be burned in the Spanish Netherlands, too.

The Margrave agreed about the fires and ruled that the printer should be banished and his goods confiscated. Van Ruremund answered back. His lawyer argued simply that subjects of the Emperor answered only to the laws of the Emperor, and not those of other countries.

He won his case and the printing went on, but the relief lasted only weeks. On 16 January 1527 the Margrave issued a new proclamation: it was now illegal to keep any copy of any New Testament in English. Every copy was to be collected and burned, and the collection was so effective that for centuries no copies of those early editions were known to survive. Still, van Ruremund went on printing; his brother Hans took 500 copies to sell in England, and Christoffel went along only to be thrown into an English jail, where he died in 1531. His widow Catherine put out much the same books when she took over the business, but she was subtler than the men; she stayed out of court.[12]

And still Tyndale stayed in Antwerp, usually poor, missing his friends bitterly, an exile who felt constantly in danger; or so he later told Stephen Vaughan, the agent of Henry VIII. In the meantime, it sometimes helped that his opponents came to town.

The old obstacle Cuthbert Tunstall was there on diplomatic business, talking of how he'd like to buy up the English New Testaments. He was approached by a London merchant called Augustine Packington, who said he knew the 'Dutch men and strangers' who had bought the New Testaments from Tyndale to sell them, and if the Bishop would just put up the money, he would buy the lot and hand them over. The Bishop was easily convinced. He dreamed of one more bonfire of Tyndale's errors.

Packington then went to Tyndale with a rather different version of his scheme. 'William,' he said, 'I know thou art a poor man and hast a heap of New Testaments and books by thee for the which thou hast both endangered thy friends and beggared thyself and I have now gotten thee a Merchant which with ready money shall despatch thee of all thou hast.' Naturally, Tyndale wanted to know who this dealer might be and he was not at all distressed to hear it was Tunstall: 'I shall get money of him for these books to bring myself out of debt,' he decided, 'and the whole world shall cry out upon the burning of God's word.'

Packington was only briefly embarrassed when New Testaments went on landing in England. He had a tense meeting with the Bishop, who said he was under the impression that Packington had bought up all the books. Packington said he'd bought what was for sale, and maybe the Bishop should spend some more and buy up the type and the blocks so no more could be made. The Bishop answered only: 'Well, Packington. Well.'[13]

Tyndale had no fixed address, or at least none that people were allowed to know, but still his work shipped out. The English clergy could argue with Tyndale's rich and stately versions of the Old Testament only on the principle of the thing, since Hebrew was hardly studied in England. Book by book, the Pentateuch in English started to land around January 1530, separate sections in different typefaces but designed to be bound together; and printed by 'Hans Luft', which was the name of Luther's printer at Wittenberg, but 'Hans Luft at Marburg'. This Luft did not exist; the books came from Hoochstraten's presses at Antwerp.[14]

The English court changed tactics. They would offer Tyndale some high position and in return he would stop his constant attacks on the ignorance of the clergy and the annulment of Henry's first marriage. When Stephen Vaughan went out as the new ambassador to the Netherlands, he had instructions to go on hunting Tyndale but with a view to persuading him, not arresting him. He sent letters to Marburg, Hamburg and Frankfurt, not knowing where Tyndale might be, and unsurprisingly he heard nothing back.

Tyndale had no reason to assume the English meant him well. His brother in England had just been heavily fined for sending him money and keeping his letters.[15] Still, he did talk to Vaughan, but on his own terms. He agreed to a meeting in a field outside Antwerp, very carefully set up by messages delivered by 'a friend', sent by 'a friend' and concerning someone known only as 'a friend'.

Vaughan reported not knowing who he was to meet until he was outside the city walls and face to face with a man who asked, 'Do you not know me?'

He had to say politely that 'I do not well remember you.'

'My name,' the man said, 'is Tyndale.'

Their talk was about how Tyndale had suffered, how he only meant to bring the word of God to the people and good advice to the King; and how he had doubts about any deal which would allow him to go back to England with the King's protection, since the clergy might always change the King's mind. Tyndale talked of the miseries of exile, how he felt surrounded by dangers, but he did not say London would be safer and happier.

It was almost night, and Tyndale took his leave, walking ostentatiously away from Antwerp as Vaughan turned back to the gates. Vaughan told the King that he knew Tyndale 'afterwards returned to the town, since there was no likelihood that he should lodge outside'.[16]

Tyndale found an address in Antwerp which he could acknowledge: a tall, gabled house where lived Thomas Poyntz and his wife. Poyntz ran the English House, the centre for the English traders who had been the foundation of Antwerp's fortune. The merchants there shared the protections that Antwerp citizens enjoyed, so inside the House residents could be arrested only for serious crimes already proven against them.

Tyndale could feel almost safe. He was also among his own kind. The chaplain was a friend, John Rogers, who was on the turn to Luther's opinions and had the Greek and Hebrew to help Tyndale with his translations. There were dinner invitations from the merchants, a social life which did not demand concealment. There was even a regular income, contributed by the English merchants, which allowed Tyndale a charitable routine. Every Monday he set out to look after the English who had fled to Antwerp for their own religious reasons.[17]

Tyndale didn't listen to rumours that someone was coming after him. He may have fancied that the merchants in town, and his Lutheran friends, would always warn him in good time. He could hardly run in any case since his rooms were full of his work and he needed the printers of Antwerp to get the words out. He would certainly not expect an Englishman to betray him.

He made friends over dinner with a man called Henry Phillips: a 'comely' man, a charming man from a good family, 'conformable' in his religion, or so it seemed. He was also a man who suddenly had money he kept mentioning but never explained, which should have been a warning, but Tyndale took to him, showed his papers and his books to him, even encouraged Poyntz to take him in as a lodger.

Poyntz was away in May 1535 when Phillips came to the English House, saying he wanted to make an arrangement to dine with Tyndale, then borrowing forty shillings to buy the meat 'because I lost my purse this morning'. Tyndale invited Phillips to go out with him to eat.

They set off down the alley, single file because the path was too narrow for two men to walk abreast. Tyndale wanted Phillips to go first – he was a modest and a mannerly man – but Phillips insisted that Tyndale go ahead of him. That made it easier for the tall Phillips to point out the shorter Tyndale when they reached the two men waiting at the end of the alley.

The plot was clear. Phillips had been paid to talk Tyndale out of his semi-sanctuary in the English House, so the imperial powers could use their direct methods against heresy. The Emperor always did insist. Charles V in the surprising journal of travels he wrote later when sailing down the Rhine, goes back again and again to the need to end the errors and disorder of Lutherans, to the way ordinary war kept distracting him from pursuing their errors, which he considered at least as important a mission as beating back his great imperial rivals, the Turks.[18]

The officers' first job was to take Tyndale to the procurator-general, who with unlikely manners gave him a good dinner before sending him the eighteen miles to the castle at Vilvoorde. He would spend a year and 135 days there.

Nobody knew for certain who gave Phillips his orders. The English authorities had no interest in having an Englishman arrested by agents of an Emperor who had long ceased to be any kind of friend. After all, Henry VIII was in the middle of divorcing the Emperor's aunt. The English merchants were furious at the breach of their privileges. Phillips himself was nervous at his own success, fretting that his servant would be caught carrying letters to London, letters to his paymaster which must on no account fall into official hands and 'greatly afraid ... that the English merchants that be in Antwerp will lay watch to do him some displeasure privily'. He went to Leuven and started bellowing publicly against Henry VIII. Thomas Theobald remembered his talk 'that Tyndale should die, which he doth follow and procureth with all diligent endeavour, rejoicing much therein'.

Tyndale in his cell was besieged by priests, friars, divines and lawyers, all of them persuading, arguing, lecturing as if he would change his mind. He suffered from catarrh and begged for a warmer cap for his head. 'I ask to be allowed to have a lamp in the evening,' he wrote to the authorities. 'It is indeed wearisome sitting alone in the dark.' He lived in a ruinous shirt, a thin coat and leggings with holes that needed patching, a perfectly poor man who was paying for his own board and lodging without knowing it; his books and goods were sold to meet the bill. He went on trying to get Hebrew grammars, dictionaries and the Bible texts so he could work for as long as he lived.

In the autumn of 1536 Tyndale was broken as a priest, the oil that had anointed him scraped ceremonially from his hands, his vestments stripped away. He became the business of secular authorities. A stake was put in the castle courtyard. In the first week of October, Tyndale was first strangled and then the brushwood, straw and gunpowder heaped around his body was set on fire with a wax candle.[19]

SELLING SECRETS

Some knowledge was meant to stay secret, especially in wartime, which was most times in the sixteenth century. In Antwerp there was a business hunting, catching and selling those secrets. You could hunt as a merchant who needed to know markets in order to bet one against another, but you could also watch as a spy – seeing who was buying armour and meant to go to war, who was raising what kind of coinage to pay soldiers on what battlefields, who was planning campaigns they had not mentioned even to their allies.

In the early 1540s the French and the Turks were fighting both Charles V and Henry VIII of England. Maître Jacques came to town in 1545, at least he said he was Maître Jacques from Geneva. He had been Claude Franchois on his way back to Bruges from London and before that he was François de la Borde, sergeant major in the French army.

You couldn't miss him. He was a man in his early forties, 'of fierce bear like aspect', according to witnesses, 'with one hand injured' and wearing gold in one ear. He'd gone to England for 'other purposes than trade' with a sidekick called Bodon and come back to Antwerp to hire soldiers. He was seen hiring sailors for the French, and paying for two Hanseatic sea captains to go down to France by land; and then he started asking questions about what arms the English were buying in Antwerp. He kept asking where it would be best to land an army in England. He was watched and reported, along with talk at the Old Beurs that certain 'canvas merchants' planned to go to London and not sell any canvas at all.

None of this watching was safe. The man who told the English all about de la Borde also said he was afraid for his life if the man even set foot again in Antwerp.[20]

That was the melodrama in an otherwise quite basic business. People could make a living or a killing in Antwerp by knowing what was happening or likely to happen somewhere else; they could turn

the difference between markets into their profit. The streets babbled
with languages. 'One can discover or even follow the nature, habits
and customs of many nations,' the merchant Guicciardini wrote. 'It is
because of this accumulation of foreigners that there is always new
news from all over the world in Antwerp.'[21]

'New' news could be much the same thing as rumour. Stephen
Vaughan complained to Thomas Cromwell that in Antwerp, 'Here
founde I a worlde of rumours the Burse and her pullettes [chicks]
brethe out.' Cromwell had complained that English merchants 'bruit
many things' but Vaughan could tell him that 'the Flemish bruit
beyond measure.'[22] Rumours circled and circled until nobody could
be sure where or why they began or how much they were worth.
Cosimo de' Medici told his man in Brussels not to worry about Antwerp stories of his bad health: they couldn't do much damage and in
any case 'we reckon it not just difficult but downright impossible you
could ever find the source.'[23]

This mattered because stories from Antwerp had a certain authority. During the Hapsburg campaigns against Lutherans in Germany,
the great Heinrich Bullinger in Zurich, successor to the preacher
Zwingli, was kept informed from Basel by Oswald Myconius. 'Someone from Antwerp was here. He told of four ships coming to Antwerp
laden with gold and silver to use against Germany,' Myconius wrote
in March 1547. He added that he had his doubts about whether the
French and English would let the ships through, but still he told the
story. He thought it would be taken so seriously that he felt obliged to
retract it three days later. 'I didn't write properly about the four ships.
Ships did come to Spain from some part or other of India, and from
Spain the gold and silver were brought little by little to Antwerp by
various merchants.' An Antwerp story had to be crushed or it would
live on and on.[24]

The Fuggers, extraordinarily rich merchants and miners from
southern Germany, had their own system of handwritten newsletters,
one or two a week, which went far beyond the strictly financial to
anything at all that might change the fortunes of merchants and
moneymen. They were written by professional hacks and Antwerp was
one of the most common datelines, along with Venice and Cologne
for trade, and Rome for God and His politics. In some years Antwerp

accounts for a third of the newsletters that survive, although that is in part because the Dutch Revolt was affecting the Fuggers' rich trade in the Netherlands and later, when Antwerp was back in Spanish hands after 1585, because they needed to know what the Spanish were planning. But we can't miss the point: the Antwerp letters don't just report what was happening in town, they collect anything known or rumoured there.[25]

Even when Antwerp was firmly back in Spanish hands after 1585, the city was still the Exchange for information. The English commander Lord Wyllughby wrote home in 1587 in a quick, wondering postscript to an official letter: 'The particularities of your secrets be more particularly published at Antwerp than (I think) the most of yourselves know them there . . .'[26]

The trick was to find good information when you needed it. Threats helped. A couple of Englishmen were sent to Antwerp in 1518 to buy provisions and ran into the 'King of heralds with the King of Denmark' and two Scottish knights. As soon as the Scots reached their lodgings for the night, they changed into grander clothes – cloth of gold, velvet lined with the fur of martens, green robes of silk and goat hair – and went to the Antwerp burgomaster to borrow money. This did not work. The Englishmen reckoned the Scots must have secrets, and they needed to grab the letters the Danish herald was carrying, so they sent one John Russell to snatch the herald on the road. His servant bolted into the woods with all the letters. It took what the Englishmen call 'kind treatment' to get the herald to tell all, how the Danes were trying to get the French to attack Sweden, how the French might be about to attack England. 'Think it would be wise to keep a watch upon Denmark . . .'[27]

There might be no need to play highwayman if you could borrow papers to make copies. The Pope sent letters to the Portuguese factor in Antwerp and 'a Christian brother of mine', Richard Herman told Cromwell, 'got a sight of them and copied them with expedition, desiring me to send them with the greatest secrecy. As I can skill of no Latin, I could not assist in the writing.' The source was 'a page that waits on the factor'.[28] Or it might pay to intercept letters that suspects 'gave to an innocent person of Canterbury to be delivered in

England', so as to know more about friars writing books against Henry VIII's next marriage.[29] Or it might be wise to keep in touch with 'the daughter of one John Silvester' who spoke to the right people 'at the sign of the Ship in the Fishmarket' and remembered who talked to whom and who had been where.

Sometimes the information came directly from seeing who bought what. Richard Wingfield told Wolsey in London that 'there are many Scotch merchants at the mart at Antwerp who have bought a number of harnesses' (which means armour).[30] Needing armour in quantity suggested war plans, and it was intelligence to put alongside any useful talk.

Talk could sometimes be trickier than usual. When the usual diplomacy stopped working the English feared the Emperor was about to make war on them in 1541. 'To verify this, Vaughan is going to Antwerp; for here no gentlemen of the Court, from whom they might learn more, have come to dine, sup or talk with them.' On the social circuit in Antwerp he picked up talk about ships arrested close to Barcelona and Cadiz, talk from Dutch and Italian and Sicilian and Spanish merchants, and put together his own narrative.[31]

Both sides used the city. In 1545 the Emperor's man at the court of Henry VIII in England told the Emperor's regent back in the Netherlands that he couldn't explain English warnings to merchants which sounded like preparations for war because he couldn't verify what his two sources in London told him. He was sure the Governor of the Hapsburg Netherlands could 'discover the truth in Antwerp or elsewhere'.[32]

Some news you could simply buy. The clerk of the van den Molens, agents and dealers, ended all his letters to clients with a note about the price of goods and money on the Beurs. At least, he did until August 1540. After that, he promised '*listini di pretio di mercati*', lists of the prices of goods, but he could enclose them with his letter and they were '*in stampa*', which means they were in print. He could buy a 'current', something like a news sheet on Twaalfmaandenstraat on his way into the Beurs, and read the commodity prices in one, the exchange rates in another. That saved him the long circuit of the trading floor.

There may have been sheets like this in Venice but Antwerp had the first that anyone mentioned. They were truly ephemeral, worth nothing after a few days, so they were not kept and filed away; a mention in a letter is all we have, along with guesses about how they could have worked based on what happened elsewhere later. Most likely they would have been organized, and later checked, by senior brokers from the market as in Amsterdam. They were lists of figures, not the newspapers which would soon appear and tell stories, nor like the pamphlets about battles and victories that were supposed to keep the Netherlands loyal to the Spanish. There was a long, long way to go to the familiar kind of market reports in true financial newspapers.

But for printed news to appear at all there had to be a market for information big enough to make it pay. The 'currents' were already a revolution of sorts: information on sale for just a few coins at a bookseller or a stationer.[33]

Any working market is information if you learn how to read it closely, and reading is the trader's skill: sensing what people want, what they'll pay, what deals are going down out of sight; being able to calculate the difference between this market and all the others. Just walking the streets of Antwerp you could see all that, if you were willing to watch and think.

See someone going to the market in the aisle of the Dominican convent church: they're buying gold, silver, jewels. Doing well or wanting to look that way. On the pavement of Wolstraat and Hofstraat – before the English were given their own fine trading mansion – someone is in the market for English wool. Courtyards along Hoogstraat for cloth, or else the halls along Maalderijstraat. The open square at Vrijdagmarkt suited some German merchants because it was close to the city scales for weighing iron and copper; later, the old clothes dealers took it over with their business in hiring out anything smart. The stalls around the Church of Our Lady used to be busy only during the weeks of the two annual fairs but now – the 1540s – they were in use all year round and the church was doing well from permanent leases.[34]

The Portuguese and the Hansa and the English had their palaces, which worked like merchant clubs and warehouses. There were offices for South German merchants in the mansions of the much greater merchant families, the Welsers, the Fuggers, the Hochstetters. Living and selling used the same kind of site. The old Beurs, close to the Grote Markt, allowed traders to meet in the open courtyard of a private house, but also to come and go from four different streets. The more it was decorated and improved, the more it looked like the kind of townhouse merchants were building. It had a courtyard, porticos all around, tall rooms and stalls on the floors above and the high, narrow tower which suggested that you needed somewhere to watch all your ships coming and going on the river.

Bartholomeus Bertels bought himself a house on Ijzerenbrug with four warehouses already on the same land, but most merchants' homes simply had cellars and storage rooms.[35] You could store your goods, show your goods, see your customers and work out deals. The surviving notaries' records are snapshots of the process, so we know that Christoffel Hochstetter was down in the cellar on Hochstetter-straat in 1544 looking at dyestuff that Jan Balbani had for sale. Notaries often recorded the name of the private house where a deal had been struck. Locals sometimes wrote contracts in the inns, which made them a little careless. Anyone passing through town would go to an inn and use it as office, home and showroom, as well as the easiest place to organize transport for anything you might buy. It helped if the inn was run by people from your own country. Heinrich Rantzau from northern Germany came to Antwerp to risk his money on the Beurs, and he stayed at the Rooden Leeuw on Camerstraat because it was owned by a Frankfurt merchant family.[36]

Deals always meant criss-crossing the city, talking credit or paying court to money, checking samples and bidding: house to inn to house and sometimes to the grander houses outside the city walls for discussions that were more urgent or more discreet. Watch the streets and you could begin to deduce who was dealing with whom. Stephen Vaughan took delivery of new loans in cash at his lodgings so that for once there should be something the all-knowing loan-broker and tax-farmer Gaspar Ducci did not know.[37] But Ducci had his ways. He found it worthwhile to keep some twenty thugs from Italy on the streets who went about in groups of three, four or six, armed with sticks, waiting on street corners or down alleys day and night.[38] They did violence, but they also watched.

*

ANTWERP

Antwerp was business, the city kept telling itself, and business was movement. Kill that life and that energy, and the city was nothing once again. The streets and squares and public spaces could never be allowed to go out of control, but it was also a port where disorder was always possible.

Local incidents were liable to have repercussions on the seas or in foreign ports. English sailors were trapped on their ships in 1546 after 'mariners and other raskall' half-killed a couple of them in town, stoned them back to the docks and then followed them on board, 'a thousand persons gaping and looking upon them'. The English fired off arrows into the crowd, and three or four, so Vaughan told London, were 'prettily hurt'.[39] Vaughan complained to the Margrave, warned him there might be retaliation in England, but he got back only polite noises.

The rules to make the streets safe were constantly expanded. In 1534, nobody could walk out without a light or with arms after curfew had rung; in 1542, foreign guests had to be told there was no going outside at all after nine in the evening; in 1552 there had been so many muggings, so many thefts of clothing, even killings, that the rules became even more specific: no gun, sword, rapier or cutlass for anyone in the streets – merchant, burgher, resident, servant or craftsman. Any honest man would want to see and be seen, so in 1566 the law ordered bread and water in jail for anyone out after the evening bell without a light.

Knowledge passed through Antwerp just as goods did. There was philosophy both practical and theoretical coming off the city's presses, and the language of angels was discussed in manuscripts being very discreetly traded. Maps of a widening world were for sale, science and medical theory and how to defend a city, the history of Rome and the detail of God. The city printed great Italian poems for the Spanish market, and Bibles – in English for heretics, in Hebrew for North Africa and later in five different languages in one polyglot volume for scholars.

Not all this knowledge was in books or even in writing. Albrecht Dürer famously came to Antwerp in 1520 chasing the Emperor to make sure of his imperial pension, and to do a little business and pick

60

up the dyes that were easier to find there, especially 'the red colour that is found at Antwerp in the new bricks'. In his two years away from Nuremberg he did rather more than that. He saw Aztec gold for the first time and 'all the days of my life I have seen nothing that rejoiced my heart so much as these things, for I saw amongst them wonderful works of art and I wondered at the subtle Ingenia of men in foreign lands.' He celebrated 'the new land of gold' not for its obvious riches but for its artfulness. He used Antwerp, and his merchant contacts, to buy objects that intrigued him. The Augsburg merchant Hochstetter was buying Indians, but Dürer was less ambitious. He bought coral, the shells of a tortoise and of snails, a magnetic lodestone, elk's hooves, a musk ball from Central Asia, and the Portuguese gave him feathers from Calicut. He had three parrots in two years, which seems careless, and his own baboon.

From Quentin Matsys, or to be exact from his mansion in Antwerp, he took back home the idea of showing his treasures in a kind of museum.[40] He also looked at the city's defences. When he was drafting his 1527 book on military architecture he thought about the roof of the circular fortress he was planning, and he wrote that the way to hold the tiles together was a hard mortar 'as I have seen so well in Antwerp'. When the book appeared, he left out Antwerp as though the mortar was his own idea.[41]

There was a subtler market than this. The magus John Dee, already courtier, geographer and spy, was drawn to stranger subjects: the occult and the ways of angels.[42] He gave up Christmas in 1562, and sailed to the Netherlands with twenty pounds from his patron Sir William Cecil. He wanted to find a printer for his own books but more importantly he meant to look for esoteric texts and men who understood them. He told Cecil 'our universities, both, in them have men in sundry knowledges right excellent', but none of them skilled in the sciences that explain the universe, the secrets of Kabbalah and the measure of the divine.

He'd been in the university town of Leuven and bought Hebrew grammars and books on astrology and the meaning of numbers. He went briefly to Zurich, to Venice, Paris, Urbino, but it was in Antwerp that 'since my coming ... by diligent search and travail (for so short a time) such men and books are come to my knowledge ... as to the former great sciences I hoped never to have so good aid.' He told Cecil this because it had cost him all the money he had and 'all that ever I could here with honesty borrow'.[43]

The book he most valued, at a thousand crowns, was the *Steganographia* of Johannes Trithemius: a text on 'hidden writing', codes and spells, and a work that stayed in manuscript a full century before it was put into print and then banned immediately by every kind of authority. It had an evil reputation even though its hierarchy of angels may be no more than a coded example of how to make a secret code. The author was an abbot, adviser to the Emperor Maximilian and a mystic in pursuit of union with God through study, knowledge, love, virtue and dignity. The same path led him to practical magic. Trithemius insisted he talked to angels, but rumour said he had devils in his service, and raised ancient heroes from their graves for the Emperor to meet. He dealt in a kind of knowledge that knew no limits: as he wrote, 'there is an chaos of infinite height in this science which no man can perfectly understand.'[44]

Dee copied out half the *Steganographia* in ten days and persuaded a Hungarian nobleman, perhaps Sambucus, to copy the rest in return for some tutorials; it was a covert, co-operative kind of publishing.[45] It was also forbidden, and it fascinated Dee, this notion of a new world of learning and new ways of knowing, not to mention talking with angels. Dee told Cecil he had learned 'manifold mo[re] sorts of wonderful science'. He drew on Trithemius' idea of alchemy as a kind of magic, and number as the key to both magic and alchemy. He turned it into hieroglyphic writing that he said God had given to him. He drew one hieroglyph and he began a book about it, the *Monas Hieroglyphica*, by explaining it 'mathematically, magically, cabalistically and anagogically' in theorems just like Euclid.

He didn't want to go home, not with a book ready to write after seven years of thinking and not while he ran the risk he would 'disdain and neglect' his chance to serve God and his country with his new knowledge. He claimed he wrote the book in Antwerp between 13 and 30 January 1564, a few rushed weeks, which is curious because there are notes on another alchemical collection which suggest he was still in Padua in January; but he wanted it known that the book came from Antwerp, the emporium for ideas as well as goods. He had used

Antwerp's particular mix of curiosity, business and dodgy freedoms to find things out and to be sure of being heard, even if nobody quite understood what he was saying.

His publisher was the printer Willem Silvius at the Golden Angel house on the Cammerport bridge, on the street that printers had just taken over from the breweries.[46] Silvius was a rackety individual who managed to get himself named the King's printer on the strength of books he paid to have printed for Charles V of Spain by Christophe Plantin. He wanted status, title and respectability so much he was ready to cheat for it even when he was bound to be found out. He may have thought the title a necessity since he was also a risk-taker; in the same year he managed the suspect oddity of Dee's book, he also produced a volume of psalms for devout Protestants which quickly went on the Index of Forbidden Books.[47] John Dee needed a dealer ready to handle goods that might be banned.

THE PROFIT IN PLAGUE

Antwerp was much like other great trading cities at the time, and like London and Amsterdam in the next century. It was a graveyard with immigrants. The death rate from plague was so high that the city's population would have shrunk without the two thousand or so new-comers who arrived each year between 1526 and 1542.[48]

But Antwerp was also an exception: they knew how to make a business out of this. They published books about plague to trade in one more kind of information, using their specialty even in the middle of pandemics. The printers put out little books in Dutch, the *pest-boekjes*, so people would know what the doctors said about the sickness, and heavyweight books in Latin so the doctors would know what to say about the sickness; and since these books mostly copied one from another, the doctors always seemed very sure.[49] They blamed the corruption of the air, and also the wrath of God, the comets and the stars. Given the sheer press of people in too few rooms, the tight, filthy streets that made such a convenient dormitory for rats, and the traffic coming in and out of the city from everywhere, both the epidemics and the endemic plague after 1574 seem perfectly predictable.

Even so, the doctors of Ghent asked Antwerp for advice in 1529 after an outbreak of the English sweats. In 1571 Jacobus Godefridus Hackendover produced a authoritative and scientific work on how to deal with plague which did not quite explain what had gone wrong when he dealt with the epidemic of 1571.

Doctors usually advised the impossible: a quiet life. Gérard van Bergen's *De pestis praeservatione libellus* of 1565 was typical: no overeating, no overdrinking, no sex at all, because it opens the passageways of the body, talk quietly to good friends, play musical instruments, clean your teeth well and shut yourself up securely to sleep at night. He tried to correct the corrupt air with rose water in summer, and otherwise with oak and juniper burned indoors. He told citizens to talk to the sick as little as possible or at least take an antidote beforehand, and if a man had to leave the house to work he should carry with him the root of white turmeric and some angelica.

The city had a simpler strategy: stop the plague moving by keeping sick people in their place. An ordinance of 1513 cramped social life by forbidding meals for more than ten people, said nobody with a death in the house could be seen out in public or go to church, and if they had to be outdoors, they must wear a white sash. The plague houses were marked out with a bale of straw by the door. A few years later three churches were set aside for people from plague houses so they didn't need to pray with healthy people. The infected dead could still be buried but outside the usual hours of church services.

Only one person from each sick house could go to market to buy provisions, and she or he had to go at the least busy hours (8 August 1534). Later, outsiders could be named to buy provisions for the sick houses, and people from the sick houses could at least tell their neighbours when they needed new supplies (3 August 1571). This is remarkable; there was nothing comfortable about living alongside plague, but the sickness did not shut down a sense of community, even among an ever-changing population. It was needed, since the poorer sick had nowhere to go. The old plague houses were far too small and the one at St Elizabeth's Hospital overflowed onto the ordinary wards, sometimes with two or three patients to each bed, in filthy conditions, with no medical help and a farting diet of rough beans and peas. Patients 'who had been in the hospital once would rather die than return there', a magistrate reported.[50]

Keeping safe depended on a mix of faith and sense. Everyone was told officially that it was important to make confession and be in a state of grace at all times, important that the city staged weekly processions of the divine sacrament to ask for God's mercy, but there were more prosaic rules: it was also important to have one ground-floor room where a priest could bring the sacraments without coming into contact with the whole infected house. As the plague settled in the city, the rules became stricter. Nobody could accept goods from an infected house for safe-keeping. Children could not go to school in times of sickness. The new rules were needed 'since,' as the order of September 1578 acknowledged, 'the previous ordinances are not well observed'.

The city couldn't begin to obey. Without social contact, movement from office to office and daily to the Beurs, bankers and merchants could not function. Without movement through the streets no goods could be landed, sold and bought or finally sent out to their customers. The city had to eat, even if the magistrates tried to ban produce, cherries and plums in particular, from any town or village where plague was reported. When the sickness was just outside the southern walls at Berchem there were guards on all the gates to stop people coming back from nursing the sick; but people still had to work in the city and still had to care for their families.

Nobody could stop the tides of people arriving and leaving, not in a place which was an emporium, so the city tried to control just the more dangerous travellers. When plague broke out in Cologne in 1553 there was a flurry of new rules. On 27 July innkeepers had to report anyone who had come from Cologne in the past fifteen days. Ten days or so later, since that ordinance 'is not being very well observed', nobody from Cologne could stay at all. On 14 August, the stricter rule was published all over again, and more than a month later some people from Cologne, and some from Coblenz and Frankfurt, were found working at the Beurs and told they had three days to get out. Anyone who had been to the Frankfurt Fair was obliged to spend eight days in quarantine at least a mile outside the Antwerp walls.

A new market opened for official, written certificates of not being deadly. From around 1571, dozens were issued to say that: 'in this house nobody has been sick of the plague'. Every kind of tradesperson from sugar dealers to saddlers, barbers, book dealers, apothecaries, sailmakers, dealers in silk and dealers in dried fish wanted written proof that they were safe. One dealer wanted a written proof that the canvas he sold was free of plague.

The city kept publishing orders, and republishing them, in the hope they might be obeyed the next time. They thought of telling the sluice masters to use the tides to clean the canals. They finally decided to try to find a place to store night soil, somewhere in the new northern streets of the Nieuwstad. And they went on banning pigs from the city: in 1578, again in 1580, again in 1584. They couldn't shut the city to save it, they couldn't change its packed, stifling nature even when the Calvinists had control and were opening up the closed lands of convents and monasteries. They had to live close to death or not live at all.

4

The Garden of Knowing

All around Antwerp, marsh and forest and polder had long ago been drained, cleared, considered and planted. In their place, foreigners noticed the fruit trees in particular, but also the ornamental bushes, the medicinal herbs, the unfamiliar flowers.

They saw country houses surrounded by grounds with avenues and lakes, space for playing games, for raising vegetables and also for contemplation. If they looked closer, there were 'more kinds and varieties of plants' than in Greece, Spain, Germany, England, France, Italy: 'countless rare and singular plants bought at huge expense from Constantinople, from . . . regions of Asia and of Africa, and recently from the New World', as the doctor and botanist Matthias de Lobel wrote. Van Gorp, assembling a history that the city could celebrate, told the Antwerp council what they already knew. Gardens were not just the pharmacists' stock-in-trade, they were for everyone. 'No expense is spared to satisfy this taste and with no purpose except delight in gazing at the plants.'[1]

The gardeners of Brabant and Flanders were much respected for their knowledge of plants and how to make them thrive. Isabella of Austria was raised in the Netherlands, a more or less local princess, and when she married King Christian II of Denmark, Norway and later Sweden in 1515 she took the idea of vegetables north, along with gardeners to raise them. The botanical gardens at Florence needed a director and appointed Casabona, who in the north had been known by the good Flemish name of Goedenhuyze. In the 1560s Philip II of Spain made his spectacular court gardens by importing men, seed and tools wholesale from the Netherlands. In 1583 Montanus, one of Philip's royal chaplains in Madrid who knew Antwerp well, was writing to the printer and publisher Christophe Plantin asking for quantities of bulbs, seeds and roots of rare plants, even though in Spain he was close to those famous gardens.[2]

The parks and gardens of Antwerp showed taste, which required a place with spare money, with traders' fortunes and traders' hopes of showing status by spending. They depended on constant access to the new and strange, which in Antwerp only meant walking down to the docks. The landscape, like the city, was built on finding things out.

The alchemist Paracelsus came to Antwerp in 1519, full of cures and mystical notions. He could buy unfamiliar and necessary things, herbs and stones and minerals that came through Antwerp in the ordinary process of trade but could be picked over and interpreted and used by anyone to practise alchemy and produce medicines (not that Paracelsus made a distinction; he thought 'the task of alchemy is not to make gold but to make medicines'.) He reckoned he learned 'more at the marketplace than in any German or foreign schools'.[3]

The Portuguese doctor known as Amato Lusitano trained in Salamanca and made his way to Antwerp in 1534, following orders from his merchant uncle Henrique Pires. He wanted to make money doing business but he also wanted to study Dioscorides, the Greek doctor to the Roman army whose *Materia Medica* had for almost a millennium and a half been the official sum total of what the world knew about herbs and medicines. Within weeks of landing he was in jail, accused of being a New Christian or a crypto-Jew, but he claimed the cover of safe conduct granted to his uncle; the city took business seriously. A year after that he was treating the Portuguese consul and a mayor of Antwerp among many others. A year after that he published his *Index Dioscoridis* in Antwerp. The city protected him, just enough.[4]

The Portuguese had noticed the uses of smilax, the shiny vine from China whose knobbly root is an anti-inflammatory like modern aspirin. The word from the east was that a smilax tea would cure the new problem arriving from the west: strains of syphilis. Supplies, according to the great anatomist Vesalius in his 1546 letter on the China root, were 'imported by the people who bring in pepper, cloves, ginger and our cinnamon: Portuguese and people sailing under the patronage of our Emperor'. It came by way of Antwerp and 'it is for sale everywhere among the people of Antwerp.' Much more importantly, the city knew how to use the convenient root; for a start you had to give up pork, beef, green fruit and fish until you were healthy again. 'The first patient to whom I saw a decoction of the China administered,' Vesalius writes, 'had it sent from Antwerp together with an empiric [a practical doctor] who said he knew its use well'.[5] Without the theory, all the dried things, the bulbs and plants and seeds, were no more than curiosities.

The unfamiliar came from everywhere. When Charles V laid siege to Tunis in 1535 he brought back the tagetes, the African marigold, with its orange balls of flower and its sharp, musky smell. The great Clusius, Charles de l'Écluse, when writing botanical catalogues, could find in Antwerp fresh cashews, white turmeric with its bitter after-taste, soursop fruits and the dried form of marsh saxifrage with its tiny yellow flower; a range of plants from cold North America to Asia to the Caribbean. He studied the shelves of apothecaries' shops and wrote in 1565 a little book about their syrups and liquors which led him to the plants that yielded them.[6]

Gardens were libraries of roots and bulbs and branches. Peeter van Coudenberghe made an extraordinary garden in Borgerhout just outside Antwerp's walls, by a stream called Vuilbeke: a botanical garden in private hands when only a handful of cities and universities and bishops had such a thing. His collection was vast, more than 400 different species when he first laid it out in 1548 and 600 only ten years later. Matthias de Lobel saluted 'the richest of gardens, full of exotic species'.[7] Rembert Dodoens, who wrote his own herbal catalogue, and Clusiuis, who published a list of Dodoens' plants, both depended on Coudenberghe for actual specimens to show. London scholars and Swiss doctors came visiting. The garden was famous even outside the network of collectors and gardeners who sent bulbs, seeds, cuttings and plants back and forth across Europe. The merchant Guicciardini put this 'noble garden' among the glories of Antwerp.[8]

Coudenberghe grew tomatoes, cotton, aubergines, gladioli, artichokes and morning glory, all exotics still, and tobacco as well, although sometimes the names arrived after the plants. He told Conrad Gessner in Zurich that he had two varieties of *Hyosycamus*, white and yellow henbanes, or so he thought. They had seed pods which reminded some of a phallus and others of red cabbage. He had to be told that what he was growing was *Nicotiana rustica*, the wild tobacco with its fierce dose of nicotine.[9]

By trade Coudenberghe was an apothecary, on the Klapdorp at the sign of the bell, but the medicinal herbs he grew were not only a matter of business. He was much more a scholar and humanist, originally a grandee from Brussels connected to all the other aristocratic collectors who were beginning to make galleries of wonders and gardens of rare plants. He sent Conrad Gessner a peony in flower while Gessner was writing his *De Hortis Germaniae*, a gift rather eclipsed by Gessner's first illustration of a tulip from Turkey. Coudenberghe was sent the black roots of Spanish salsify; the dragon's blood tree from the Canaries which reached him by way of a monastery garden in Lisbon; the century plant from Mexico which was sent at the same time to his fellow collector Charles de Saint-Omer, but only Coudenberghe's survived. He had devised a 'temperate or Flemish' frame much like our cold frame, and he knew the practical trick of putting delicate plants in pots in the basement so they could live through the winter.[10]

Out of all this, he made the manual for medicine which stayed constantly in print for the next hundred years: his *Dispensatorium*. Plantin wanted a new edition of the pharmacopoeia that the German scholar Valerius Cordus had published in 1536, along with notes on his lectures on Dioscorides. Anyone who approved of authority would have to approve a standard text resting on an older standard text which was dressed with famous names. He asked his friend Coudenberghe to make the revision.

Coudenberghe had his garden for reference, especially for plants newly arrived from the New World or from Asia. He could meet people with foreign, even esoteric information on the street. He had his knowledge as a drug-maker, his experience from the apothecary business, and he knew the Greek and Latin sources for his science and something of the Persian and Arab literature as well. He also felt free to question and correct, breaking from authority. He cut chunks of Cordus and added material; he used what he knew of the history of pharmacy, and what he handed to Plantin was close to a new work. To it, we owe such recipes as how many scorpions it takes to make oil of scorpions (twenty to thirty according to size). The subtitle proclaims the book '*infinitis erroribus liberata [et] vindicata*', 'freed and released from countless errors'.[11]

For a hundred years it was the definitive text, reprinted fourteen times with editions in Leiden and Rotterdam and Paris. It was obviously needed, because the first Antwerp print run of 1,200 sold out briskly, doctors hurrying to catch up with everything new from a wider and wider world. Coudenberghe might have managed this in some other city but it would have been much harder without access to all the living and dried specimens, and the connection with doctors and collectors. It would also have been much less known; his book went everywhere that Plantin's system of sending and selling books worked, through the Frankfurt Fair, to the booksellers around Europe who bought and traded his books. The machine of the Antwerp book trade made the learning and cures in the *Dispensatorium* not just remarkable, but also truly useful.

5

The Lesson

Antwerp made a business of teaching. The scale is astonishing: one out of every 200 men in work was a teacher, compared with one in 4,000 in a city like Lyons which was also rich and grand and busy.[1]

There were parish schools in all five parishes which more or less ignored number and science and were known very exactly as Latin schools: they taught Roman classics, the Church Fathers and some theology. They also taught chants, because four of them were founded 'so that the churches might be better adorned with the singing of choirs'.[2]

Many more schools were private, run by 'free teachers' but regulated strictly by the teachers' Guild of St Ambrose. No school could open without the Guild's licence. No school could change address without telling the Guild and hanging out a sign. 'Inappropriate books' earned a fine. Schools could be punished for having both sexes in the same classroom. Some private schools did teach the sons of merchants, took them aged between five and seven and sent them off at ages between ten and twelve to work and to travel abroad, but practical maths and languages were taught in the warehouse, the office, the ship and on the dock. There were other schools for the daughters, who would one day be the women whose power and penchant for kissing were sometimes so shocking to foreign newcomers.

Peeter Heyns took in fifty girls at a time, mostly fourteen or fifteen years old, in the house called De Lauwerboom or the Bay Tree on Augustijnenstraat. He was a poet and a playwright for one of the literary and dramatic societies, the Chambers of Rhetoric: *De Bloeyende Wijngaerd*. He liked to teach through plays and performance, not least because he had fifty paying actors waiting in the schoolroom. He promised the girls fluency, self-confidence and flair and he knew their performances would make sure his school was noticed. The business of schooling was competitive, after all.

His texts were moral, almost political, always high-minded. The 'joyous tragedy' of Judith and Holofernes could be a manual for loyal women dealing with newcomer Spanish commanders by cutting off their heads. Yet his was a school grand enough for the daughters of senior civil servants from all the richest provinces of the Spanish Netherlands, along with the daughters of all kinds of merchants. The girls might grow to be the women who took over businesses from their late husbands, or started firms in their own right, or set up as art dealers or painters. They might marry well and still have lives. But Heyns' kind of education was a control on all that: a mixture of moral purpose, basic knitting, how to play the harpsichord without excitement, how to speak in French and how to write an elegant hand, along with just enough arithmetic to buy and sell on a decent, domestic scale. He taught counting with *jetons* – counters or pennies. He taught how to keep household accounts in both Latin and Arab numerals. He taught sums, not mathematics. He taught nothing beyond the rule of three, which is handy for working out the cost of eight yards of cloth when you know the price of six, and is easy to learn by heart. It hardly sounds like the training of clever, independent women, but then schools for upper-class girls often don't.

The law made a woman's way in the world seem peculiarly difficult. In theory Antwerp's women were legally incapable and needed a male guardian to do anything. Even a single working woman, living alone, needed to find a man to make a legal agreement. A woman could not hold city office. A woman could not be anyone's legal representative, although she could defend herself and argue her children's rights. Very occasionally there were exceptions, as when Margriete Meyererts managed to defend a lawsuit about land against Magdalena van Wesenpuele – a widow taking on a single woman – but usually women were meant to know their place not choose it.

But they could choose if they married. Husband and wife were 'of one mind as they were of one body', as the clerk Jan van Boendale wrote. If the husband was away from his business, maybe travelling for trade or doing his civic duty, the wife could simply stand in and make all the decisions. Ruth Beyerlinck was married to an adviser to the city council and while he was away on official business she signed contracts, collected interest, rented and sold houses; actions all vital to the family fortunes.[3] A wife could also be a *koopvrouw*, a female trader in her own right with no need to answer to a husband, if the husband did not object to her being in business. As long as she didn't share a trade with her husband, or work out of a corner of his shop or warehouse, she could work independently. When it came to common property in a marriage, city houses were defined as 'movable property' so they went into the common fund. If the husband died first the wife got half. All through the century, household wealth was redefined, first to make sure the wife would have first call on her own best dress, then by 1608 to allow her some 300 physical objects to which the other heirs had no right at all. Sons and daughters had equal shares in the rest. All that meant women had the money to buy time to decide what they wanted to do, and a fair degree of liberty to do it.

As parents they shared responsibility, and if a widow remarried she kept her property and her children. The same went for her apprentices. Bernaert Tymbach was a trader who decided with his wife Margriete Kareets to take on an apprentice jointly, and after Tymbach's death Margriete went on organizing the boy's education. The law might growl a patriarchal message – men rule, women follow – but life and trade required co-operation.[4]

Heyns made a hard living. Usually he was paid, but quite often he took sugar, soap, beer, wine or vinegar from the parents' stock-in-trade. The printer Willem Silvius, not a famously scrupulous man, paid in books for the schooling of two daughters. Heyns' income was so uncertain that in the Calvinist 1570s he took on other jobs: clerk for the wardens of a district, which increased his income by half; and when Antwerp was under siege he managed the grain rations. Other teachers worked as gaugers, measuring how much wine was really left in barrels, which mattered because Antwerp was the turntable of the wine trade, moving Mediterranean wines to the Baltic, selling Rhine wines and French wines in the Low Countries. Gaugers might be merchants in their own right or accountants or calligraphers, or in the case of Michiel Coignet a maker of fine mathematical instruments.

Circumstances – war or plague or religion – could upset the school

business. Students might simply go home in bad times: Anneke Geer-
aerts went home from Heyns' school on 15 November 1576 'because
of the rioting' and returned only on 14 May 1577.[5] Heyns himself
was suspect as a Calvinist, since he taught French and therefore most
likely heresy, and was a vocal supporter of the Prince of Orange. He
thought it wiser to get out of town in 1568 when the Spanish threatened a 'religious cleansing' of the guilds. He went with a thousand
others to hard times in Cologne and then on to Gdansk. When finally
he could come back to Antwerp in 1571 he opened his school again
only briefly before plague shut it down for four long months.

The schoolbook Heyns bought more than any other was Gabriel
Meurier's *La Guirlande des jeunes filles en françois & flamen*: a
whole set of ready-made conversations in both French and Flemish,
for the instruction of young ladies.[6] Meurier added a brisk four lines
dedicated to the Bay Tree College of Nymphs ('*Nymphes gayes en
abry du Laurier / Mille saluts vous envoye le Meurier* . . .'; 'Brilliant
girls in the shade of the Bay Tree, Meurier sends you a thousand greet-
ings . . .') and another to Peeter Heyns, who offers to help the nymphs
as they learn French. After that there's Meurier's own version of the
Ten Commandments, rather longer than God's.

As a teacher, Meurier had some idea of what students knew, what
they felt and what they feared, so it's tempting to think he based his
dialogues on reality. Here are the girls in their bedrooms looking for
rats, mice and bedbugs that bite. They have a kitten that drags combs
and bracelets around the floor. They debate who should do the clean-
ing and nobody does. They need water, they go to the well, but they
get the servant to help; they have never lived without servants. They
meet a girl with no Mama, no Papa, just a penniless uncle who lives
on 'bread, wine and the grace of God'; but then they hear her uncle's
name and decide with relief that he's at least from a good family.

They know what school is for: they're enrolled because of the talk
about the matron, her very good name, and the fact that 'She teaches
us to fear God, to honour our parents and our teachers. Then to read
and write.' The schools are obsessed with order, the social order all
around but also everything from the hour-by-hour timetable to rules
for dress and talk. A girl must take off her hat 'or is it stuck to your

head?' Girls have to speak clearly 'because you're just biting and grinding your words'. When writing, they need the sand that blots the words so all the good moral lessons do not get dirtied or rubbed out and they need to sharpen their quill points if the ink doesn't flow properly. They then discuss, for the sake of vocabulary, whether the feathers are from a goose, a swan, even possibly a heron.

They tell each other: 'A child of two could do better.'

The food is unreliable, or perhaps that is Meurier's joke at Heyns' expense. The girls take their hot soup and they find it thin and tasteless: 'it just tastes of smoke and the chimney.' They are also nervous of the discipline. One girl says, 'a good caning does no harm to anyone', to which her friend answers, very reasonably, 'Then you take my punishment for me . . .'[7]

Claude Luython made the same kind of book for boys, but it's clear their punishments were rather more serious. A father asks the teacher to get hold of good sticks, and his idea of mercy is to ask him to 'be careful about hurting his bones, but go hard on the skin and the flesh.' The boy sensibly arranges to intercept his father's letter to the school begging the teacher to hand out punishment before the father starts to hate his own son. He changes the most important details, so his father now asks for no punishment at all, especially not to use a stick, and asks the teacher not to hate the boy.[8]

Boys at least knew what school was meant to instil: either good Latin or good business, or both for the scholar merchants of the city. Heyns had to fight about what girls should be taught and whether they should be taught at all, which accounts for the conservative tinge in his teaching. Both issues seem dusty in a place where women had so much ability to act and trade and decide for themselves, but schools are often the places where dead ideas struggle furiously against reality.

Everyone was still supposed to agree that the point of educating women was to keep them chaste. The humanist Juan Luis Vives said so in his book on teaching Christian women; Heyns got Plantin to print the French translation, so the ideas mattered at the Bay Tree school. Vives suggests the best tutor for a girl would be a woman or else a man whose wife is really attractive so he is 'less inclined to conceive a passion for other men's wives'. He also warned girls to be careful what they did in public, especially dancing and playing music because they only heated the body, inflamed desire and made the heart beat faster. He thought learning was good for girls, might even keep them away from lust and lighter pleasures. He quotes Plutarch: 'Never will a woman dedicated to literature distract herself in dancing.'[9]

And yet Heyns did not promote this self-effacing kind of girl, private and discreet. When his last play was printed – *Le Miroir des mesnagères* (*The Mirror for Housewives*) – he dedicated it to one of his ex-students, Abigail Fagel, daughter of the sheriff of Bruges, and wife of a counsellor at the court of Holland and Zeeland. He remembered her performances on stage, how she was 'always playing one of the main characters so simply and cleanly that the memory will stay for ever with the audience who saw her'.

She was not just his star; she became his proof that girls with the best connections really should be schooled. He sets her against 'those who hold it is better to have an idiot than a learnéd woman, who also say schools for girls are not lawful because young women are ruined by them and become shameless and too bold'.[10] He contradicts himself affably, a student of Vives who puts women on a stage, a defender of teaching women who tries not to teach them too much.

Schools did not teach boys much of what they would need in the outside world, either, so the girls' disadvantage is subtler than it might seem. In the real world, women were stallholders or shopkeepers, one in ten of the city's merchants. Anna Janssen was a printer, Jozina van Dale loaned money to entrepreneurs. There were women, not many, in the spice trade and in marine insurance. One woman sold armour. There were at least two female surgeons: Lynken van Gelder and the widow of Jan de Menuwey. The city could hardly work without them.

Women didn't paint, but Catharina van Hemessen, daughter of an Antwerp mannerist painter, did. She had to do unwomanly things, looking at naked men and dissecting corpses to learn anatomy. She managed. She worked at the court of Mary of Hungary, and made it in the end to the Guild of St Luke, an official painter like her father. She painted a gallery of women who might otherwise have been invisible. She painted herself sitting at an easel, the first known signed self-portrait of a working artist, a woman insisting on being seen.

There's a little book of poems from 1529 which says on its title page that it's 'beautiful' and 'unspoiled', that it contains many 'charming' and 'skilful' verses to answer the errors that come from the accursed sect of Lutherans.[11] This is not what makes it remarkable. It was written and first published the year before in the vernacular but then translated into Latin by Eligius Eucharius, who was once house chaplain to Charles V. Even he is not as singular as the fact of any translation at all from rough Netherlandish to academic Latin in 1529.

Even more remarkable is the fact that the author, Anna Bijns, a woman in Antwerp, published under her own name. She couldn't join the rhetorical societies and be part of their very public shows and parades. If she'd competed in the rhetoric exercises her father loved, she'd have been obliged to be anonymous so as not to give away her gender. In print she didn't have to be reticent or self-effacing like a man, although the poem that is her dedication asks readers 'to tell yourselves it's all just women's work'.

She allowed herself strong satire against bossy women and henpecked husbands and marriage as slavery, although she never married. These were themes in the repertoire of the male rhetorical societies, but she was the one with the readership.

Her main campaign was against Luther and all his works, against Protestants who disputed Church authority and wanted to read the Bible and think about it for themselves. 'Scripture these days,' she complained, 'is read in the ale-house, with Gospel in one hand, in the other a Pint.' She was especially tart about women who dared to think they could teach scholars. These orthodox opinions won her not just her translation, but also the support of the local Franciscan friars, who agreed with her anger at the city's excessive tolerance. She was also, creditably, judgemental about monks if they didn't take their vocation seriously.

There was less reward for this independent brilliance than you might expect. Anna Bijns ran a primary school with her brother for a while and then founded a school of her own where she taught simple catechism, reading, writing and arithmetic. Her poems were known around Europe in their Latin versions and went through five editions in her lifetime. In 1575, in her eighties, she went to a pauper's grave.

*

Antwerp women were famous for speaking six languages or more, even if they had never left Brabant. Language became another of the city's trades.

Printers already turned out books for business, keeping it international: books of exchange with woodcuts of coins in circulation and their relative values, books full of useful arithmetic, and later books that explained in tables the mysteries of compound interest. They produced business-like language books, a whole parade of them. There were dictionaries for six or even eight languages, like the one that Cornelius Valerius wrote in 1579 for anyone wanting to learn German, English, Latin, French, Spanish or Italian. It was a guide to what merchants needed when they were working the docks or the exchange, which assumed the same men might have learned letters to read.[12]

Joachim Trognaesius sold Jesuit texts in Antwerp and a line of minor pornography with pictures. He also put out a dictionary and phrase book of seven languages in 1586. It says you need seven languages to do business: Flemish, English, German, Latin, French, Spanish and Italian. The English section asks: 'how many are ther becom ryche, without the knowledge of divres languages?'

His book was much more than a word list; it tried to help with buying, selling, and above all with demanding or avoiding payment of debts. It was helpful to a single man passing a woman in the street: how to find out her name, how to answer the even more important questions about her prospects: 'She hath a good dowrie' is translated into seven languages. It also helped the traveller, maybe the travelling salesman, when he's staying at an inn. He learns how to say he doesn't feel well, wants a warm towel round his head and his bed curtains pinned shut, and a serving girl follows to light him to bed. The stratagem does not work. His new 'she friend' refuses to snuff out the candle until she's safely out of the room. She says flatly: 'You are not sick seeing that you speak of kissing.'[13]

Books like this may have begun with local needs, understanding the foreigners in town, but in the sixteenth century a large majority of all the new language books printed in Western Europe were published in Antwerp.[14] Claude Luython writes in his 1552 dictionary of French and Flemish that he 'knows no town in low Germany where such care has been taken to teach the young French' (Luython was a French teacher in Antwerp, but you guessed that) because French is used so much in 'the town best known in all Europe for doing business'.[15] How that French sounded is another question; Gabriel Meurier felt the need to add a whole section on pronunciation to his 1562 book on conjugations because 'nobody can deny that languages can be ruined by bad and barbarous pronunciation, and French more than any other.'[16]

The best-seller of all these helpers came out in 1536, written by the schoolmaster Noël de Berlaimont: *Vocabulare van nieus geordineert ende wederom gecorrigeert*, a book of conversations reprinted more than a hundred times in the next century and a half. Like the others, it seems at first an opening into a real social world: table talk over dinner, ten people sharing soup, salad, and then salted meat served with radish, capers, carrots. The menu is a little more varied in Luython's 1552 dictionary: bread white, brown and leavened, biscuits and potage and salad, milk and buttermilk; meat fried, grilled and boiled, from tripe to gigot of lamb, including goat, beef, roast capon and boudin and an item labelled 'fish'. That was true plenty in a carnivorous culture, more meat than bread, and there were pickles and mustard to go with it; in every way the books tend to celebrate how good things are.

So naturally they make language a matter of manners, keeping things smooth. One of the men at de Berlaimont's dinner is asked why he says so little and admits he does not yet know how to speak French well: 'What should I say? Better be quiet than speak badly.' The schoolboys in Luython's book are being taught their place. 'When you pass an older person, or a magistrateè, priest or noble or a learned man, take off your hat at once,' the boys are told. If they're sitting, get up and bend the knee to the new arrival and 'Keep your feet together when talking to him.'[17]

Some of these books were for the docks or the road, and some were quartos so they could be doubled up and carried under a belt, or stuffed into a rucksack. These were made for Spanish soldiers as they made their way across Flanders, wrecking or bringing order according to your point of view. They often seem like early guides to the art of chatting up: 'I am doing well', then 'I give you pleasure', then 'I give

1. The money changer's wife is distracted from her holy book by the pearls and gold he is examining: money takes over the city and then the world.

2. Fire: the night watch has one constant enemy.

3. Plague: the city needs immigrants to replace the dead.

4. The glory of Antwerp in 1540: a river full of ships, the tower of the Church of Our Lady.

5. Pieter Bruegel paints Babel twice: in Brussels as an official monument …

6. … but first in Antwerp as a furiously energetic building site with a tyrant ruler, busy with every kind of machine.

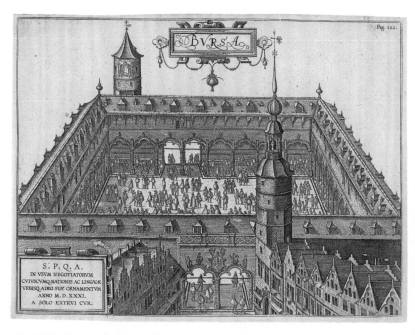

7 & 8. The Beurs or Exchange of Antwerp (*top*): the trading heart of the city where the men wear swords. At the gates (*below*), selling fowl, monkeys, a falcon and bread.

9. On the top floor of the Beurs: the market in art.

10. Joris Verzeleer, who sold gilt to Kings who could not afford gold.

11. Joos van Cleve's assembly line of kissing babies, Christ and John the Baptist.

12. Katharina, African servant to the Portuguese factor: Antwerp had more black faces than any other European city except Lisbon. It also sold the goods to buy slaves.

him a drink'; then 'I thank you' and 'I bring us a drink'. You can see the half hour in a dockside pub. If the half hour had consequences, you might need 'Go away, what are you doing here . . .' and 'I won't talk to you, I say nothing to you' or even 'all you're doing here is grazing.'[18] These were sad, bloody books about a bit of human contact in the intervals of fighting; they hardly ever survived to be kept in a library.[19]

Others open a schoolmaster's window on the city, a reality slightly adjusted by the need to conjugate things. Gabriel Meur dedicated his book *Vocabulaire François-Flameng mis en lumière*, published through Plantin in 1562, to all the youth of Antwerp. He tells his readers in a preface why they should choose a teacher for their children's minds as carefully as they choose a doctor of good reputation for their bodies.[20] He doesn't – quite – need to say they should chose Meurier. His other audience, he knew very well, was Antwerp merchants; by the 1568 printing he filled empty pages 'so as not to sell white paper' with business letters about debt and exchange.[21] After all, de Berlaimont ends his book with all the important mechanics of life, like lending and borrowing and debt collecting. He gives instructions on how to write leases and suchlike documents, and only then does he include the text of the Lord's Prayer and the Ave Maria. The priorities are clear.[22]

Before that he stages little familiar dramas. One man walks in on another and menaces him: 'you know why I'm here.' He's waited long enough for his money, he says, and the debtor has to promise to find someone to guarantee his debt – and in both languages. There are model letters for dunning a debtor when you yourself have debts to pay: 'Dear David, send the twenty florins you owe me because I need them to pay a man who will not leave me in peace night or day.' The debtor answers, but to say he can pay only in eight days, and only when someone else pays back the money he owes.

It's not just that everything is about money; it is about the anxiety of being tangled in a whole chain of credit. There were no banks in the North to handle cash or move it to your creditors, so everyone had to use written bills, proof of other people's obligations to pay back other people's debts. They were as good as cash, but they put a man in his place in a nerve-racking chain.

6

The City Published

Simone Turchi rode in two processions.

The first time he rode, he was 'triumphantly and magnificently mounted' on a fine trotting horse with gold harness, dressed in violet velvet with embroidery of gold and the occasional pearl; he was among the forty merchants from Lucca who led the procession of foreigners welcoming Prince Philip to Antwerp in 1549.[1] The second time, two years later, he was in black and his journey started in the prison at the Steen. He was put in a chair, his own special chair, and the seat fell in under him and two iron bars shot out from the armrests to trap his thighs. He had a bag of gunpowder tied on his back and one on his chest. He was going to die for the murder he did in this chair.

He was put on a cart and was tugged through the streets by two horses to the Grote Markt. The chair, with Turchi locked in it, was set down in the square and his executioners built a fire all around it. He was kept close to the fire so he would burn, but not so close that he would burn quickly. It was an hour before the authorities decided they should light a straw torch, set off the gunpowder and let him die.[2]

His body was hung on a high stake outside the city; after which his name, his crime and his death became news. The story travelled with people who hadn't been there, was heard by people who hadn't known his name, and told and retold across Europe by merchants who were expected to carry sensations to pay for their dinners as they travelled. Anything from Antwerp had glamour, and anything about money in Antwerp was easy to believe, so the story started with advantages.[3]

This story is exceptional, though, because we know what people knew about the case from two published versions written within six years of the crime, and the archives more or less confirm the details they give. For once, we can watch news moving.

Niccolò Nettoli was a merchant from Florence doing business in Antwerp, so naturally he had to travel. Some time before 1553 he went south to Paris for a few days, and then on to Agen in the wine country south-east of Bordeaux. He knew that people thought 'you can't leave Paris without being stuffed with news, however little time you spend there' but he had not been in the city very long. So when he was asked in Agen if he had anything new, which was a usual opening line at any dinner according to the conversation manuals, he told a story from just before his time in Antwerp: Turchi's story.

Matteo Bandello, Bishop of Agen, was one of those who heard him. The Bishop was a political exile, not overworked, and he listened hard to stories like anyone in a provincial town; they might be useful and in any case they made the wider world seem closer. He also wrote them down, and we owe to him the first printed story of Romeo and Juliet, and that other tragic lover, the Duchess of Malfi. He was about to publish for the first time: his *Novelle* appeared in Lucca in 1553. His merchant sources, at least for the stories with a French and Flemish setting, are clear from the settings, which are all along the route of the old Flanders wine trade between Agen and Antwerp, by way of Bordeaux, Saintes in Poitou, Poitiers, La Rochelle and Paris.[4]

Now, a story could cross Europe without harm if it was spoken at the right tables, but a printed version could reach the wrong people. Bandello meant to include the Turchi case in his 1553 book, and he had already sent the manuscript to the printer in Lucca when the Turchi family objected to a reminder of a crime with their name on it. They 'managed to persuade the Censorship that it should not be printed, because it would do them such damage as though someone else's crime ruined the reputation of someone who had no part in it'.[5] Bandello offered to add a note that its villain was not as closely related to the distinguished Turchi family as the name might suggest, but he was not eager for a fight. He was already mildly suspect, accused of hints of the occult and even heresy in his stories.[6]

So we can be sure the full sensational story was written in detail and ready for print in 1553, only two years after the events. This

ANTWERP

matters because it finally appeared only in 1573, twelve years after
Bandello's death, from Alessandro Marsili, a Lyons printer who at
least could not be accused of heresy since he was trying to get himself
a cash reward for having a Protestant beheaded during religious
riots.[7] Marsili included a preface supposedly by Bandello to his 'honest' readers, which makes the dead man sound defensive. He writes
that there was no point in any censoring, because the story was far too
well known all over Europe, and in any case he would not be the first
to put it in print; the 'most learnèd Cardano, in his admirable *De
subtilitate rerum*, mentions such a notorious case'.[8]

Gerolamo Cardano was in Padua, and his encyclopedic *De subtilitate* first appeared in 1552, which would show the story moving
briskly on the trade runs out of Antwerp and towards Northern Italy.
But Bandello, or his publisher, didn't get the right book. Cardano was
fascinated by technology and he put the trap chair into his *De rerum
varietate* of 1557, under 'concealed weapons' and filed between 'glass'
and 'sailing aids' with some sensational details which are remarkably
exact. He knew that the murder was done in a suburban villa, that a
business meeting was involved, that Turchi held his victim for a time
and was finally executed by fire in the chair he had used for the murder. But his main interest was in the chair, one more wicked device,
although 'as I believe, few inventors of wicked devices will get to take
any joy in their inventions'.[9]

The machine had a fine literary afterlife, a mention in the revised
editions of Jean Carion's *Chronicles* at least as early as 1553 ('and the
same Turchi was burned alive in the same chair') and even in John
Ford's great tragedy *The Broken Heart* almost eighty years later, a
play which starts by claiming that older people will know that its fiction is in fact truth.[10] It was a persistent sensation, which makes more
remarkable what else Bandello bothers to get right about its 'unheard
of and horrific' story – as though Dracula was fact-checked.[11]

It shows how Antwerp's reputation allowed its scandals to travel
well. Cardano thinks of the city as the most famous emporium of Europe.[12] Bandello has a general view of Antwerp as 'the most famous, the
richest commercial and sociable land'.[13] In one of the *Novelle* he tells
about the decline of Bruges and the rise of Antwerp. He sets another, a
trick story about a wife, her lover and how they manage to convince

her husband that he can't trust his own eyes when he finds them in bed together, in an Antwerp so detailed that the plot turns on the timing of the river boat back from Brussels on a Saturday evening.[14] The city was full of copy.

The Turchi story is the kind of light on the life of an ambitious banker in Antwerp that no financial records could deliver, and an account of what it meant to fail.

Simone Turchi arrived in Antwerp as a banker, after which he was an intermediary and a freelance sponger who survived at times from the money of Maria van den Werve, the rich and distinguished woman he was courting for fourteen years. He needed her money to keep giving her the lavish presents that she loved. He was famous for his vicious tongue and his tendency to set friends against each other with just the right rumour, but he was plausible enough to get hometown banks to use him to run their Antwerp affairs. He didn't waste time or effort on those affairs. When representing the Gigli, a solid Lucca trading house, he handed all the work to his nephew.

The man he killed, his fellow countryman Geronimo Deodati, was a much more genteel banker and trader, slapdash, fat and rather odd-looking with his startlingly pale face and his brown goatee.[15] He must have seemed a proper victim. When Turchi was at a low ebb Deodati salvaged him with embarrassing loans, and later he sent Turchi to jail in Lucca to encourage him to pay them back. Turchi never forgave either affront. Deodati said out loud once too often that Turchi was a failure who'd be lucky to work again as a runner let alone a banker. When Turchi was attacked in the streets close to the Beurs and his face slashed one January morning, he blamed Deodati. He didn't think in general terms of unsafe streets, he looked for the merchant who might commission violence.

Niccolò Nettoli told his fellow diners in Agen about a 'way of life more open and more informal' in Antwerp, where women had a degree of freedom and were not shut into early marriage like Italian girls. Young women, unmarried and living at home, could go out with young men. Parents approved, sent the pair off during the day to eat, drink and dance 'all unwatched' and welcomed them back at night with thanks to the suitor for the honour done their family. 'Kissing is permitted there to everyone at any time and in any place.' That openness was what made possible the first meeting between Turchi and Deodati, at the house of Maria van den Werve. She was a true Antwerp grandee, famous for her grace and loveliness, and thought in town to be a likely wife for the imperial general Philibert of Châlon, Prince of Orange, until he was killed at the siege of Florence. Nettoli said her house 'was like the residence of some ruler or office holder of high rank'. She was now a prospect with a mansion and a fortune of her own and her fortieth birthday in sight. Gentlemen callers were expected.

Turchi was already well established when Deodati arrived and, like the 'youths of every nation that were brought to Antwerp on business', went to pay his respects to Maria. The men were rivals of a kind, but among a whole system of rivals. The lady insisted each of her suitors give her a portrait of himself, done by a known artist, and already she had a gallery of more than forty pictures. Turchi, however, was the only man the town thought was sleeping with her. She had started to trust him with her money, selling off farm and city land from 1543 so he could make her, as she hoped, a better return.[16]

Deodati made friends with Turchi, knew the street talk about Turchi's affairs; and given the man's reputation as a troublemaker it is not likely the street was kind. He knew how easily credit could be lost in a place where people wanted to know everything, and the talk would undermine Turchi's chances of doing good business should he think of any to do. Various merchants from Lucca were already warning Maria that Turchi did not concentrate, that his affairs were going sour. She was worried. She turned to Deodati for advice since he had just married, and counted now as a friend rather than a suitor. He had his own experience with Turchi and money, so he gave Maria very clear advice: either get the man's employers to acknowledge her money and the interest due as a debt of the firm or else take the money back.

Maria was Turchi's one resource, so he had to know who was giving her advice and spoiling his position. He asked directly and, unfortunately for Deodati, Maria answered directly.

Turchi plotted. He probably borrowed the trick chair with the iron bars that made it into a snare, but he may have invented it for himself.

As the murder story travelled it seemed more and more important that Turchi should be diabolical inventor as well as murderer.

He had the device in his suburban home, the pleasure house with a garden where he gave generous parties meant to maintain what was left of his credit. He invited Deodati on various pretexts including the promise of some truly lovely cauliflower plants, a gift proper for a gardening city. Deodati took his time responding, so Turchi offered better bait: business talk, very discreet, with some newcomer from Lyons who did not want to be seen around town. Fresh information from a distant market was always worth money.

The man from Lyons, being one more invention, was not there when Deodati arrived. For a while Turchi and Deodati walked in the small salon where the chair was standing. A servant called Giulio, a big man from Perugia, came to announce that the merchant had finally arrived. Abruptly, he lifted the sizeable Deodati and stuffed him into the chair. The seat collapsed, the iron bars shot across his legs. The servant walked out, bolting the door behind him.

Turchi picked up a dagger and made his terms clear: Deodati had to sign a paper or die. He might have been making Deodati admit to owing Turchi money, which would have been convenient, or forcing a confession of malice in Deodati's actions for debt in Lucca which left Turchi in jail. He might have been demanding a confession that Deodati organized the street incident in which Turchi was cut. The town talk covered all those possibilities. What we know is that Turchi struck at Deodati's face and cut him slightly on the cheek, which made Deodati wail and shriek for mercy. Turchi threw down the dagger and walked away.

Giulio found his master. 'We've opened the ball, we have to dance,' he said. Giulio picked up the dagger, ignored Deodati's howls, battered him on the head and stabbed him in the chest. Master and servant couldn't carry the dead body, so they dragged it to a cellar and buried it.

A merchant's disappearance made all Antwerp talk. Deodati's wife and family didn't understand why he had not come back to supper and to bed. Turchi needed to know what the city officials meant to do, and since he often saw the most senior of them, who happened to be cousins of Maria van den Werve, he went to dine and to listen. He discovered that a whole district was to be searched the next day, and it included his summer house.

Turchi left dinner early. There were walls and a chair to be washed free of blood, there was a body to be dug up and dragged to a well where it could be hidden; and for all this, Turchi saw that Giulio needed help, so he called in another servant from Piedmont. This man knew the clothes and the face of Deodati as the two men carried the corpse out of the garden by the heels and by the head, and the moment they were out of the garden, he panicked and ran. Giulio chased him in the dark, but he lost him, and when he got back to the body, he found he could not move it on his own as far as the well, so he dragged it back into the house.

The servant from Piedmont went about the streets all night. Turchi was also tormented: should he escape, or would that be a confession to murder? Giulio was rather more practical. He said he'd take the blame and grabbed all the money in Turchi's purse and two heavy gold chains. At dawn, when the gates opened, he was gone.

The man from Piedmont went to Deodati's family and told them what he knew. Turchi got to know about this, or maybe he simply guessed it and meant to give Giulio's disappearance a useful meaning. He told the law officers that his servant had done the murder. Deodati's family asked advice on what to do next and one of the law officers asked a lawyer uncle, who told him to arrest Turchi at once. When Turchi was confronted with his servant, he couldn't deny he had ordered the man to help Giulio. The body was brought, and Turchi was made to face it, because there were people in the city who were sure the body of a murdered man would bleed again in the presence of his murderer. But Deodati had lost too much blood for that.

Giulio was now in Aix, and in Bandello's version he writes to Turchi to tell him what to do: to say he knew nothing, but if the body was found in his summer house then to say he was quite sure Giulio was the killer. He handed the letter to a peasant who was headed for Antwerp, the usual informal mails, but this carrier could not read and had a bad memory. When he reached town, he had to ask around for someone called something like Turchi, and he explained too much and he mentioned Giulio's name. The letter reached the magistrates. This time Turchi was told he would be tortured, which was the usual form of questioning when there was already unquestionable proof of a murder, and he sobbed and he confessed.

Nettoli published Antwerp to a Bishop's dinner table, and the Bishop published the city to the reading world, its easy ways, its violent ways, its uses for information, including laying traps. He even told, between the lines, the unspeakable story of what it was to fail in a city that moved on so relentlessly.

Away in Alsace, Georg Wickram also heard stories about Antwerp, and he wrote them into a new kind of novel: no knights, no chivalry, but the life of the middle classes and their children. In 1554 he produced *Knaben Spiegel*, 'The Mirror for Rascals'. Close to the start he preaches in verse that if young men want to go to Antwerp they have to beware of 'sexual liaisons, filth and wicked pastimes'.

He thinks that barbers conspire there with the bathhouse workers, the ones who provide such a convenient space for any kind of liaison – dinner, bath and bed – and know how 'to cut open purses and bleed them dry'. His characters, the boys for whom he's making his mirror, find themselves lodgings with a smooth operator who is delighted when they claim to be nobility, but who soon finds they know how to fudge and wangle. When the landlord wants his bills paid, the boys say they're leaving to find another host who trusts them more. They drink well, which is what everyone did in Antwerp, and they have good times with beautiful women and they run off when all they've paid is a few token bills, the ones from the tailor and the cobbler, and they barely have the money to get out of town. One of them surrenders his 'lovely new coat' and gets away cold as well as broke. They can't even pay the shoemaker's daughter for the drinks she stood them, and she scolds them because it is 'shameful to cheat a woman, as though you were trapping a fox'.[17]

The boys would have found their women easily enough. They could have looked around the docks; when the men who loaded hay wanted a shelter against bad weather close to the Scheldt they told the city that merchants and citizens would otherwise have to hunt for them in all the 'taverns and bawdy houses' there.[18] Prostitution must be confined to a special area, so the diocese said in 1576, which suggests that it wasn't. Lepelstraat was notorious, and even a tourist attraction.

It was round the corner from the grand Church of St Andreus and the street where the washed and polished godly passed on Sundays on their way to the newly built Church of St Joris, opened in 1529 to serve a burgeoning population of the righteous, or at least the penitent. A holy walk was ambushed by tarts and boozers. The city made an attempt in 1530 to clear out 'men and women of dissolute and lively ways, running low-life taverns' from the 'better' or at least more handsome of the streets between the churches. A hundred years later, nothing much had changed: Constantijn Huygens found on Lepelstraat 'a lovers' lane, nothing but pleasure and very friendly nymphs'.[19]

Men who wanted men left fewer traces, despite the bugger hunt that broke out after 1500, and women who wanted women were only very rarely taken to court, and most usually when they were dressing like men. As the century went on, ideas were a more immediate issue than bodies. Fewer cases of murder or assault came to court, and even fewer accusations of prostitution or adultery or sodomy.[20] What worried the city was heresy and begging, offences against authority and propriety. But then sodomy was itself a kind of heresy, a refusal of orthodoxy, which made it more than a local incident. The Margrave of Antwerp took it on himself in 1569 to send a messenger to Brussels to warn the city council about an Italian who had committed 'certain buggery in Antwerp' and who should be arrested at once.

The baker Mathyus Guser still burned alive in 1531 for sex with other men, men like Frans Back and Jacob Gase in 1533 had their hair burned off with a torch, and at least one, Jacomo de Rossy in 1556, was beheaded. De Rossy's end was unusual, but his situation was perfectly usual: he had no goods at all for the bailiff to confiscate. Few men punished for sodomy had any kind of serious money or property. They belonged to the alarming class of poor people who were always suspected of being over-keen on begging, thieving, rioting, prostitution and crime in general, newcomers who dared to find a way to keep themselves alive.[21] Rich men could always arrange to have some money confiscated by the bailiff to avoid unnecessary trouble. Those who couldn't, and who suffered, were often foreign to Antwerp, even if they came from only a few miles away. There were group trials and the lists of defendants were a mix of nationalities and origins; it seems the strangers had no great difficulty in meeting local men. Italians did not always stay with Italians or Spaniards with Spaniards.[22] How they met is quite another question.

Being comfortable didn't save you from bad neighbours. We know that from the novel that Georg Wickram published in 1556, a new kind of story about quite ordinary merchant life in Antwerp. If Wickram knew anything about Antwerp, if he had witnesses, we're looking at the street life of the city.

In *Von guten und bösen Nachbarn*, 'Of Good and Bad Neighbours', he introduces the Portuguese merchant Robertus, who has a kindly, literate Holland man living on one side, and on the other a cunning troublemaker with a crowd of foreign servants. Robertus stops his children talking to his bad neighbour's wayward son, and the furious neighbour comes after him with a sword. The neighbour says he doesn't believe a word Robertus says and besides his wife is a mean woman, just scum. The neighbour's wife hits a child with a bucket and the scream is so loud people come to see what's happening.

Robertus is careful about trouble, as outsiders have to be. He keeps to the back of his house to avoid the neighbour, but next door's maid takes to throwing dirty dishwater over his shop and next door's manservant throws the garbage outside at night. The good neighbour tries to comfort Robertus when he loses all but one of his children and has to bury them, tells him about all those other families that have lost and suffered, and in the middle of their talk a messenger arrives from Lisbon with an invitation to go back to Portugal to be heir to a fortune. Unsurprisingly, Robertus decides to go.

He comes back to his street one last time, but he's not anxious now about his bad neighbour and his malice. He is still, despite everything, a member of a community which takes in more than one nationality and one language; he wants to say goodbye to that community. He lays out tables with splendid food and drink in the open street and invites everyone except the bad neighbour and every one of them is sad to see him go.[23]

Young Lazarus is assembling his qualifications to get married and he's told to travel and learn French. That means going to Antwerp, where 'you can find schools that teach any language' – French, Spanish,

Italian and more. He also hopes to find a good master who can teach him the subtler arts of working gold, and he knows he has to ship out to Brabant to become a 'noble and skilful man'.[24] There are the usual warnings against brazen women and getting into fights, and the wicked young men who hang about in taverns. (The same message is in Willem de Volder's play *Acolastus*, published in Antwerp in 1528, a school play by a teacher trying to cram morals into boys: except that boy goes abroad from Antwerp to his ruin, and the thoroughly good time involved in it. Enough people wanted the Prodigal Son rewritten to make *Acolastus* a Renaissance best-seller.)[25] Wickram could hardly leave out the warnings.

But Lazarus' ship docks at Antwerp and after that it seems that Wickram, who never travelled more than the twenty-two miles from his birthplace in Colmar to his job as town clerk in Burkheim, has other people's memories to use.

Lazarus sees the city and he finds it wonderful, the buildings unlike anything he ever saw. His travelling companion Reichart knows where to go to find good food at night and meet people from the Beurs. Lazarus also has a friend from Lisbon called Ferdinandus who has been living in Antwerp for a while and has his own idea of what is worth seeing. They look at churches, they go on the water, they see the shooting range and they walk by the impressive façades of the guild houses. They are invited to communal meals where everyone, Wickram says, praises God and then eats with the best breeding, after which there's talk of business which is not interesting enough to be remembered.

Lazarus is promised more joy in a day in Antwerp than in a month in Lisbon.[26]

Wickram wrote as though he knew the town. He writes about the details of everyday middle-class life expecting that people will want to know such things about Antwerp. Its scandalous reputation allowed a quite new kind of fiction, a view of real city life. But did Wickram invent the habits of the city or did he just report them? If he was reporting then how could he possibly know what he was talking about?

Consider three groups who set off overland from Antwerp in 1547 by way of Brussels and Mons, heading for Basel. Each group had two carts, bundles of clothes, some money and *laissez-passers* issued in the Low Countries, nothing else. They were *novos cristianos*, or *conversos*, Jews who had been forcibly converted, had fled the Inquisition in Portugal and found life in Antwerp congenial until Charles V had one of his imperial tantrums about heretics and tried to throw them all out. Since they left with assets, even though it was illegal to leave Portugal let alone take anything they'd need to make a life somewhere else, the Emperor appointed the thuggish Johannes Vuysting to chase them down, and he found one party just before Colmar.

They were first searched for money in front of the city's provost and court clerks, who found cash in boots and shoes, or sewn into the linings of trousers and shirts; and most of it in the waistband under the clothes of Caterina Lopes, a woman in her sixties. She had some 740 ducats or maybe six times the cost of moving a group safely from Antwerp to Zurich and then on to Ferrara, Ancona, Salonika or Istanbul. Then the local goldsmith, Caspar Henschelot or Hanshel, was brought in as interpreter because he spoke Spanish, and the questioning began.

It was soon clear the questions were producing nothing of great substance. Colmar didn't want to move to the next stage and torture the people they were holding, because they didn't want the expense. They told the imperial court 'it seems very doubtful to us whether we should try them at all' because the *conversos* held at Milan had been released, in Antwerp they were allowed to move freely and were exempt from taxes, and many groups had passed through Colmar with no trouble at all. 'Not one of them was ever arrested except for these poor people, who have many small children and otherwise nothing but their provisions.'[27]

For almost ten weeks they were held until proper arrangements had been made to make sure their money did not get away. On 12 September 1547 they were released, most of them broke. There is no evidence of where they finally landed, how they got there or what happened next. But during those weeks in jail they were talking, and their chatter was written down.

It exposed the little snobberies of the group. Their occupations were discussed: a ship's captain, a jeweller and a blacksmith, the rest being in the cloth or leather trades. A cobbler said nobody richer would tell him if they had any bales of merchandise travelling after them. A tailor complained he was kept out of meetings to plan the journey. The unmarried women were mostly widows, the married ones talked of their own trading in the North: Isabel Lopes, wife to a tailor, had sold shirts and linen, and the widow Gracia Dias complained she could never make a living in Antwerp from selling fish 'and other things'.

They were all made to list their contacts in Antwerp; a few had family there, sugar merchants or ship insurers. They wanted to go to Italy, maybe Venice, maybe Ancona, and maybe they were on their way to Salonika and Ottoman territory. The ambiguities may have something to do with what they really knew about the world. Isabel Dias thought Italy was one big city.

They had certainly spent time in Antwerp, although it's hard to know how long. They had done business there, seen business being done. Wickram could have talked to them, used their stories as copy for his *Von guten und bösen Nachbarn*, which is about the life of families who are Portuguese, like the *conversos*, and living in Antwerp as many of them had done. More to the point, Wickram starts his book with a letter of dedication to his 'dear friend', the goldsmith Caspar Henschel, who had translated the evidence the *conversos* gave. He thanks him for all his favours.

Wickram meant his book as a lesson for Henschel's sons, who needed to travel to learn the goldsmithing business. He teaches how to conform just enough to find a master and how to avoid the embarrassment of having to sell off decent clothes in order to eat. Besides the boys, he's writing for an audience that reads rather than listens, a middle class who could judge how useful were his stories and how plausible. So we have something unexpected: a sixteenth-century novel of merchant life in Antwerp with proper sources. Even the life on the city streets was published now.

7

The Unsettlement

Cities are settlements, but Antwerp could unsettle anyone; that might even have been the point of going there. The city changed the lives that passed through, and sometimes saved them.

When Damião de Goes first arrived in 1523 he was official and important, nothing more: the new secretary of the Casa de India in Antwerp, the royal Portuguese trading firm that bought and sold much of Europe's essential black pepper as well as other spices. He was just 'a kid', as he told the Inquisition many years later in Lisbon: only twenty-one.[1] He'd been trained in the Portuguese court to be quite a good musician, the mannerly kind of boy who might become a diplomat, but he was already full of wonder at the way the world was opening. He was fascinated by the King of Portugal's elephants and his rhinoceros; he saw the rhinoceros fight the elephant and win.[2]

Antwerp was something quite new to him: a city where he could hear unexpected ideas, openly meet people who would be masking their identities at home, and see the goods of the world for sale. He also had money. Netherlandish art was fashionable in Spain and in Portugal, and in Antwerp de Goes did some looking for himself. He bought works by the respectable Quentin Matsys, painter of rich persons, hideous duchesses and holy scenes, a pious satirist, but he also bought the phantasmagorical visions of Hieronymus Bosch. He owned a startling St Anthony set in a landscape of fire and devastation, attended by demons with funnel hats, ice skates and beaks, by walking fish, screaming monkeys, goldfinches under beds, musicians with the faces of hedgehogs. The picture has a sinister underlying reality: it shows all the apparatus for curing the terrible disease called 'St Anthony's fire', the necessary supply of mandrake roots and the essential laboratories, but that disease was ergotism, a toxic fungal rot of rye that the Portuguese knew only by rumours out of Mallorca. De Goes bought the picture without needing any familiar or significant subject beyond the saint who justified the wildness of Bosch's mind. He just wanted the image for itself.[3]

In the Portuguese *feitoria*, their headquarters, hostel, warehouse and office all in one, he listened and argued at table. Some of his companions were *novos cristianos* or *conversos*, the New Christians from Portugal, whose conversions were brutal and not heartfelt. He knew who they really were. He wrote history later and he called them not the general 'heretics' like other writers but the more exact 'Jews'.

He told the Inquisition examiners he'd heard people talking Lutheranism many times, that he'd begun to fall into error himself: thinking that Indulgences had no value, that confessing out loud was not necessary.[4] The factory had its own Lutheran connections. The senior factor and even more his secretary had made a great fuss, only two years before de Goes arrived, of the artist Dürer, whose attitudes to God and Emperor were clear. It was in Antwerp that Dürer heard the news that Luther had been arrested by imperial powers and he passed judgement: 'traitorous' he said, meaning the empire not the preacher.[5]

De Goes could let his mind pitch and stir in a way impossible at home. He was consul of the Portuguese nation, chief executive officer if you like, the representative of the Portuguese merchants in Antwerp; he served a very Catholic monarch who was keen on having his own Inquisition; but still he went to Wittenberg and heard the reformer Luther's Palm Sunday sermon, and ate dinner with Luther and his fellow reformer Melanchthon. He chose to make friends with Cornelius Grapheus, town secretary of Antwerp, who had been jailed for his Lutheran opinions and only just let out. Grapheus wanted to make a humanist of him, taught him Latin, which he learned assiduously, set him on the road to studying at Leuven in 1532 and giving up the career in diplomacy he had begun.

The kid turned down the job of running the whole Casa de India in Lisbon in 1535. He was the house guest of Erasmus himself in Freiburg at the time and even Erasmus worried whether he had made the right decision.

Back in Antwerp he was still working for a 'most Christian' king.

He was also riding hard for the imperial court in Brussels to save one of the great Antwerp merchants, Diogo Mendes, from charges of heresy and living as a Jew. His world had nothing simple in it, because he must have known that the charges were true.

The coming of the Portuguese spice ships in 1502 began the reinvention of Antwerp, but the Portuguese did not have an easy time of it. Think of them as the Vikings of the South: living in a narrow country with far too many lords, going out to sea because there was never enough land to go round, investigating all the world because they had no reason to stop. They had been coming north for a time, often men in their twenties from good families, but also from the dirt-poor inland valleys of the Beiras. They came to rebuild family fortunes, or raise a dowry for their orphan sisters, but nobody in Flanders needed the cloth and linen they brought, and pedlars selling door to door did not have a good reputation. They were watched. They were particularly anxious not to be suspected of being Jewish, so they went to notaries to swear they were proper Christians 'going through the world working and sweating' on behalf of their families.[6]

The first official *feitoria* was in Bruges. It sold sugar from Madeira and São Tomé, then ivory and gold and the fierce red malagueta peppers from West Africa. The merchants retreated at speed from the politics of Flanders, and the Hapsburgs' violent impatience with rebels, and crossed into Antwerp in Brabant in 1499. They moved just as the trade routes across oceans were opening wide. Portuguese caravels were sailing beyond the coast of West Africa down to the Cape of Good Hope and the Indian Ocean and opening new ways to Asia which did not have to go overland through Ottoman lands or risk hostile fleets on the Mediterranean. Their basic trade was black pepper but they were also hauling cinnamon, cloves and ginger round the Cape, diamonds from Golconda, silk and porcelain from China, the kind of luxuries, low weight and high value, which were already a famous specialty of Antwerp.

The first spice ship brought a new trade and a new class of person: the merchant assistants, junior partners, men in their early twenties who would represent great men and great fortunes back in Portugal. They did not plan to settle in Antwerp, unless of course they made a

truly useful marriage into some rich and established family there; they
were on assignment. After them came the barbers, apothecaries and
musicians, who followed the Portuguese as the tailors and booksellers
followed the Italians. There were craftsmen who were welcome
because they could teach skills the city did not yet know, like the making of buttons and perfumes, the spinning of silver and gold to make
filigree, the boiling of sugar for conserves and pastilles and jams. Their
community helped to shape Antwerp. When Albrecht Dürer was in
town in 1520, it was the Portuguese nation which honoured him most
with feasts and dinners and social breakfasts, which bought his pictures and gave him presents such as barrels of wine and a live parrot.
The Portuguese factor sat for his portrait, and so did the factor's servant, Dürer's first black model. She has the still, resigned look of a
woman who knows she can never go home.

She is a reminder. Spice is what fixed the riches of Antwerp but the
slave trade helped its special character: somewhere to sell pepper, buy
silver, sell wool or fish or grain and then buy the trade goods you
needed to buy slaves – all the very various currencies that the many
local slave markets required. The price of a human being was brass
and copper bangles on the Benin River in West Africa, and the copper
ones from Antwerp did best of all, but on the River Forçados only fifty
miles away you had to have the cowrie shells, which were shipped
from the Malabar coast. If you went to the wrong river with the bangles, you could get only palm oil and yams in return.

Almost everyone was ready to do a deal for fine cloth, though.[7]
Cloth, even used clothes, bought gold in Africa, and gold, back in Europe, was good for buying German silver to make coins. In the first
twenty years of the sixteenth century, Portugal managed this way to
get one-tenth of all the gold mined in the world, and a stable silver
currency at home. The Antwerp *feitoria* bought cloth from all along
the coastline of Northern Europe: bright-coloured linens that were
made in Brittany, wool cloth from Flanders, and rough hemp fabric
for sails and sacks. Agents went out with a contract to bring back to
the factory a fixed amount of cloth by a set date. The cloth they
brought back did not always end up being changed directly for gold.
Some was traded for other fabrics from North Africa which used to
go along the old caravan routes over the Sahara and now could be

carried briskly down the coast.[8] All this circuit of trade had its centre in Antwerp, where human beings were not sold.

And yet more Africans lived there than in any other European city except Lisbon itself. They weren't as obvious as the Lisbon class of black ferrymen who so startled the humanist Nicolaes Cleynaerts, a man who knew Antwerp well and could make the comparison, but then Antwerp was an even more variegated city. Some of those Africans must have been slaves when they arrived, because the city gave slaves the right to petition for their freedom, but hardly any did. Many lived as merchants, maybe sailors, sometimes craftsmen. Antoine Rodrigues from Cabo Verde, '*negro oft moriaen*', 'black or Moorish', was given a certificate of good conduct in 1566 after twenty-four years working as a dyer in Antwerp. Black babies were baptized. Some black faces were recorded, and not just because artists wanted exotic models. Jan Mostaert painted a Renaissance gentleman who happened to be black, perhaps someone from the court in Brussels or Antwerp or Mechelen, or just possibly an African merchant.[9]

Antwerp was full of people passing through, just as almost everything bought or sold or promised in the city was only passing through. The goods were not the point, they did not feed, clothe or decorate the place; the point was the deals and the profits. And the world came to pay for everything in bills payable in Antwerp, the world's creditor.[10]

The passing trade was the city's great advantage, and it could be used.

EXODUS

A woman walks the Lisbon docks, being careful. She's with her daughter, and they very much want to speak to someone but the two are not there for the reasons some women sometimes want to talk to sailors on the docks. These two want to save their lives.

She hesitates, but the light is fading and she knows she has to act. She goes up to a ship's captain and mentions, just mentions, the possibility of finding passage out. She's watchful. She notices a couple of guards coming onto the quayside and at once she runs off with her daughter. They know the Inquisition *familiares* keep circling the docks to find people like them. In one operation the guards needed four boats to carry off the people they arrested, and all the goods they were confiscating. Anyone with them would be jailed.

The ship's captain remembered the women when he gave evidence to the Inquisition in 1544.[11] He makes it sound as though they were nothing unusual: more Jews trying to get out of the path of the Inquisition. The women just didn't know how things worked. To get away there had to be organization: someone to explain the route, fix ships, letters of credit and guides. There had to be a fixed point on the escape route, so people coming different ways out of Portugal could find their way onto the routes up the Rhine and over the Alps to Venice, to the friendly Italian states of Ferrara and Ancona and beyond to the mercifully unchristian Ottomans in Istanbul. They needed a turntable town to protect the escape committee just well enough, a place where the Portuguese were long established and too valuable to dislodge, a place which was willing on occasions to defy the Emperor.

Antwerp found a complicated new place in the world. The city was quietly tolerating a wholesale defiance of heresy laws, making it hard to arrest or prosecute anyone suspected of keeping to Jewish ways. It was also making the connections which made it possible to manoeuvre between the great rival powers of Eurasia, the Hapsburgs in the west and the Ottomans in the east.

Ottomans in Istanbul talked of a Muslim caliphate, a holy purpose, and also of being heirs to Timur of Persia or Genghis Khan. Hapsburgs in Madrid talked of the Holy Roman Empire, the one true Church, and remembered Charlemagne. Each wanted the role of God's will on earth. Charles V had himself crowned as Caesar, but Sultan Suleiman could dispute that from what had once been the capital of the Roman Empire in Istanbul. In the campaigns of 1532 Ibrahim Pasha told Hapsburg envoys that there could be only one true sovereign in the world, either emperor or sultan.[12] He showed as well as told, in terms the Hapsburgs would understand. Other sultans never had orbs, sceptres, crowns or golden chains, all Western and kingly things, but Suleiman had a golden throne, a parade helmet and a sceptre, mostly bought from Venice. The Ottomans could play the same imperial game as the West, but with rather better bling. This had advantages in diplomacy. A Hapsburg delegation trying to talk peace were so overcome by all the pearls and jewels on the golden Ottoman throne that they stood like 'speechless corpses'.[13]

Antwerp worked both sides of this divide. Portuguese ships brought spices from round the Cape, but spice also came from Alexandria along the Ottoman routes well into the 1530s and the Antwerp Beurs dealt in coral and pearls from Egypt. The city was tied to the trade routes that ran south across the Sahel so that when the Turks grabbed Tunis in 1535, there were Flemish ships at anchor in the harbour. The Bey of Tunis, Mulay Hasan, fled to Antwerp as his natural refuge. He was a model for painters, of course – a useful exotic. He liked to be blindfolded to listen to music, he was keen on peacock for dinner and he went hunting with the Duke of Tassis in full Arab robes.[14]

The Ottoman offers were always enticing: use our ships, be the next Venice, trade through the Mediterranean to the world. But the Hapsburg guns were closer.

Francisco Mendes was Francisco Mendes Benveniste at the Portuguese court, known by the Jewish name he had brought from Spain. He was supposed to mask his identity and his faith, but everybody knew exactly who and what he was. He might have no clear right even to be in Lisbon but he kept a king and a nation afloat by running the spice trade for the Portuguese Crown.

Mendes was head of by far the largest trading and banking organization in Europe, the last resource of kings and sometimes sultans: the House of Mendes. He deposited more silver at the Lisbon mint between 1517 and 1534 than any other merchant, which suggests he had much more silver to spare. He also must have known the secret and illegal synagogue, the right people to make unleavened bread and the special dishes for a Sephardic Passover, and the men who could kill animals in the proper *kashrut* fashion; his life was doubled. Like all Jews in Portugal he lived an epic of insecurity.

Isabella of Spain cleared Spanish Jews from her lands in 1492 and some 120,000 of them crossed the frontier into Portugal at once. Anyone who paid an entry tax could stay. Those who couldn't pay or who stayed more than eight months were to be enslaved, their children taken away and made into Christians. Some of those children were sent off to the Gulf of Guinea to populate the hot, wet islands of São

Tomé and Annabon, if they survived. They did not get much help with survival. There are Hebrew inscriptions on those African graves.

Six hundred stayed anchored in Portugal, if they had the riches, the influence or the skills to make themselves either invisible or indispensable. But when King Manoel wanted to marry the Spanish Infanta in 1496, Isabella insisted that all heretics be 'cleansed' from any land her daughter would rule. Manoel had once been kindly but now he waited at the Lisbon docks with priests and soldiers to arrest the refugees and forcibly baptize them. They immediately learned discretion, and made their rules of life quite secret, which reinforced an even stronger sense of community. For all his posturing, Manoel could not yet allow himself to be distressed by their presence, because he needed to borrow money, and his Christian subjects were forbidden the sin of usury.

The street sensed insider outsiders, people both official and completely improper whose beliefs needed correction. The vicious old habit of blaming the Jews returned as virulently as at any time since the Black Death. In 1506 Dominican friars in Lisbon stirred up a mob and found enough Jews to need bonfire piles for the corpses in the Rossio square.

Everything in Jewish lives was now conditional.[15]

In 1515 Manoel asked Rome for permission to open the Inquisition in Portugal, but he did nothing more. Under his successor, João III, a practical man, the Portuguese Crown was too busy in Brazil for sugar and brazilwood and in India for the spice trade, but João did find time to set up a secret inquiry into the New Christians in 1524. He was shocked to find how many Jews were living like Jews.[16]

Mendes Benveniste had to live with this dangerous balance, always knowing how easily it could be upset by a King's enthusiasms or any political shift which might block off an escape route. He invested in an expensive and forceful campaign in Rome to keep the Inquisition out of Portugal, with few illusions about his chances of success. In December 1531 he bought a Papal 'brief of protection' against any future charges of heresy for himself, his wife, his household and his unborn children. Within two months, the papers for setting up the Inquisition reached Lisbon.

Mendes had everything to defend. His family controlled the India trade in spice and was able to lend to Emperors. He had a brilliant wife, Beatriz de Luna, later known as Dona Gracia. He had a young daughter whom the Portuguese would love to marry away from her family so as to divide the Mendes fortune. He also had a younger brother, Diogo, in Antwerp whose problems were even more immediate.

The Emperor Charles V was supposed to be firm against heretics and equally firm against the Turks, but each campaign seemed to distract him from the other, or so he came to think.[17] He was especially anxious about anyone who worked with the Turks, those who sold them arms and other goods, those who helped *conversos* make their way east, taking their wealth out of his lands.

Johannes Vuysting was set on to hunt down anyone trying to get away. Vuysting ambushed and arrested and found, he said, a fabulously wealthy conspiracy: a rescue committee of Jews determined to clear the way from Hapsburg to Ottoman territory. Charles was most enthusiastic. It was a nest of heretics working in Turkish interests and also a hoard of great fortunes wide open to an Emperor in money trouble. It was everything he wanted.

Vuysting even had names. A young man, himself anonymous and disillusioned, said he had abandoned Salonika in 1531, talked to Inquisitors in Rome and taken their advice to go at once to Flanders to tell his story to the Emperor's confessor. He named the men who had given his mother money to go east from Flanders in the first place, and provided her with the itinerary she was to follow and the contacts she was to trust. They were: Manoel Serrano, Gabriel de Negro, Loys Perez and one more who was already suspected of harbouring refugees in his Antwerp palace: Diogo Mendes.

Serrano was arrested and jailed and one of his servants gave evidence against him, but the evidence was so incoherent that Serrano was set free; the imperial authorities did not even manage their usual trick of making him pay for his own interrogation. De Negro went into hiding, his books and his goods were confiscated, and the merchant Erasmus Schetz, whose dealings went from Brazil to Russia, was set to work out his net worth. Like a true friend, Schetz reported that de Negro had nothing except liabilities. The authorities lost interest.

That left Diogo Mendes, the most powerful of the Portuguese merchants in Antwerp and the main man in the spice trade in the North, along with his Italian partners. He was charged with monopolizing the spice trade and keeping out local merchants, which was true although not quite what it seemed. Thirty years earlier, Schetz himself along with other Netherlandish merchants had managed a monopoly to buy spices directly from the Portuguese for gold, silver and quicksilver. The Italians took the trade over, then Germans, then Francisco and Diogo Mendes and their associates, but they did not shut out the others; Schetz still had spice to sell on the German markets.[18]

The other charges were much more dangerous: Mendes was accused of being a practising Jew, persuading the recently converted to take back their original faith, and secretly helping them and their goods to go east.

Diogo Mendes' Antwerp palace, his *hostel*, was surrounded by wide gardens filled with medicinal herbs; it looked a very settled place. He had a 'very large family' there, sixty or so valets, clerks, cooks and cleaners, people to run the business, people to manage life, sometimes members of his own family. In this house almost everyone was Portuguese, which must have helped with discretion, and the size of the household made it unremarkable how many people came and went.

The mixture of business, private life and careful secrets was ordinary in the great houses of bankers and merchants, but Mendes had a way of life he could not be caught living. He had books in Hebrew – they were seized in 1532 – and he was known later to correct the Hebrew conjugations of his nephew Bernardo Micas, who was a rather slow student. Any Hebrew texts raised suspicions. Nobody official in Antwerp could read them, for a start, so the imperial powers had to send to Leuven to find out that Diogo owned a book of psalms and a prayer book with prayers rather tactlessly asking God to send the real Messiah as soon as possible.[19]

He could follow dietary rules easily enough since such a large household needed its own arrangements and was not simply buying from the market. He was allowed his own chaplain, by special dispensation, and he had a chapel in his house. Gaspar Lopes, son of his half-brother, was caught in Pavia on his way east and told the torturers that Mendes' chapel was a synagogue where a young girl dressed all in white 'in the manner of Jewish priests' sang in Spanish the psalms of David.

Mendes was arrested and his mansion and warehouses were seized, along with all his papers and books. On 19 July 1532 he was taken to jail.

Within weeks letters started to arrive. Henry VIII of England wrote, or so the official summary of the case says, but the letter itself is missing.[20] Other letters survive in Spanish and Portuguese archives. They told the Emperor what he had really done when he jailed Diogo Mendes, how even an Emperor sure of his holy mission had to consider the world.

First, Catarina Queen of Portugal, the Emperor's sister, wrote to her 'most Exalted, most Excellent Prince and Most Powerful Brother'. She wanted the case of Diogo Mendes investigated, 'so that his rights are fully respected with no account taken of any unfavourable report concerning him'. She was concerned for all the merchants who had goods deposited with him and couldn't afford to have them locked away, but more than that she wanted Charles to know who Diogo was: the brother of Francisco Mendes Benveniste, '[whom] I consider a very loyal servant of the Crown', 'one of the leading merchants' to be found in Lisbon and a man who manages the business of many other merchants because of his 'sterling reputation'. The Queen says Francisco has lived in Portugal for forty years, which is since the Jews were expelled from Spain and many crossed the border, and she uses both his Spanish and Jewish surnames. She knows exactly who and what he is, and she wants the facts ignored.[21]

That was 26 August. On 28 August the King of Portugal also wrote that Francisco had 'accumulated enormous wealth here [in Portugal] as well as in your realms and domains and particularly in Flanders'. He was 'a person of very great reputation', who had done business 'in the Indies trade ... on behalf of my Exchequer'. The King was 'most beholden to him'. His brother Diogo had been in Flanders 'with his entire estate' for the last twenty years and he represented many merchants from Portugal. 'They put themselves into his hands, in consideration of his great trustworthiness.' But now Francisco had been told of Diogo's arrest, that his possessions have been seized including 'the merchandise ... belonging to Francisco himself or entrusted to him by many other merchants of this kingdom, a considerable sum'. Francisco had asked the King 'as a special favour' to write to the Emperor.

The King gets directly to the point. He writes that Francisco along with all the other merchants he represents, 'owe me an enormous sum of money, deriving from purchases and contracts of pepper and spices in my Indies trade'. Like anyone with a state to run, João needed early and reliable money. In Antwerp he found a consortium of merchants prepared to pay for spices at once, take a risk on the price and sell the goods later. 'I most especially entreat you,' he writes, 'to see to it that the sale of the spices they bought from me is not delayed, nor by the same token, the payments.'[22]

King João also wrote to his chancellor in February 1533 to tell him not to send full loads of anything to Diogo in case they were confiscated. He warned Francisco Mendes not to send large consignments on Diogo's own ship.[23] He saw the state income of Portugal being confiscated for Charles' own reasons.

For once, the Emperor hesitated. After all, he was pursuing Diogo Mendes, the man who had made a huge loan to his grandfather and predecessor, Emperor Maximilian, and had once bailed out the Portuguese *feitoria* in Antwerp on which his royal brother-in-law depended. Mendes was accused by the Emperor of a wicked monopoly, but that same monopoly had been the support of the Crown of Portugal since 1525.

The city of Antwerp resisted and set its lawyers dancing around the imperial orders. First Mendes denied everything, in writing. Then his lawyer, Jasper Stinen, ignored the evidence altogether and went to work on the commissioners that the imperial governor, Mary of Hungary, had appointed to investigate. He agreed that heresy was an imperial issue, but the commissioners had no expertise in questions of faith so the case should be moved to a Church court. That would take all the spoils out of the Emperor's control and the Emperor was not ready to agree. Stinen then argued that the whole supposed conspiracy to help the *conversos* move their goods and lives to Ottoman territory had nothing at all to do with questions of faith, which meant the Emperor had no jurisdiction anyway. The city would have to settle it.

De Goes rode to Brussels to persuade the court to retreat, and the commissioners did leave town, but Diogo Mendes still had to be bailed out in early September for 50,000 ducats, which was useful money. The Portuguese had to campaign for an immunity against prosecution for the monopoly they quite clearly owned in the spice trade. Mary of Hungary as governor had to be told to show special favour to the Portuguese Casa de India factory, which she had no intention of doing. But Antwerp's way of thinking did prevail.

Then, in Lisbon in 1535, Francisco Mendes died.

Within a year, the Inquisition had the force of law in Portugal. It could still act only on the basis of solid evidence, not talk or rumour, but that protection had a time limit and would soon lapse. Other laws were coming. *Conversos* would need a royal licence to leave Portugal. They could take nothing with them. No captain could allow them on board his ship.

There would have been a crisis even if Francisco with all his courtly contacts had survived. His death meant the whole House of Mendes was at risk, its loans and trades and deals across Europe. Its future now depended on one woman: Francisco's widow, Beatriz de Luna. She inherited not just his half share of the business but also something much more important: the unquestioned authority to run it, as head of the largest banking and trading organization in Europe. She was very powerful and very vulnerable. In time she would put away her Spanish name and take back her Jewish name as Dona Gracia Naçi, but for now her Jewishness could be used against her and against her baby daughter Ana. For the woman who later 'helped the Jews when they did not have money to leave, comforted them in Flanders and in the bitter mountains of the Alps and Germany', as Samuel Usque wrote in his *Consolaçam*, her duty was becoming clear and it could not lie in Lisbon.[24]

Ana was the immediate issue: a baby who would have two-thirds of the other half of the firm's capital if and when it was divided. Francisco had left orders that the division must never happen. His executors asked for a four-year delay in making an inventory of the estate, without which it could not be settled, but King João refused because, he said, he needed to know more about the widow's motives, and he doubted if she was going to help him to marry Ana off to some shopworn noble.

In May 1537 the inventory of the estate was complete and the King said he wanted Francisco's daughter to be taken at once into the Queen's household, given a royal upbringing and then married 'with the fortune left her by her father' to 'an honourable person'. She would be lost to the family, there would be no possibility of returning to Judaism, and she would be a hostage to keep the Mendes family and the rest of their fortune where the Portuguese court could use them.

Diogo Mendes chartered an English ship at Antwerp and sent it south.

You had to take a ship to safety, of course, but the first problem was how to get on board without being seen. It was best to go to the docks after sunset or before sunrise, and have any boxes and bags sent ahead so you didn't draw attention. Some people took dinghies out, so they could board on the side away from the quay. Some had the luxury of private cargo ships which would wait in the mouth of the river, and they slipped out to meet them on little fishing boats. Diogo Mendes could carry his family north with greater ease but he must have known that once or twice a ship had been stopped by cannon shots at the mouth of the river, just out of the port of Lisbon.

The fare north for a Christian was three or four ducats, eleven at most, but *novos cristianos* knew they would be asked for twenty-six or even fifty. Complain, resist or refuse, and it was simple for the crew to land a difficult passenger where the Inquisition could find them. Accuse a captain, however justly, and you were unlikely to win your point on shore. Diogo Fernandes Netto found someone had broken open his wife's jewel case: he accused the ship's captain, Manoel Carneiro, and also said the fare demanded for his wife was downright extortion. Carneiro did go to jail, but Fernandes Netto joined him there in a couple of days, accused of judaizing. The imperial officer for New Christians ruled that there was no solid evidence the captain had walked off with 400 ducats' worth of jewels, but he said the fare should at least be reduced to eleven ducats. It was minimal justice.[25]

Everything revolved around Antwerp, however you got there. Some people landed directly in the Netherlands, usually north of Antwerp in Veere or Middelburg. Dona Gracia sailed first to England on Diogo's ship. When the spice ships docked at Plymouth or Southampton they were met by Christopher Fernandes, whose job was to know what lay ahead in Antwerp. It might be worth going on, it might be worth waiting long months for the Emperor's religious enthusiasms to calm down. In London, any 'false Christians' coming from Portugal would go to the house of Alves Lopes, which served as synagogue for the very unofficial colony of Jews. 'The said Alves,' the Inquisition was told, 'helps them to go whither they want.'

They had a banker of sorts, Antonio della Rogna, 'a tall Jew with one eye, a master of Hebrew theology'. He would arrange letters of credit on his distinguished relations in Antwerp, the Mendes family, so the refugees had resources to move on. He had spent time in prison in Brabant while Vuysting tried to extract from him the details of how the escape route worked.[26]

Although they had to be discreet, since Jews had supposedly been banned from England for more than 200 years, they did not feel unwelcome. Henry VIII had a talent for spending money, and he needed to borrow from the Antwerp merchants from the first decade of his reign; the Mendes firm had an agent in London by the 1520s.[27] Diogo Pires, otherwise Didacus Pyrrhus Lusitanus, thought he'd seen Henry VIII in person welcoming the newcomers and offering his protection around 1535; he said so in a letter he wrote a decade later.[28] All this had to end when the Spanish Ambassador denounced the community in 1542. Henry VIII at last remembered his duty to suppress heresy even if that meant a very musical king putting most of his musicians in prison.[29]

Once she was in Antwerp, Dona Gracia had her work: the Mendes empire of money and trade, but also the escape route to Italy and beyond. She was away from the imminent threat in Portugal but she needed every connection possible, the authority of her name and family, and a city where the sheer volume of trading made it easy to move money. Antwerp also made sense because of its ambiguity. The Emperor sometimes condemned the *conversos*, sometimes excused them, sometimes chivvied them and followed them across Europe; but at least his moods shifted. There were chances to get away if you knew how.

Dona Gracia was too visible to move quickly, but others were already on their way and she helped to engineer their escapes. We know a surprising amount about how it was done.

Someone, Diogo Netto said it wasn't him, left a paper folded in three in his Antwerp house. The commissioners, with difficulty, translated it. 'Always behave as decent people and God will help you,' it instructed. The rest was the timetable for moving on.

The carriage would leave Antwerp before dawn, no need to advertise who was on the move, and the travellers were to stay at the Vier Escara inn when they reached Cologne. The carter would then go off to hire the boat to go up the Rhine. 'A man called Pero Tonnellero who speaks good Spanish' went along at his own expense to cope with the officials who checked to see if there were goods on board the boats as well as people. They were harmless, the guide writes, but on no account try to bribe them. Some of the stronger travellers went off with Pero along the way to buy provisions because the group would carry most of its own food. It was best if everyone also slept on board to avoid being questioned.

All this was planned in Antwerp, the port through which passed the people, their assets and also their experience of making an escape.

In Mainz, the refugees slept at 'the inn with the sign of a fish' and then hired wagons to go overland across Switzerland, first to Lucerne and on across the lake to Altdorf 'along the old route'. After the water they hired horses to cross the Alps. 'Those who are in better shape can go on foot in order to save some money.' The main roads were too conspicuous in the mountains so they had to take the narrow, steep and stony side paths. The walkers could always make themselves useful if a wagon overturned. And all the way 'the less you talk, the better.'[30]

Someone who had already made the journey wrote back to Diogo Netto in Antwerp to fill in the details. At each stop there would be someone to give 'information about the way ahead', so the route was fixed. Horses for twenty people meant hiring from different stables, but if you wanted to see your wife at all while riding across the Alps, make sure both horses came from the same farm because horses like to travel as a family. Be careful about passports, carrying them in a box so the wax seal does not get lost. The writer says their seal was dislodged when they got to Magadino, a port on the banks of Lake

Maggiore, and they had to pay a huge fine. 'Robbed,' he says, 'and with no remedy and all because of women's fancy.' Local officials worked on the principle that 'rich people can pay' so 'on this road . . . always behave like poor people.' He blames the daughter of Diogo Fernandez who wore a showy hat (*barete*).

The Emperor was against heresy and in favour of strong central powers, which was more or less the same policy from two points of view. After the 1540 revolt in Ghent had been crushed, he made moves against heretics and also to shore up the machinery of his government, because both issues were pressing.

He sent Dr Boisot from the Privy Council to Antwerp in November 1540 to deal with the *novos cristianos*. Boisot reached town in the early evening, summoned the Margrave and the city officials to his lodging for six the next morning and did not get the reply he expected. The Margrave sent word that he had a fever and would come if he could, the others said they'd come but they saw no need to start so early. The sheriff arrived before six the next morning to say the Margrave was much too ill to come at all and the others thought it would be better to wait for daylight so as not to upset the population. Boisot summoned them all to the Margrave's house for six-thirty. At seven he was still waiting.

When they did arrive they complained that two of the men he meant to arrest were residents long before the latest rules were made and the third was 'a rich and powerful man with many friends in the town'. They said there was a rumour among the merchants that once the New Christians were questioned it would be the turn of the Lutherans and they were already shipping their goods and their families to other countries. The Margrave said that seizing the goods of the men they were about to arrest would only make the merchants think 'the present chase was more about goods than punishing persons'.

The city went back to its habit of making it as difficult as possible to ruin or dislodge foreign merchants, a process which had begun in March of that year when the Emperor sent a marshal to hunt out heretics and the Antwerp authorities arrested him for infringing city privileges. This time Boisot sent marshals to Gabriel de Negro's house to make sure he and his goods did not disappear, which they did the moment the men told de Negro what was happening. The sheriff thought he'd spotted his man on the Beurs but he couldn't have been there, he told Boisot, so he must be hiding. Since de Negro was the community's rabbi, and the *mohel* who performed circumcisions, he had every reason to fear a charge of heresy. Manoel Serrano, a partner in the pepper consortium, was too rich and important to the city to be molested; he was judged 'not guilty' at once, but had to go into hiding. Manoel Henriques was the one who found food and beds for new arrivals and planned their onward route, so he knew how to vanish, which he did.

Dona Gracia was not settled in Antwerp. She had been there less than a year when she began to talk about moving on in 1538, perhaps to Ferrara, the Italian duchy so famously sympathetic to Jewish new-comers. Antwerp had its own explanation. In 1539 Diogo Mendes married her sister Brianda and not Gracia, his brother's widow: she must be jealous. Never mind that Diogo was not obliged by the rules of *yibbum* to choose Gracia, because she already had a child by Fran-cisco and the line of inheritance was quite clear. He was staying in Antwerp for the spice business and he was not obliged to marry Bri-anda either. He chose, which was his offence.

Dona Gracia had more reason to be disturbed by the shifts in imper-ial attitudes to people like her and by the marshals hunting heretics. Diogo, for all his power, had to make a show of conforming. His daughter with Brianda was named Beatriz, a graceful compliment to Dona Gracia's gentile names, but she had to be christened, very publicly, in the Church of Our Lady. Gracia could never forget the Hapsburg interest in marrying off her daughter, and controlling her fortune and her share in the House of Mendes.

That fortune was, on paper, a matter of connections, and it was quite alarmingly portable. Diogo Mendes needed to be in Antwerp to check the ships arriving and deal with the merchants who bought the spices and sold them on across Northern Europe. That left Gracia to do business with the Sultan, the Emperor and the King of France, and to find the money when the Mendes were forced to make a loan to the Emperor. She could move with her business.

For a while she was waiting for written safe conducts to Ferrara. Without them the journey was risky since she would be travelling with riches, and that would interest imperial authorities as well as light-fingered travellers. She needed the company of a ducal envoy from Ferrara, but the papers went astray and the envoy had to leave, so Dona Gracia and her capital stayed in Antwerp for the moment.

Diogo died in 1542 and he chose to make Dona Gracia his executor; at once she was the whole House of Mendes. He charged her with the firm's capital and obligations 'disposed in many places'. That might well include the schemes to bring Jews out of Portugal, but it certainly meant all the deals and arrangements across Europe, the business that Francisco had entrusted to Dona Gracia and not to Diogo. Diogo's widow did not even inherit Diogo's share of the firm. The man's death divided Gracia and her sister Brianda even more than his marriage.

It also left an immediate threat: Diogo's reputation. Within a week of his death he was once more accused of having been a secret Jew, a charge almost impossible to defend, especially for a dead man. Dona Gracia and her lawyers argued strenuously that he should have been charged while he was still alive, but they knew the real issue. If Diogo was found to be a Jew and a heretic then he lost his whole estate to the Crown.

All his papers were impounded and a court official was set to sleep next to the boxes so nothing could be taken away or hidden. Dona Gracia had to talk and spend her way to a pardon with a 'gift' of 40,000 ducats to the imperial court. The pardon was strong enough to clear Diogo, Dona Gracia and any future generations: one more paper which might avoid trouble for as long as trouble was not what the Emperor wanted.

The calm broke almost at once. There was talk that Mary of Hungary thought Dona Gracia's daughter Ana should marry the rather nondescript aristocrat the court had found for her. Her Majesty wanted to talk about the marriage, La Senhora said she was indisposed, and not inclined to leave Antwerp for Brussels. When finally she did agree to travel to the court she told Mary she'd rather see her daughter drowned than married off. It might be coincidence that Mary quickly turned tougher on the newly arrived *conversos*.

A year later, in 1543, Gracia at last had a papal safe conduct to take herself, her widowed sister, their children and their servants to Rome or anywhere in the Papal States, which included Ferrara. The paper was meant to protect against charges of 'heresy or Judaism'. She could have gone in November, but she waited and worked. In June the next year she was again sheltering dozens of new arrivals in her house and making sure they were not taken off to jail.

In the brutally dry summer of 1545, with plague raging and people eager to find someone to blame, there was no more time. She said she had decided to take the waters at Aix-la-Chapelle. She was a martyr to stomach pains and very keen on the waters, and since she usually went for weeks at a time it was a perfect excuse to pack up a household and send trunks on ahead. Brussels did not have to know she was going on to Lyons, among other places, to clear up the business of the House of Mendes – she needed to collect a huge and virtually uncollectable loan to the French, which required Dona Gracia's particular skills – and then on to Venice, and after difficult times there, to Ferrara.

The Hapsburgs wanted her fortune and did not mean to give it up. It took two years of bitter negotiation for the Mendes cousin João Micas, later known as Joseph Naçi, to agree what could be taken away, and all that time the empire's rivals were circling. Dona Gracia was in Italy but Italians knew the useful talk about her fortune was still in Antwerp.

In 1546 Giorgio Dati, the Medicis' man, reported home in late October on the 'fresh matter' of the Mendes fortune. He'd found in Leuven a 'confidential' man who knew a man who knew the Mendes, and who could maybe pass them an invitation from a fine Italian prince who did not need to be named or connected with Florence, not yet. It took some time for Dati's confidential man to get past the natural doubts of the Mendes' friend, 'they are a suspicious people and very afraid of being found out at present', but then he was very interested to talk about Florence and especially Pisa, where houses were cheap, the sea routes were open to Spain and Portugal and Naples, and there might be a chance of Jews studying at the university. Dati was bidding for the Mendes.

He thought New Christians might be glad to come directly from Portugal if they were promised safety and nobody kept too close an eye on exactly how they chose to live. The question was urgent because in just a year they would lose the protection of the Portuguese law that insisted on actual evidence before they were prosecuted. Dati's contact wanted money for his services, and since he was on Hapsburg territory working against Hapsburg interests he said he wanted to be paid very well, like anyone doing 'death-defying' service.[31]

As for the other New Christians, they kept coming, as Dati reported in March 1546, landing in Antwerp on Portuguese vessels and going on to Venice, Ferrara, Salonika. The Duke of Ferrara was secretly trying to persuade them to stay, but they found the duchy too expensive and they wanted the greater freedom of Salonika and then Istanbul.[32] Governor Mary told the Emperor that they came daily and in such numbers they must be the ones under suspicion at home, but she could not see a reason to accuse them. She said they were heading for Salonika and 'it is to be feared the business of your country will lessen, because some of them handle great loads of merchandise.'[33]

This is not at all where the story ends. Dona Gracia finally reached Istanbul in 1553, and settled in the European quarter. Joseph Naçi became both counsellor and provider of strong drink to Suleiman's grotesque son Selim as he came to rule the Ottoman Empire. Those heretic connections gave Antwerp a fantastic moment, when it almost seemed to have its choice of empires. It is a ghost story to be told in its proper place.

8

Money

The banker and merchant Erasmus Schetz tried to explain money to his 'most special friend', the 'great and most learnèd man', the philosopher Desiderius Erasmus of Rotterdam. He was not doing well. 'I was certain,' Schetz wrote, 'that within a year I would have rendered you capable of understanding all this.' He added: 'I would prefer that you were more capable of grasping this matter than I see you are.'

Erasmus was expecting income from a parish in England, but the coins seemed to have different values in different places. Schetz had to tell Erasmus that there was money in coins and money on paper and the value of the two could shift, that other people could take the difference between the markets in money 'to their own gain, and your detriment'. The great philosopher had a rather simpler view: he assumed he was being robbed.[1]

That would once have seemed reasonable. Cash had to be shipped, its price could change if there was trouble on the shipping routes and it could disappear and reappear on the way thanks to thieves, carters, pirates, light-fingered porters or brigands in the woods. You could imagine money moving on a ship or a cart. But money now seemed to move in stranger ways and kept changing as it went. It had a life quite separate from any goods it priced or bought. That looks uncommonly like the first version of the financialization that makes us set values in money terms as though money were somehow an objective gauge and gives an almost mystical power to markets which are really the sum of people's mistakes, crimes and enthusiasms. It is a radical change of mind, and Antwerp has to take some of the blame.

*

For in 1532, the same year Schetz was trying to explain money, Antwerp was opening its new Beurs or Exchange, the model for the engines of the world that Erasmus could not understand. It was not just a convenient place to do business, but a celebration, almost a hallowing of the 'community of trade'. For the city didn't only make a living from commerce; commerce was its identity, the energy which held it together, made the grand old landlord families into a ruling class that was usually willing to co-operate with the artisans and merchants who were paying them rent, made the locals value and protect the foreign merchants who thrived among them. The first great civic monument of the glory years was the Exchange. The much-needed new town hall had to wait another three decades.

Money's physical address was very separate from the goods landing on the docks and stored in the basements and warehouses. Money had its own market and when Charles V made it the single place where all letters of credit were tested, and paid, the new Beurs was even more than a market; it was its capital, in every sense.

There was an old Beurs, of course, a place to do deals. It had begun to annoy some merchants, who petitioned in 1526 for a new building, but it did have advantages. It looked like the house of any great merchant: a courtyard, porticos, a tower to watch the shipping on the river. It was almost domestic. It also suited traders whose life revolved around their contacts with trading groups from different cities or kingdoms, individual deals made on the move, constant attention to whatever they could hear on a street corner about wars, treaties, other markets. They liked the way the old Beurs opened tactfully onto more than one street, in more than one direction.

The new Beurs was a monument, not a house. It wasn't easy to find a site that was central enough, big enough and available. It would not do to confiscate land from anyone unduly powerful, so it helped to find a gap which happened to belong mostly to the city and partly to a city magistrate. This produced a solution which was brilliant but also surprising, because it meant the great new monument could not dominate a square or a street and stop passers-by in their tracks. Instead, it was built in the space between existing streets, and its boundaries were the backs of houses. You had to seek it out, to walk down one of two new straight streets, Twaalf Maandenstraat, which

led in from the market at the Meir and was already stuffed with notaries staying close to business, or Borzestraat, which led north towards
the most important of the city's canals. A press of fine gabled houses
ended at a great seven-storey tower with a high look-out balcony, and
then the double arches of a gateway across the width of the whole
road. Climb the steps, dodge the sellers of live hens and dead rabbits,
cross through those gates, and you were standing in the very heart
and engine of all trades: the market for money.[2]

The architects, the Spillemans brothers, made something quite new
but with comforting reminders of the older Beurs: the same central
courtyard, covered porticos for dealing in the rain, more than one
way to come and go. This new version had two clocks and two towers
instead of one, just to emphasize how much business there was to
watch on the river. It was on a scale grand enough to justify the stone
tablet set above one of the entrances which said the Beurs was 'for the
use of merchants of whatever nation, whatever language . . .' Much
more than a place where merchants might usefully happen to meet, it
shaped their days and spelt out the city's influence. The Italian mer-
hant Guicciardini reckoned the Beurs linked exchanges from London
and Lisbon to Augsburg and Nuremberg, from Rome and Venice,
Genoa and Florence to Lyons, Paris and Medina del Campo. More,
the Beurs was 'an ornament to the city'.[3]

It opened a new district, it made new boundaries between the very
rich and everyone else. It made over the shape of the city in its own
interests. While it was being built the shopkeepers in the old city,
around the Grote Markt and the Church of Our Lady and close to the
wharves, brought a law case to stop it because they were rightly afraid
their trade would walk away to a new centre.[4] By 1556 when Volcxken Diericx and Hieronymus Cock were setting up their hugely
successful business in selling prints, they didn't honour the old trade
geography of the city by opening in the traditional printers' district.
They followed the money and opened close to the new Beurs.[5]

Once inside you stood in a 'square', as Guicciardini wrote, the most
beautiful of all the twenty-two squares, big and small, in Antwerp. It
was 'free of people going through, of carts and horses and any kind
of obstacle or disturbance'.[6] There was a wide, covered walkway,

elegantly tiled, with stores on all four sides. There were more stores on two floors above that, with dormer windows in the roof; a steady, elegant rise of equal doors and windows which was intricately decorated, sandstone, brick and other stone, with stone trefoils and armorial bearings. It looks a little like the *plaza mayor* of Spanish cities, Madrid or Salamanca, which are big and ceremonial market squares closed in by baroque ranges, but Madrid took its familiar form decades later and Salamanca only after centuries; this was something new.

The city was mad for chance and lotteries, but all amusements were banned in the Beurs. The ragpickers and fruit pedlars who crowded the more formal side of business in the first years were quickly thrown out, although you could still buy chickens and cabbages from the stalls on the steps just past the gates. The Beurs was to be as dignified and overwhelming as the rush of business would allow.

It enforced routine, which was not always the essence of business. It opened at ten when the Carolus rang, stayed open until midday, and reopened from six in the evening. It closed, devoutly, for Holy Week, Whitsun and Christmas. It claimed even to organize the information which bred profit. A man who wanted to buy or sell letters of exchange could ask a money broker in the square for the going exchange rates. The big firms didn't need to bother, of course, since they were the ones who fixed them. And every merchant had to follow these routines, because absence was conspicuous and it started talk; if a merchant wasn't seen, he must be in trouble, on the brink or maybe already bust. Letters of credit were all honoured and all paid, never mind the names on them, because nobody dared be the one to refuse. The Spanish merchant Simon Ruiz was warned about making a fuss, because 'on this Beurs, however it happens, that can look bad', and looking bad was a catastrophe.[7]

Merchants had a timetable so fixed that Guicciardini could put it in print. In his day, 'evening and morning they go to the English Beurs', which was a place of business on Wolstraat for the English trades, 'and there they stay for an hour at a time, doing business buying and selling every kind of merchandise with the help of translators for each language (of whom there are a great number)'. 'And a little later,' he continues, 'they go to the new Beurs, which is the main site of their activity; and there, for an hour and with the help of the same interpreters, they talk and trade exchange rates and deposits, mostly.'[8]

In pictures like the one in Guicciardini's book, the market floor is full of gentlemen talking in decorous twos and threes and fours. It takes a moment to notice all the swords.

The twenty-second of February 1545: Gilbert van Schoonbeke went twice to the Beurs. Gaspar Ducci, his uncle by marriage, had his eyes everywhere in the city. He noted the names of the men who were with him. He also noticed that van Schoonbeke had no weapon.[9]

It was almost dark and van Schoonbeke was ready to leave. Just outside the gates of the Beurs stood Ducci's nephew Antonio Rensi and his servant Rousseau, one on each side. As van Schoonbeke came down the steps, the pair threw themselves on him and tried to cut him across the body with a sword, but Gilbert's servant blocked the blow. Ducci's men hit hard enough to break his head open, but his hat saved his life. Van Schoonbeke ran. Ducci's men went on attacking the servant, throwing a sword at him. Van Schoonbeke ran straight through the Beurs and took refuge on the other side in the house of a merchant.

He told a court later that he was sure Ducci had told his servants: 'Go and finish him for me.' He heard that some assistant of Ducci's had tried to tell them not to go, but Ducci had said: 'Do as I told you.' He'd said, so van Schoonbeke reported, that: 'I will have my revenge on Gilbert even if it costs me ten thousand ducats.'

These men are not outsiders, not thugs or criminals. They are two of the great powers of Antwerp. Ducci raised money for the Hapsburgs' wars and the running of the Spanish Netherlands, kept the King of England in jewels and was helpful to the French even when they were supposed to be at war with the Hapsburg Emperor. He and his company traded in anything movable. Van Schoonbeke was an engineer, builder and speculator who remade the walls of Antwerp and reshaped what was inside, including in time a whole new district to the north.

They came to blows over a load of onions. The old Antwerp weigh house was far too small for purpose: most items had to be left outside and there was a strict limit on how many could be weighed at one time. Leaving a cargo outside and weighing only a part of it was a perfect occasion of fraud. Van Schoonbeke accused Ducci of dishonesty over some onions and all their old antagonisms flared.

Some of this was a matter of sour business – van Schoonbeke and Ducci had done property deals together; some might have been Ducci's sense that van Schoonbeke had so many friends in the city hierarchy that he was a rival and a threat; and some was perhaps family malice since Ducci was married to van Schoonbeke's aunt-by-marriage.[10]

It was certainly personal. Ducci promised out loud that he'd sleep with van Schoonbeke's wife, so van Schoonbeke told the court, and that was an insult to his honest and very beautiful young wife Elisabeth. It was the kind of insult van Schoonbeke said he couldn't avenge or even answer 'except by acts that could cost him his life'.

Violence was in any case part of the culture of commerce. Only one year earlier someone had tried to kill Ducci on the street, and everyone knew the reputation of Rensi and Rousseau. A few weeks before, they had beaten up the house of Maria van der Werve, the woman in the Turchi affair, grand and connected in every way. They had broken down her doors, smashed windows with halberds and picks, but Ducci kept them on. Their notoriety was worth a lot to him.

Everyone knew about Ducci, too, because there seemed to be no limits on the man. When van Schoonbeke walked away from the very public attack, Ducci asked a senior foreign banker – Lazarus Tucher, head of the Hochstetter house – to warn van Schoonbeke that the assassins were still in town and he should be on his guard. Months later, van Schoonbeke was still more or less confined to his house, able to walk the streets only with a guard of citizens, 'a great cost and expense', as he complained, 'and not without just cause'.

Ducci ignored at least five summonses in a month to appear in court to explain the attack. He saw no need for a defence; he was defended already by the powers that depended on him. That left van Schoonbeke, who went to court only twice, free rein to denounce his enemy. 'A man of quarrels', 'never staying on peaceful terms with anyone who had dealings with him', 'putting out malicious calumnies to colour or disguise the murderous and treacherous acts he committed'.[11] What's remarkable is that this tabloid language was addressed to those who knew at first hand who and what Ducci was. They were expected to agree.

'He has been the inventor and the author of all the wrongs and abuses that infect the Antwerp Beurs – introduced for his own good and the ruin of others.'

The charges were not unfair. Even so, the Hapsburgs had wars to fight and a certain style to maintain, and they gratefully used Gaspar Ducci. 'It seems he is allowed, under the cover of some clout or favour he has at court,' van Schoonbeke complained, 'to make himself the Lord of Antwerp and keep the people under his thumb and say "go kill that one", "cut up that one", "grab his arms", "give a couple of slaps to that one there".'[12]

He told the judge how Ducci argued in church with the prebendary Nicholas Maes, then had his servant wait at the door to try to kill Maes as he was walking out and how Ducci went to court to get Mary of Hungary to punish the merchant de Baros as proof of his own power and influence, and then boasted that he had paid to get the man condemned. He arranged a beating on the street for de Baros, who finally decided to quit Antwerp because he could not stand being constantly watched by armed men.[13] Ducci's men, twenty of them, were 'here only to attack anyone Ducci wants to attack', the court was told. 'He has his servants and a great band of mercenaries with him at the Beurs and elsewhere, making such a commotion that the little children run after them.'

'What security or protection is there for the poor, ordinary, good and peaceful foreign merchant,' von Schoonbeke asked, 'against the insolence, tyranny, force and violence of a powerful and vengeful enemy like Gaspar Ducci?' He seemed to upset the machinery of the city, its open idea of commerce and its need for foreign merchants to keep it rich. He was suspect to the people who used him most, and who depended on him. They waited years until he had faded and failed and his mansion was being rented out for weddings and banquets before they said out loud what they thought.

Then, 'There's nothing that happened to Gaspar Ducci that was not foreseen long ago,' Cosimo de' Medici wrote in 1550 to Bernardo, his ambassador in Brussels, 'and we predicted it all because of his inordinate greed and avarice. 'We should weep for his ruin, as they say, but he got exactly what he deserved.'[14] You'd never guess how essential this same Ducci had sometimes been to Cosimo: the man who could deliver letters and pay expenses when the chivalric Order of the Golden Fleece was honouring its royal dead, the man who could be told in the same letter to fix a loan of 100,000 scudi from German merchants and buy Flemish bloodstock horses. In those days Cosimo was happy to thank Ducci for his 'good work', hoping to reward him 'with something more than words'.[15]

Ducci, according to Henry VIII's agent Stephen Vaughan, was an 'exceeding troublous fellow'.[16] He was a man who 'works all things for his own commodity', 'who will often speak more than he can do'.[17] 'I find [him] often devising things which he cannot perform.'[18] Nobody could be sure of that. His reputation sometimes made people think there was nobody else able to help them, but sometimes made his help impossible. When a King's money man could not talk directly to the great house of Fugger, bankers and merchants, he had to talk to Ducci. In May 1546 the Fugger factor was 'taken with a dangerous palsy; his life is now despaired of' so Vaughan was 'driven thus to devise with Jasper Dowche how to know . . . the Fugger's mind'.[19]

Fernando de Assa and Marten Lopes defied Ducci's official monopoly and sold alum to England; Lopes told Vaughan that Ducci was 'in a great rage' and meant to buy it back, which infuriated de Assa and Lopes. 'They hate the said [Gaspar] so that if the King were to sell it him they would never bargain more with his Majesty.'[20] Some merchants, Deodati for example, would not let their bills go to 'any house of the Dowche' (which was how the English usually wrote Ducci) 'after experience of their evil dealing' and they were happy to deliver any cash the King needed to a private house 'lest Jasper Dowche should hear of it'.[21] That might or might not help. When Vaughan patched together a very discreet loan he had to tell London: 'As to "keeping counsel of th'exchange", [Ducci] knew of it twelve days ago.'[22]

For all his irritation, Vaughan also knew that 'unless some way is devised . . . for [Ducci's] contentation, he will hinder all Henry's affairs here.'[23] 'I think no thing to be done by the merchants in no place of Christendom that 'scapeth his knowledge.'[24]

Even the imperial court could be irritated by their necessary broker. Charles V wrote to Philip II in November 1547 explaining that he'd heard how Ducci was putting pressure on his associates to pay a new loan two-thirds in gold, one-third in silver 'despite the fact that with letters of exchange they are not obliged to do any such thing'. The associates were asking Madrid to pay the two and a half per cent that Ducci's demand was costing them. The Emperor was furious.[25]

If Ducci's clients mistrusted him, his neighbours hated him. Mary of Hungary relied on Ducci to keep the cash flowing by any means necessary. She always depended on such local help. She knew what it was to be half-ignored by her brother Charles as she ran the Netherlands for him, to know he never saw her letters except in some secretary's summary, to have to threaten constantly to resign to get attention. She built her local authority on handing out jobs so she could trust those who had them.[26] She herself was admired, but as Bernardo Navagero reported to the Senate in Venice 'she is not much loved by the people.' Some of them might resent being ruled by a woman, he thought, and some called her cruel, but the real cause of their hate was all the money she took from them. Gaspar Ducci was hated 'because they think, and they're right, that he is the one who reminds the Queen of assorted ways of extracting their money'.[27]

Ducci was once banned from the Beurs for three years for cornering the city's money and stopping trade dead; but he came back with his usefulness intact, with his street-corner toughs but also his manners so courtly he served the Queen gilded oysters on dishes crusted with pearls.[28] He bought his country estate and the title that went with it from the agents of William of Orange, an imperial favourite before he became leader of the revolt against Spain. He could hardly have made a career anywhere except Antwerp and the obvious question is: how could he happen at all?

The Duccis quit a tiny mountain village between Florence and Lucca sometime in the mid fifteenth century and moved down to the silk town of Pescia in the valley. At the end of half a century there, they had a few good positions, mostly to do with the cathedral. But Gaspar Ducci did not mean to be any kind of clerk. He had only basic schooling in grammar and arithmetic, and he found work very young with merchants in Lucca, which was a good social move. He was in the same position as the sons of even the richest merchants, learning on the job just like they did after only a few years of school.

The house of Niccolò Nobili thought highly of him, enough to send him to their Antwerp branch at the age of twenty. It was a classic young man's job, making things happen in a distant market and keeping Lucca informed; but Ducci was exceptional. He did the diplomacy so well that within a couple of years, by 1517, he was representing Iacopo Arnolfini and Bartolomeo Condecini and various German companies, dealing for them in wool and spices and metals. By 1526, when he first makes an appearance in notarial records, he was accepting letters of credit on behalf of the great trading house of Welser.[29]

He was a man who knew things and knew who knew things, and could talk to them. He had nothing for the moment that he could keep in a warehouse, so he had to understand the relationships between other people's deals, how things moved, who was trading what, where there were differences in prices between markets. He had to check the fluctuations in exchange rates and also the supply of money, the literal question of how many coins were on hand and how safe it would be to bring more. His thinking was so financial it looks almost modern.

It was 1532 before Ducci felt confident enough to launch into his own kind of dealing, and he did it using his Welser connections, allied first with Alexius Grimel, who was the Welser agent in Antwerp, then with Bartolomeo Welser and his son-in-law Hieronymus Seiler. Their company was dissolved but somehow Ducci walked away with the profits. The Beurs was already nervous.

In 1540, at the autumn fair, he went too far. He cornered money, like other people might corner a commodity on a market. He controlled all the solid cash in Antwerp, the silver and gold, and brought about the ruin of the Portuguese factor who had good enough credit but no cash to pay bills. This hurt almost everybody, from the great German dealers in metals who wanted to sell to the Portuguese, to the English and French who needed African gold, to the English and Flemish who wanted to sell their wheat and their cloth. The Portuguese factor had to be able to do business, or there would be no raisins, no sugar, no salt, no olive oil, no spices and pepper – black or the red malagueta – no copper and no silver for European markets because this was before the New World riches began to arrive by way of Seville.[30] Ducci was not just playing on official terror of running out of cash to pay restless soldiers or to buy proper, lavish princely display. He was proving to Antwerp that all its business, its life, could be stopped dead by one man.

You could look at his offence in two ways. Either it was a scandalous threat to the commerce of Antwerp, or it was proof he knew all the possible ways to collect money. It was clear which mattered more to the imperial court. It helped that Ducci was always willing to agree a deal which would make his usefulness quite clear. When the Governor, Mary of Hungary, imposed a 1 per cent tax on exports, Ducci bought the right to collect it for 200,000 gulden, which was rather more than even he managed to collect.[31] On the other hand, while he was collecting duty on anything sold to the enemy France in 1542, he was also lending to the King of France through the markets in Lyons.[32] He understood the new power: money.

With money he could be more or less impossible, boasting about his contacts 'for that he is a little glorious and glory is his heaven', as Vaughan told the English Privy Council.[33] He talked about going to London but complained 'like a princely babe' about the seas, his weakness, the demands of the Emperor and his need for a properly grand escort. Vaughan could hardly decide what Antwerp thought of him. He told London that 'all here cry out upon him and would "eat him" if he had not the Emperor's favor.'[34] Or perhaps not, since eight days later he wrote that Ducci 'ruleth all the rout of merchants' in Antwerp and yet is 'easily beloved amongst them'.[35]

When Henry VIII needed 300,000 ducats on the Antwerp market in 1546, expecting to raise it from the great house of Fugger in Augsburg, Vaughan had to talk first to Ducci because of the man's ego. Otherwise, he would complain that 'whereas he had bruited that the King would always use him in such services, the using of other men demonstrates that he is disregarded.'[36]

He turned down a fee of 1,000 crowns for helping the English, and everyone assumed the Emperor had told him not to accept it; but then he said he could do no more for Vaughan unless the 1,000 crowns was paid to his son.[37] He wanted favours from London 'for the damages he suffers and the pension which he refused'.[38]

Everything was negotiable, even when it was cash that was needed. Ducci did deals in which a quarter of the money came as fustian cloth to be delivered in London.[39] He did deals where half the money was coming as copper, and 'unless copper or some jewel were taken, no money could be had.'[40] Sometimes there were jewels: a 'dagger of gold garnished with stones and pearls', a collar and a basin with the same embellishment, which were useless for paying an army and, worse, they weren't finished, so there was the possibility they might hold up the whole deal.[41]

If he agreed to provide cash he needed to know 'when and how Henry means to employ this money, so that he may provide the kinds that may serve best'. This was information that could tell an enemy where the next war was planned and who was to fight it, but the borrower had to give it; the money had to be trusted where it was going to be spent – made of the right metal, with the right ruler's face on it. 'The sum must be received in more than a hundred divers coins, and every gold coin weighed,' Vaughan told the Privy Council.[42] Vaughan complained, as he collected a new load, that 'with 20 helpers, [I] could not weigh every piece in a month.'[43]

There was then the question of how the money would reach those who needed it. Vaughan's money was put in sealed bags and locked in a chest in the Fugger house until someone could work out how to move it. Vaughan feared 'the Emperor will hardly grant the conveyance away of so much', and Ducci agreed there were real problems in shipping it to Calais and then to England. 'The Queen', meaning Mary in Brussels, 'will hardly grant it,' he said. 'It might be sent in some great vat with merchandise, by ship to [Calais], without licence either of Queen or Emperor; but if the Queen know that licence is desired she will "sett streight wayte that it shall not passe".'[44]

A few weeks later the Margrave sent for Vaughan, each message more urgent, to say he understood the English were 'about to undo this country' by setting men to buy up all the good gold and ship it to the English mint. Vaughan said Henry had 20,000 mercenaries waiting who required 'a heap of money', and besides the King paid out 'infinite sums' for goods bought in Antwerp, but still the Margrave insisted that gold was not to leave town. It took a deputation of the Fugger's men, Vaughan and Ducci, all pointing out that if money couldn't change hands then there would be bankruptcies and the city would come to a halt, to persuade the Margrave to lift the embargo.[45]

An exasperated Vaughan had to tell London that 'this morning the Margrave of Andwerp sent and arrested in my hands all the money' he'd received from the Fuggers. He was especially aggrieved because the day before he'd been at Ducci's house in the country, and he'd met the Margrave, who had said he could certainly move any money which was not imperial coins, an agreement between gentlemen.[46] A year later his annoyance was sharper still. He suspected 'that [Ducci], finding men here unwilling to emprunt [lend] to the Emperor, and having always boasted to the Queen that the Emperor should never want it among the merchants of the Bourse, has informed her that English merchants and others have conveyed away most of the valued gold.'[47]

Vaughan took the blame for the wrong Ducci did him.

Ducci played kings against each other, and looked for a deal in woad or herring for himself while he helped finance alliances and wars. His money could change sides overnight if need be. He had no nationality that mattered, no loyalties to a king, a duke, a state, a city or a flag; he needed Antwerp but he defied its rules. A bit of disrespect for national boundaries was quite usual; any working sailor could choose sides, too, even sail for navies that were fighting against his own country, but once he chose his ship he had to listen to his captain's orders. Ducci listened to nobody except his own particular interests.

This was not the proper, old-fashioned notion of trade, where you made money if you did work, bought materials and added value, the moral case for profit that Aquinas argued. This was a new-fangled trade with no apparent rules, and at its heart was the Beurs. It was not much help that the Church had ruled in favour of the business of the exchanges, or so a panel of Paris jurists promised the Spanish merchants in Antwerp as early as 1530. Merchants worried. Guicciardini thought that the exchange was useful for keeping trade moving, but the malice of some merchants, usually the richer ones, 'with a gross, insatiable appetite for extraordinary gain', led to great fortunes based on lending for interest. Interest was allowed, and always demanded in

Antwerp, but it could yield 'unjust profit', as Guicciardini wrote. You could gain very little at great risk, or lose everything.[48]

He worried about the whole basis of Antwerp's success: a city where goods were passing through. The artificiality of all this struck him – buying and selling for people and places half a world away – as did the effect of bringing together so many dealers and traders and keeping them in a narrow place. He wanted to approve, but 'rich Merchants moved with desire of unsatiable gain, having gathered together great Masses of money do either by giving forth to interest when there is need of money, or taking up when there is no need, make money either scarce or plentiful at their own pleasure and to their own gain particular, but to the great prejudice of the commonwealth.'[49]

There was grudging acceptance that exchanges were useful. Thomas Wilson, once English Ambassador and fundraiser in the Netherlands, knew exchanges were 'very good and most necessary, without further talke, if they bee honeste and good themselves that use it'.[50] He knew his world couldn't do without places where money could move; without them 'how should travailers do, namely scholers and studientes, if they had not their billes of credite and the exchange readie for their most safety and ease of carriage. Or how could any man deale betwixt country and country to have hys turne served for great masses of mony.'

Yet exchanges were blatant and monumental before they were understood, and they were appearing all across Northern Europe: the high stone gates in Antwerp, the squares in Frankfurt and Cologne and Hamburg and also in Lyons, or the London Royal Exchange, which needed Flemish stone and Flemish builders to put up a facsimile of its Antwerp original.[51] Antwerp and its Beurs were imitated even as they could so easily seem a moral hazard, one that could spoil the reputation of decent men. A Mr W.S., who was probably not William Shakespeare, wrote *The True Chronicle History . . . of Thomas, Lord Cromwell*, published in 1602. In it, Cromwell goes to Antwerp to manage the books of the Merchant Adventurers, the great English trading company, and he stays straight, with his books nicely balanced. He knows other people will say otherwise. If they do, then 'Antwerpe for all the wealth within thy Towne / I will not stay here not two houres longer.'[52]

Markets were becoming abstractions, less available to careful moral judgement. The change of mind goes further than cash and deals and arbitrage. It took art and music from being a service to being a commodity, putting angels in oils on the walls at home, giving everyone tunes to play on the lute and filling bookshops with everything from theology to pornography. Money took over the role of Church, courts and grandees in shaping a culture.

9

The Art in the Deal

On the trading floor at the Beurs, in between the arcades, there's nothing much to see except people. You have to imagine what is being bought and sold, how all that money would look in sacks or chests, the warmth of wool, the crystals of alum, the dry-packed sacks of spice, the timber, the diamonds, silver, copper and gold, the grain that may not yet have been planted and the fish which has not yet been caught. But look up to the second storey. The floor looks like an afterthought, which it was – added to the plans while the Beurs was being built in 1531, a late decision to add one more trade to the centre of trading.

In its deep stalls and stores there are goods you can see, even touch: paintings, sculptures, maps, prints of one kind and another, 'small stuff', which might mean silver or other luxury goods, and later the essential kind of artists' supplies: vermillion cooked in town, brilliant red cochineal from Mexico, the lovely ultramarine made from lapis lazuli mined in Afghanistan – the blue that Albrecht Dürer bought in Antwerp and almost nobody else could afford. Up here, art isn't a relationship any more, a matter of patrons commissioning work or painters working at courts or in churches; it is a commodity.

It has dealers, for a start, although the dealers seem to have taken their time to move into the Beurs, to judge from when they started paying rent.[1] The first of them to leave any written trace was a woman called Heylwijch Swandeleeren, a good thirty years before the Beurs was built. She called herself a 'saleswoman'. She was married to a painter called Jan de Pape and in March 1502 he was working on a retable for a church altar which Jan Baruzeel was sculpting. Baruzeel wanted his money. On 29 March, Heylwijch promised to pay nine

Flemish pounds at the time of the Whitsun market in the *pand*, the market attached to the great Church of Our Lady, and she'd pay earlier if she sold the piece earlier. This single written agreement shows Heylwijch with stock that she hoped to sell, ready-made art in need of a buyer, and she was not just standing at a market stall, because she hopes to make a deal before the market. She is dealing, sixteen years before the first official art dealer (*beeldvercopere*) is registered with the Saint Luke's Guild.[2]

Artists' wives and widows, sometimes the artists no longer in so much demand, followed her to invent the new profession. The artists' market on the second storey of the Beurs, the *schilderspand*, was theirs. Patrons once used to go to an artist's workshop, discuss the work they wanted with the man who would make it (and they were almost always men). Now they could go a dealer and see what she (and they were often women) had in stock. Dealers were needed. Art was being domesticated, paintings brought home to bring on holy thoughts in an alcove, or to hang in the dining room to start a conversation – the Bruegels at Jongelinck's table, for example. These were paintings the artist had already chosen to make, maybe a product line since they were easy enough to copy convincingly, and not individual works a patron ordered out of the artist's studio to dress a church, a town hall, an almshouse or some other public space.

You could have art without talking to an artist. Such was the demand that by 1515 there were more than a hundred workshops in full production in the city.

The new trade was worth stealing away from the church markets. Art was serious business. A fine decorated retable to sit behind the altar of a church could cost as much as a solid clinker-built cog ship, or if it was truly ambitious even twenty-three times as much.[3]

This happened first in Antwerp for good reasons: habit and money. The city had become the market for luxury. The Medici came to buy horses, but also paintings on cloth which they hung in their villas alongside Botticellis. Antwerp had men with money who allowed themselves showy things, diamonds, tapestry, books, silk, paintings or sculpture, portable things for the home they might not see for another few months or even years, goods to fit the great person they were determined to be when they got there. If they were Portuguese or Spanish they had an added motive: they knew that Flemish art was already fashionable at home. Their bosses, more settled, thought in terms of giving art to – say – a church in Genoa, a great man's public gesture. They did not need to go far to buy a painting. They all knew how to ship from Antwerp, because they did that for a living.

Dealers had to know what people wanted, or sometimes needed in order to keep their status. Joris Vezeleer understood this well; he had himself painted with a signet ring and a glove of fine leather, clear signs that he was a high-class merchant. He had dealt in wool and leather, in dyestuffs like vermillion and blue copper sulphate, but his core business was making kings look like kings. François I of France had been a prisoner of his closest rival, the Emperor Charles V; he was short of cash and still trying to find the money to ransom his two sons who had stayed in Spain when he was let go. François needed to look royal again. The fact that Charles was also his client did not bother Vezeleer at all.

He travelled to France whenever he was called and this courtesy, or maybe flattery, appealed to François, who made him a present of 192 French pounds (or *livres*) for the 'various journeys he has made to the King here'. He dealt in stones from Antwerp which were finer than anything on sale in Paris, given the city's connections from Mexico to Golconda. He dealt in quantity, quickly, shipping to Rouen and then overland to Paris; buying barrels at Boulogne which he stuffed with jewels wrapped in hay and cloth for the last, risky leg of the journey. More than anything, he understood that François wanted what he could not afford. He made wonderful cups with diamonds, rubies, pearls, with the heads of Roman emperors and ancient gods and even versions of Roman coins. But discreetly he made them in gilded silver, not gold. He knew that François still had to give the impression of living in a world of gold.[4]

Antwerp was the market for all kinds of images and fine goods. The city's name was on prints which went out to the new territories in Mexico to guide painters filling the walls of churches with holy images.[5] If you were a Suffolk wool merchant burying the dead you could order a weeping widow in alabaster and the proper number of weeping children for the tomb. Funeral monuments went out as kits to be assembled on arrival, sometimes with trained assistants to help the buyers. Sometimes the alabaster panel with its figures and story arrived with only a drawing to show how it ought to be framed, and sometimes the customer was left to improvise.

These ready-mades were desirable because they came from the same towns, sometimes the same workshops, as the monuments made for kings and princes. Tombs in two kinds of coloured marble with pure white alabaster figures were a specialty of Antwerp and Mechelen. They were meant to be almost imperial, like the interiors of Roman palaces, with forms that were properly classical out of books of architectural theory and also the details that came from looking around on trips to Rome: the scrolls and strapwork and cartouches and even candelabra that fit between the columns. The detail fitted the complexity of the Gothic, and the Latin forms kept its tangles roughly in order. All this work *all'antiqua* kept workshops so busy they had a perfect excuse to hire foreign craftsmen; or so sculptors like Cornelis Floris claimed when the local guilds in Antwerp complained in 1538.

When William Cecil needed 'little pillars of marble' for his show-off mansion Burghley House he found them in Antwerp along with an entire classical gallery in stone, ready-made. When Thomas Gresham was building the Royal Exchange in London, he not only followed the plan of the Antwerp Beurs, he shipped almost all the materials he needed across the North Sea, the intricate ironwork and the stone columns, the slate, bricks and wood. He even shopped there for the statue of Queen Elizabeth to stand above the grand main entrance.[6]

The city had become a school of style. Jacob Binck came to Antwerp in 1549 as court artist to the King of Sweden and to his brother-in-law the Duke of Prussia. He was supposed to ensure the sculptor Cornelis Floris was actually making the promised grand monument to the Duchess Dorothea, but he stayed far too long and needed an excuse. He told the King he was properly employed: he was making a careful record of 'buildings, fortresses, walls and moats, pleasure houses, gardens and fountains that could no doubt be useful to his Majesty'. He knew the King would not turn down the knowledge he had drawn.

Knowledge also moved by itself. Long before Antwerp lost its certainties – before the churches were stripped, before there was a

revolt against the Spanish which threatened business – the craftsmen
and sculptors and stonemasons of the Low Countries were travelling.
They were on the move at least from the 1540s. War and unrest may
have started the process, but business was the real point. There were
plenty of places – Hamburg or London, Emden or Norwich – which
needed their skills, but where competition hardly existed. When Antwerp finally had its new and splendid town hall in the 1560s, the style
was shipped north almost at once; Laurens van Steenwinkel and his
son moved to Emden, where they built a town hall just like it, for homage, pride and profit.[7]

Every kind of skill travelled. There were water engineers, the ones
who knew how to lay foundations in a swamp or a marsh, and they
were versatile. William de Raet became a citizen of Antwerp in 1558,
known for his skill in distilling herbs and flowers, but out of the country he had quite different ideas. He said he knew how to run a foundry
to make metal sculptures, but also guns. He was your man for artillery, fireworks, deadly war machines; he invented a light wooden
cannon and also fireballs that would stick with pins to a ship or to city
gates. His specialty when he was on the road was draining marshes,
building canals and being disappointed; he never did get to turn Florence into a seaport and Pisa managed to spoil his plans for draining
the ground north of Lucca. But he did draw and build the walls
around Wolfenbüttel, and he started work on a canal to lead from
there to the sea; not everything failed.[8]

Others were more aggressive, and less tactful. Paul van Hof, not a
name that has come down the ages, wrote to the city fathers in Lübeck
in 1548 with a proposal to 'make here some buildings in the antique
manner since the antique style which is now generally regarded as the
highest art is rather absent in this town'. No reply survives, which is
hardly surprising since Lübeck to this day is famous for its distinct
Hanseatic style.

Antwerp had lines of product for the market in art and the start of
brand names based on artists' reputations.

Consider the painter Joos van Cleve. He'd worked in Bruges before
he moved to Antwerp around 1511, a craftsman following the buyers
and the market. He set up a workshop like any other trade. He had

apprentices, journeymen, brought in specialists for special tasks, such as adding the expected kind of background landscape with the back-lit mountains and the watery horizon in between, the ships at a three-quarter angle, the windmills, the city walls broken by towers, all nicely contrasted with vivid sea and bright sky. That is often said to be his innovation, but somebody else normally did the painting, the pictures going back and forth from workshop to workshop to fill in the detail.

Van Cleve drew the image in the strong lines of woodcut. It was often marked up with notes on which colour to use where, a sophisti-cated kind of painting by numbers. He specifies, for example, the mix of purple and yellow which will give him the pink he needs, which means no need for second thoughts and a painting which is dry and saleable much more quickly. He'd store away drawings of scenes that might fit other paintings; Christ's body being carried into the tomb turns up in several pictures.

He kept the cartoons, outlines of an image which could be laid over wood or canvas with holes pricked along the lines, then dusted with charcoal which would sift through the holes to make an exact guide. 'Pouncing' made possible a kind of mass production, and a nice econ-omy of ideas. Then he checked the product before it left the shop, sometimes with the clients alongside him. If he didn't like the face an assistant had painted, which happened quite often, he wiped it and started again. Other times, he forgot children in family portraits – he had to add a couple of young sons to one picture when the paint was very nearly dry. When he sold to Pompeius Occo, the agent in Ant-werp of the house of Fugger, he forgot the great man's coat of arms altogether. He had to find another painter to put the mistake right.

Holy pictures were also coming into the home. Around 1520 van Cleve's workshop started to turn out two main lines: a Madonna with cherries, and a curiously passionate kiss between fleshy babies who represented Christ and St John the Baptist. You could order them facing right or facing left, smaller or larger, vertical if you had the money or horizontal if not; the horizontal versions were noticeably less well finished. 'Pouncing' made the images standard, and the brush of the master, or a very good assistant, gave the quality. But when van

Cleve saw fashion shifting to classical figures in the 1540s, he was suddenly fascinated by the virtuous Roman matron Lucretia. He shows her choosing death over dishonour with a knife that somehow never does harm to her lovely breasts.

This flexibility went much further. Van Cleve was linked to the Antwerp mannerists by his vivid colours and his loyalty to the detailed landscapes in the background, but he modified and compromised. Style mattered when making a sale to foreigners, and it helped to make a picture seem familiar. He could do an Italian accent for Genoa, German for Cologne; subtle changes. He knew Italian merchants wanted the kind of pictures that they might have bought at home if only they knew enough good local painters. So he arranged his saints in the regular geometry they knew, the Holy Family as a neat triangle. He included details in half-moons above the main image, in the Italian manner. He paid tribute to the prints that everyone knew of Leonardo's drawings of grotesque heads.

Going north his figures break loose and cross each other with an eye-catching energy, even when his subject is the Death of the Virgin. They have a lovely, calculated disorder. And when he worked in France, even though he got to the French court because the Queen had been raised in Flanders and wanted familiar art, he put proper French stiffening into his portraits. The bourgeoisie could be at an angle but kings were upright. He was, after all, doing the heavy work of making François I of France look like a king again.[9]

Flexibility was one of the city's talents. Its later star, Frans Floris, was one of the three Antwerp painters that Carolus Scribanius later put up to match Italian Titian and German Dürer in his boosterish little book *Antverpia*; but after five years in Rome, Floris was also trusted to paint a great triumphal arch for the Genoans in the proper Italian manner.[10] This way of doing good business was shockingly radical in a sixteenth-century context, like being a double agent.

For there was supposed to be a war of the soul as well as a commercial war between Italians and northerners. Giorgio Vasari claimed that proper art began in Italy, or to be exact Tuscany. For him 'some subtle influence in the very air of Italy' allowed artists to leave behind the gross mediaeval styles and find again the elegance of antiquity.[11]

He had to be answered. Johann Fischart, the Strasbourg satirist, used a preface to a book of papal portraits to accuse him of 'inopportune love for his fatherland'. Germanic cultures, from the Netherlands east, all righteously insistent on their worth, 'present and offer to the Italians the restoration, completion and renewal of the true art of painting'. Even Vasari, he writes, will admit 'the Italians display disreputable habits and manners that permit them to hate and persecute all foreign artists to the utmost extreme.'[12]

Michelangelo, among others, fought back, at least according to his associate Francisco de Holanda in his 1540s book *De pintura antigua*, on ancient painting. He thought Netherlandish work will only 'appeal to women, especially to the very old and the very young ... to monks and nuns and to certain noblemen who have no sense of true harmony'. But de Holanda has his reasons for reporting such sunless opinions. In his native Portugal Flemish artists were all too fashionable, so it helped that the great Michelangelo called their work sentimental, liable to bring people to tears not through their own merits but 'due to the goodness of the devout person' contemplating them.

Flemish style was influencing the best known of Portuguese sculptors like Diego Pires. Royal tombs had been made by what de Holanda considered the wrong kind of foreigners: northerners, Flemish or Walloon. The wonderful Vasco Fernandes, Grão Vasco, was painting St Peter in heavy robes, figures twisted for the rhythms they made in the pictures, foregrounds with tiles to emphasize depth and detailed landscapes behind; he was using elements of Flemish painting. He put his signature on at least two paintings, which was a very foreign habit. True, Vasco obviously also knew about Italian designs for telling stories, there were plenty of prints on the market in Portugal to tell him, and the story went about later that he had trained in Italy with Pinturicchio; he was another one in the vivid circulatory of the language of images. But men like de Holanda, Vasari and Fischart wanted to take sides, to impose unreal boundaries: Italian or Northern, make your choice.[13] The issue was the identity of cultures without nations to arm or police them; there would not be a German or an Italian nation for another four hundred years.

Money was the other issue: the painter as economic asset. Philip II in Spain had image problems and a failing economy, and one of his courtiers, Felipe de Guevara, drafted in 1563 a book meant to help: a *Comentario de la pintura y pintores antiguos*, a commentary on painting and ancient painters. De Guevara knew about art from Flanders and Brabant; he was born in Brussels, his father was a formidable collector, and he had a Bosch and a van Eyck of his own. He also knew about the Antwerp art market and its new workings. He says the real issue with pictures is how they last and how much other people want to collect them. He tells the story of a friend who was offered a job lot of two dozen paintings on canvas in Antwerp for only a ducat each, which was half the original price and around a tenth of the price for painting on wood. He says the work would never have been produced except for fools who think more is always better.

So when he comes to make suggestions to King Philip, he doesn't just talk grandly about how art is like farming because it nourishes the people and imposes order on nature. He talks money and markets. He wants Spain to produce art because it will help the economy and provide work for 'labourers and mechanics, who sustain themselves and their families only by their sweat'. He argues for new ideas, new styles in art because they will bring in the customers, for as long as the work is good enough. He talks about competition. He is talking about the Antwerp system. It helped that he saw national advantage in this, that the Spanish might 'stop being in awe of the Germans'.[14]

Not every artist could manage the Antwerp shuffle, and a shift in taste could be painful. Van Cleve's own family knew that. His son, the unfortunate Cornelis, offered his work in the Flemish style to Philip II expecting to make a career, but he was turned down in favour of the newly fashionable Italians. The change meant ruin because he had let himself depend on the court. In despair he went out to parade in the streets, his clothes and cape varnished with turpentine varnish, all shiny and bizarre. He was painter and picture all at once. And nobody was buying.[15]

10

Listen to the City

Walk out and listen: bells, carts, shouts in the city, sometimes dogs, cows or geese, sometimes horses, whistles, builders, market cries and pedlars and, according to Guicciardini, much more. He wrote of 'hardly a corner of the streets not filled with the joyous sound of singing and the playing of instruments', 'instruments of all sorts which everyone understands and knows'. The Hanseatic merchants had a band to play to them daily on their walk to do business at the Beurs. Street processions, civic and holy, were showy with 'great costly gold pole-candlesticks and their long old Frankish silver trumpets; and there were many pipers and drummers in the German fashion; all were loudly and noisily blown and beaten,' as Dürer noticed in 1520. The Church of Our Lady was 'so vast that many masses may be sung there at one time without interfering one with another'.[1]

The music of the Netherlands was already famous. It was Flemish singers who went with the distraught Queen Juana of Spain all around Castille in 1506, singing the Office of the Dead each day for her dead but unburied husband, whose coffin travelled with them. The *capilla flamenca*, the choir from Flanders, travelled with Charles V on his journeys round the Empire; he hardly ever took musicians from Spain.[2] Queens, kings and emperors paid for the soundtrack of court life and the dignity of their prayers, a kind of patronage which ran through the machinery of the Church and the grand houses of dukes and princes. Music was a household service, like art or cooking.

Antwerp, being in Brabant, was rather different. Erik, King of Sweden, on his way to woo Elizabeth of England in 1560, stopped off in Antwerp, where his people spent 'a huge amount of money ... on hiring musicians and singers to go with him'; what's more, his spending was notorious enough to be reported to the Medicis in Florence.[3] In Antwerp even kings went shopping for their music.

There was a music business, developed enough for a simple kind of merger and acquisition. Georges Lohoys, a musician with a fat contacts book, made a deal with a newcomer, Jean Hobreau or Petit-Jehan, on 20 March 1541. The two would work together, keep joint accounts, provide the music for weddings, banquets, any kind of party any time and for anyone, merchant or citizen or plain resident. They agreed to pool the tips and the incidentals along with the fees. They gave lessons in playing and lessons in dancing, sometimes at their own hall. They also needed apprentices who could play various instruments, and Georges Lohoys was much too busy to do without them. Two of the boys, Didier and Pierre, ran home to their father and it was such a crisis that Lohoys called out three sheriff's men to bring them back.[4]

There was high-minded music, as in the booklet the Antwerp bishop wrote which set the Ten Commandments. There was carnival music, raunchy as you like, about bodies and drink and not being able to pay the rent. There was music as a demure evening diversion. Girls had their portraits painted sitting before keyboards with their families, playing the virginals.

In Gabriel Meurier's *La Guirlande des Jeunes Filles en François & Flamen*, his book of conversation 'for the instruction of young ladies', music is one more game to play when you manage to get stern teachers to give you a holiday; it comes after making a pretty doll, bragging of your skills and being told you're qualified now to teach the fish to swim. In the dialogues the girls learn how to say the spinet is out of tune, the clavichord needs tuning, and once they have told each other not to sing worldly songs their enthusiasm dims quite quickly; and they find that playing this game too much, like any other, leaves a girl likely to let herself down and spoil herself.[5]

The great Erasmus worried about the dirty songs that girls might learn, such as those about cuckolded husbands, the secret meetings of lovers, a girl getting away from her vigilant parents. 'A lot of people, especially in Flanders,' he complained in his book on Christian marriage, 'earn a living from such stuff. If the law were more vigilant, the authors of these lullabies would be flogged by the hangman . . .'[6]

Arguments about pleasure quickly turned hot and biblical. Dance was either filthiness or ordained by God, nothing much in between. Huguenots from Paris declared it a sickness; it 'must infect the dancer', Thomas Chesneau said in a bad-tempered pamphlet. He acknowledged that some saintly persons had been known to dance – King David leaping and dancing, for example – but he said that was as different from modern dancing as proper marriage was different from fornication, or chastity from filthiness. The coming of Jesus had, in any case, wiped away the importance of all those Old Testament examples. He insisted on sobriety, on seriousness, and when people told him there was not much left to reform in Christendom and dance was 'a matter of indifference' he thought of dances 'which enflame the flesh of men as well as women'. For once, it was not only women whose arousal was an issue.

The answer to this came from Antwerp, in a loud, anonymous blast of print. The Bible showed, again and again, that it was possible to dance without vice, so the unnamed writer said. That meant that to attack dance in general was 'to offend the honour of God'. 'You might as well forbid eating and drinking because that can produce greed or drunkenness or corruption.' The pamphlet was written as a young person's apology for dance, and dance was a 'holy, ancient and laudable recreation'. 'In the grave and decent and careful movements of your body, which are dance, you glorify the main Author of the things around us.'[7]

Girls shouldn't indulge in music but always did, shouldn't heat themselves with dancing or public display but then Dürer couldn't help noticing at the official civic welcome in 1520 the 'beautiful maidens in tableaux whose like I have seldom seen'.[8] Meanwhile, there was such life in the music which came off the streets: the breath of the city, flashy like a carnival, meant for people who knew life with 'a flat purse' and the worry that the landlord was about to throw you out. 'What shall we do?' The songs were in print from the same publishers as the holy stuff. In Tielman Susato's *Musyck Boexken*, for example, there's a wife who beats up her husband because he gambles. There are also tarts in short skirts, women with 'hard breasts' and a girl who sings: 'Come tickle me now, I'm not shy. But don't tear my dress . . .'

*

Tielman Susato made a business out of all this. He came to town from Cologne in 1529 at the age of fourteen.[9] A year later he was being grossly underpaid, half the going rate, for copying music; his employer was the powerful Confraternity of Our Lady, a brotherhood of merchants and citizens that maintained a chapel within the huge parish church, along with six military brotherhoods, three rhetoricians' chambers, which were a kind of literary society, and twenty-seven trade guilds. A year after that, at sixteen, he was hired to play for the city band. The band loaned him a sackbut (*trompet*), field trumpet (*veld trompet*), crumhorn, recorder (*pipe*) and flute. In 1531 he was paid for playing the sackbut, a shouty kind of wind instrument with a slide like a trombone, nineteen times during Mass in the Confraternity's chapel.

He was a professional, not a servant. In religious processions where the city band played, Susato was paid by the authorities. He was paid in church by a lay brotherhood, men who took a close interest in the form of the music and the instruments that played it. They remembered their dead with requiems, sang votive Masses on days which were not official feast days, used songs to honour Our Lady. As Dürer noticed, 'the altars are richly endowed; the best musicians that can be had are employed.'[10]

So the Confraternity of the Holy Sacrament sang Mass to their organ, 'a pure, sung Mass' that began at seven each Thursday morning with half an hour of bell-ringing; the Confraternity of Our Lady sang Masses and praises 'in fine music to the accompaniment of a perfect organ'; the hosiers' guild of St Anne sponsored a Tuesday Mass; the Confraternity of the Holy Cross needed fifteen singers for some of its votive Masses; the Confraternity of St Andrew kept an organist and a bellows assistant, a bell-ringer and a chaplain on annual retainer, along with nineteen singers.[11]

These brotherhoods commissioned holy music, but not the same kind as the priests. They ordered motets, settings of words in various voices, which the priests could not easily fit into their services. They liked and used polyphony, music made up of different voices following different lines, when plainsong on one line was the proper and official church music. One of the first known sheets of printed polyphony was made in Antwerp for the visit of Charles V in 1515; it was already the city's secular style. They paid the best singers to sing duets and trios and they were keen on hiring instrumentalists to double the voices of their singers. They paid top money for wood-wind players, sackbut or shawn or cornet, because there was a distinct hierarchy of instruments. String players were needed at weddings, and dancing masters had to have lutes and guitars, but strings were not quite serious.

Susato had a place serving this merchant world, but he didn't want to stay on the margins. He married into the class: Elizabeth Peltz, sister of a successful merchant who would later become the head of the Confraternity of Our Lady. He started to think about a business of his own, but perhaps not on his own, in the complicated craft of printing music.

It seems an obvious idea. Antwerp was already the centre for making musical type, but that was on a small scale. The city was soused in music, and the demand for new material was too great for scribes to satisfy. 'Scribes are in such short supply', as the music publisher Hubert Waelrant says in one of his dedications, and in any case they were inaccurate and dishonest. The amateurs in town were writing for themselves. Waelrant wrote: 'This is about the second year a number of learnèd and sacred songs have been submitted to us. Their harmony was so well received by musicians, incredible as it sounds, that they all wanted the songs to be published.'[12]

Look at the title pages of the music that survives, and you can see that people simply wanted new tunes to play and new songs to sing. Antwerp publishers often sold anthologies with no composers' names, so buyers took a risk on unfamiliar material. They also included pages on the basic skill of reading music, in Netherlandish so anyone could understand, and sometimes also prefaces on exactly how to play the guitar, the lute or the cittern (which was an easier, smaller, less fragile and more portable version of the lute.) Beginners were welcome. The printing was careful to end lines neatly, to put in all the sharps and flats, to place word and tone so playing would be simple; the publishers Hubert Waelrant and Jan de Laet were famous for that. By contrast, in Venice publishers sold the new works of particular composers to players who knew precisely what they wanted. There might be learnèd notes on how to improve your playing technique, but nothing more.

Printed music in Venice was for professionals. In Antwerp it was everyone's.

Susato sold his own instruments to the city, a tenor sackbut and a bass sackbut, and in 1542 he joined a partnership to print and publish music. The city granted him subsidies two years running for 'bringing a new trade to Antwerp' ('*van buyten comende ende nyeuwe neeringe brenghende*'), because, oddly for a city already famous for print and full of music, this was the first firm to specialize in the business. One of his partners was a printer, and the other already owned the privilege, the protected right, to print a book of '*modulationes*' in four voices, a book of variations. Susato was simply, so it seems, the editor for the music.

Yet within a few months he'd bought out his first partner, and two years later he got rid of his second after a long lawsuit which had to do with a contract Susato drew up rather carelessly in an inn called Het Beerkin. He was good at being a merchant when not drinking. He set himself up close to the new Beurs on Twaalfmaandenstraat. He meant to show he was some new kind of musician, composer, publisher.

He was a merchant who took all kinds of risks, some of them as respectable as taking part in lotteries, which we know because he won big in Middelburg, the first prize of a silver-gilt cup filled with cash. He borrowed jewels from a merchant called Hornick so he could show them to possible buyers, secured their value against some polder land he had in the north and did not bother to return what must have been a spectacle of gold, pearls and stones. He was taken to court. Then he didn't get round to paying taxes on the land he owned in the north. Again he was taken to court, as he was for sundry unpaid debts.

None of this broke his close connections with the merchant class. His *Cincquiesme livre des chansons* (1545) is dedicated to 'my dear Lord and friend' Gaspar Ducci, the banker and speculator. The *Sixiesme* book is dedicated to a German money man called Keltenhover because 'nobody pursues the noble and liberal art of music with greater love and affection'. In his *Treziesme livre*, Nicolas Nicolai, known as Grundius, was praised assiduously for his 'perfect knowledge of music', but then he was an imperial counsellor and the main Brabant tax-gatherer and he had sold Susato his land in the north. When Nicolai was arrested for embezzling from the Imperial Treasury, Susato witnessed the document that appointed his defence lawyer.

He made the best of a city with a storehouse of patrons. The composer Orlando di Lasso, chapel master at the Church of St John Lateran in Rome, was already known in Italy, but famous only there. He came back to the Netherlands to see his dying parents, who were dead before he could get home to Mons; so he went on to Antwerp in 1554, where he stayed for two years. There he met the merchant Stefano Gentile from Genoa, one of the cultured circle of Genoese in Antwerp with serious money. They bought tapestry, they commissioned holy pictures, they had their portraits painted, they did business with the goldsmiths and jewellers.[13] Gentile helped Lasso find Susato, and then Gentile subsidized Susato.

Lasso learned well. For his next work, a book of motets, he had for patron one of the most powerful men in the Empire: Antoine Perrenot de Granvelle, the right hand of the fading Charles V, the essential adviser to the governors of the Netherlands, and counsellor to the newcomer Philip II. Susato had dedicated a book of his own motets to Granvelle but with nothing like the fervour Lasso found for a man who was now his 'sole patron and benefactor'.[14]

Susato tried to fly even higher, at least according to his son-in-law, who told a friend in letter of 1565 that he was trying to marry the deeply problematic Erik of Sweden to Elizabeth of England and, when that failed, to Christina of Lorraine. Christina had a claim to her father's throne in Denmark which she, at least, found interesting. If Susato really was involved, he chose the wrong cause. Christina had no interest at all in Sweden and Erik, quite apart from the ominous, grumbling meetings of his angry nobles offshore, wanted only to marry the sensible, comfortable barmaid with whom he was living.[15]

By that time Susato was out of Antwerp and away on his polder land, a bailiff and a sheriff in North Holland. He moved perhaps because of his Protestant ideas – he was publishing books of psalms in Dutch, which was dangerous with the Inquisition paying attention – but more likely because any time the city economy turned down, so did the music business.

He used the old kind of patronage, grandee paying a musician's bills and sponsoring a brilliant new career, but he was using a quite new system. Print changed everything. When music could be printed efficiently it could be distributed more easily and more widely. It was available like books, patronized by the great but not controlled by them, made for the streets as well as the palaces. Anyone could have the new tunes.

II

1549

The morning of 10 September, in the rain. There is an army standing by the walls of Antwerp. They're not looking at the walls, so they can't be planning to attack the city. They're outside the walls, so they are not defending it, either. There are 4,000 of them, all citizens, line after line of pikes, axes, halberds, arquebuses, all so neatly parallel to the road south that if an attack does come they will need a sharp right turn to stop themselves falling over each other.

They are waiting for an audience, not an enemy.

Antwerp is greeting its rulers. The Emperor Charles V has come from Madrid to present his son Philip so he can make his entrance into the bothersome city he will inherit. The citizens of Antwerp are expected to swear an oath of allegiance. They are not rebelling, not yet, so they have to put on a subtle show, fulsomely deferential but still insisting on all their special rights and privileges. The city has to do this in the language of the Hapsburgs, which is all theatre in the streets, rather like ancient Rome after a satisfactory war.

The show lacks some conviction. The triumphal arch outside the gates was supposed to have two façades, a second one on the hidden side, to show the city made an effort; but it is not finished. It was meant to have four square columns that would have carried the names of emperors back to Charlemagne, weather permitting, which the weather does not.

There is a little round church, also unfinished, where grand citizens and foreign merchants all in their ceremonial clothes, gaudy velvet and gold and silver thread, make a procession out of the city along with a 'huge multitude of priests'. The Emperor takes official possession of the city there. Then the citizens lead the way into town, followed by the splendid foreign merchants. The men from Lucca go first.

They pass city walls that have been rebuilt, mostly. The plans come from Madrid, the costs stay in Antwerp, which is one more reason to resent the Hapsburg rulers. There is grievance talk about being governed by a foreigner, about the oath of allegiance to be sworn in the city when Antwerp has 'so many and such privileges won in ancient times that it rules and governs itself almost like a free city or a Republic,' as Guicciardini wrote later. Antwerp 'is a city on every measure and every count among the principal cities of Europe, but the most principal of all when it comes to trade'.[1]

There is also the question of succession, about Philip following Charles. Some citizens are 'scared by the difficult personality of the prince who makes no effort to cherish them', who is all too obviously impressed by the opulence of Antwerp and the fine paintings and the scholarship but above all the money. Even his father is finding Philip difficult: they aren't talking, which means their ceremonial arrival is a show of solidarity as doubtful as the army posing at the walls.

City and Emperor have a strenuous relationship. He has paid too little attention to the Netherlands even though the territory is what makes his Empire work, with its available taxes and loans. Antwerp insists that imperial laws don't always fit a city which depends on heretics for its riches – Lutheran Germans, *converso* Jews from Portugal only theoretically converted and often inclined to Calvinism if they are, and local merchants all too taken with Calvin. It was better not to mention Anabaptists or the deliberately invisible and rather suspect group called the Family of Love, with their troublesome notion that all these struggles were unimportant since truth would be made blindingly clear in the end. The Emperor wanted the death penalty once for dealing in the wrong kind of holy books; Antwerp saved its printers by ignoring the order, and then reducing the penalty to a theoretical kind of banishment. The Emperor wanted to interrogate various of the *conversos* but the city somehow couldn't find them, and besides, it seemed rude to wake them too early in the morning. When Madrid comes visiting, as today, the Emperor's victories over Lutheran rebels are celebrated without mentioning who was defeated.

The Empire is sure it is Holy and Roman, the city is making itself a new and secular world. Charles wants to keep off the Turks and beat back the tides of heresy in Germany, and he needs to resist the possibility that some newfangled religious enthusiasm will break up his richest territory. Philip will have the same problem in the decades to come. His commander, the Duke of Alba, will look at the city's rich collection of the unorthodox and call it Babylon.

There ought to be carts smashing over these cobblestones, porters pushing and pulling the world's goods from all the water to all the land, merchants bustling from one appointment to another in the hopes of a deal, and twenty gentlemen from Italy, all with knives, watching the traffic in the interests of the Emperor's mortgage broker. Instead, there are roadblocks of lumber, canvas, papier mâché, paint and tinsel. There are girls standing about on shelves built for the day, and moral lessons being mimed on makeshift stages.

The streets aren't usually clean and monumental, but today there is room for processions from the gates to the core of the city. There are great arches that only look like stone which are supposed to prove how welcome are Charles and Philip. The Empire doesn't need to know that the craftsmen's guilds took a whole year before they felt welcoming enough to agree to pay their part, that the defence forces and the legal community refused; the city is nothing like unanimous. At the end the decorations had to be collected and sold to help settle the bills.[2]

The various trading nations – *natie* meant guild as well as trading bloc – know they have to get their place exactly right to show their standing. The Portuguese and the English, the men from Genoa and the men from Florence argue so strenuously over who will go first that the Emperor bans the lot of them.

It is also raining, 'rain without stopping', so 'it was not possible to see many of these things live.' And many things 'of great consequence' were not done at all. To avoid uncertainty the town clerk, Cornelius Grapheus, published a book in several languages to explain what should have been. He says he will treat the shows 'as though they were completed'. He forbids all other images or pictures or accounts, and he insists that his is the true description, never mind what people saw.[3]

*

The city had to be mobilized to make the show. Some 1,716 craftsmen were working on the streets – Grapheus counted them meticulously – and 'all of them from within the town'. They were the city's resources, but they had to be hurried along. Workmen were threatened with fines if they didn't work quickly, and then on 3 September there were threats of heavy punishment for anyone who stopped work before seven in the evening, or rested more than the one permitted hour in the afternoon. Antwerp was told to clean the streets, take down the stalls that might get in the way: hide its life away. The girls who were to decorate the *tableaux vivants* on the great arches along the way were told 'not to fail to turn up'.

The audience for all this was an Emperor and his heir. It made perfect sense as a political statement, not just some carnival show, because the Hapsburgs inhabited a world of theatre in the crudest sense, of painted flats, symbolic actions, special costumes. Philip came to Antwerp from days of pageant at his aunt's castles at Binche and Mariemont in Hainault. He had seen a designated hero storm the castle of the evil enchanter Norabroch, which meant challenging the Knight of the Red Gryphon, the Knight of the Black Eagle and the Knight of the Golden Lion on a mission to pull a sword from a pillar. Armed with the sword, the official hero had only to touch the wizard's soldiers for them to fall down. With one more blow he could smash a great phial, full of all the enchantments, left carelessly hanging at the castle gate. As for the enemy Norabroch, he was left on his throne quite unable to move. He was wonderfully dressed in cloth of gold to show he was a proper, noble and maybe royal enemy, very likely French.[4]

In the real world you couldn't pin down enemies just by going through the Fortunate Pass, skirting the Perilous Tower and visiting the Prosperous Isle as in the game at Binche. There anarchy, unrest and disturbance were all pent up in the Castle of the Savages with its sham walls of board painted to look like brick. Around Antwerp, sixty miles or so to the north, Calvinists were meeting, considering the need to revolt against a rigidly Catholic Empire. The French might make trouble any day. The English were not reliable. The theatrical games showed only what ought to be.

So Emperor, Prince and their two Queens understand perfectly the palace the city built in the Grote Markt to give them supper and a banquet and a balcony to watch the shows and jousts. It was a false town hall, deliberately bigger than anything more solid in Venice, made of wood but so brilliantly worked and painted that it looked like stone. It was built 'with almost unbelievable speed', Grapheus wrote. It was an eleventh-hour claim on greatness.

Down by St Elizabeth's hospital, where the Spanish and Italian merchants have their mansions, just before the odd little triangular 'temple' that hides a well, there's the biggest roadblock of them all: a philosophic argument one hundred feet high, fashioned out of stucco, wood, canvas and gold paint with just enough marble columns to anchor it. The merchants from Genoa have spent 6,000 gold florins to build it, kept 280 artists and craftsmen working for seventeen days. They paid the great Frans Floris to paint some 200 muscular and significant figures of gods and heroes, all more than life size, in five weeks. It is special pleading by a loyalist maritime city, but it stands in the very different city of Antwerp.

The glory of Charles fills the arch, with the promise that Philip will continue it. Philip beats back the harpies and wild beasts on the front side, the Fates weave his destiny, the gods equip him; Athena hands over her spear and shield for wisdom, Jupiter gives the thunderbolt he used to put down the revolt of the giants by making their bodies explode into flame. The giants are a general version of Charles' enemies, which makes the most likely particular candidates the Protestant Schmalkaldic League, defeated two years before at Mühlberg. The Genoans disapprove of heresy almost as much as Charles does.

They also want war against the Turks, which is why Victory is surrounded by Turkish soldiers in another panel. Philip, like his father, is expected to win. The god Terminus gives up the world so Philip can have it, especially America and especially the silver coming from America. Janus seems to be closing the temple of war, which is curious, but he is also the god of beginnings and changes, peace as well as war, and there is a promise underneath his statue in grey letters to look like carving: 'The Return of the Golden Age'.

The street is full of reminders that the sea matters and Genoa is a sea power, that Charles is to be honoured for putting down heretics: a panel shows him 'liberating faith'. This is not at all the message

Antwerp wants to hear, but then this monstrous arch is covered with so much to see and read that almost nobody is expected to understand it. It is designed for an audience of one, the Emperor, an invitation to come and decipher its mysteries through his interest in mathematics, in astrology and astronomy. He does come several times to see it and talk with the man who invented it: Stefano Ambrogio Schiappalaria, merchant and humanist from Genoa, living and trading in Antwerp. It was a design, Schiappalaria wrote much later, entirely to do with the harmony of the world, the harmony of a man's personality; 'if it would be able to move one would also perhaps be able to hear a harmonious sound.'

He meant to publish a book explaining all this, but he never did, and when he was writing the life of Julius Caesar and reflecting on the parallels with Charles V, he saw the nature of the Emperor not in the arch's pictures, or the words written on it, but only in the measurements. 'I who was charged with the invention tried my utmost to make visible, particularly in the principal measurements the musical proportion that it seemed to me could be perceived in the virtuous soul of such a valorous prince.' These are things nobody could hope to see from the street: the show was not useful without the book.[5]

The Antwerp fathers, too, are telling Emperor and son stories that citizens cannot be expected to grasp; their minds as well as their worlds are too far apart. On the stage of the arch of the Guild of Coinmakers, the god Saturn is busily making coins, which he hands to the goddess Juno Moneta, who throws them out in quantity to the crowd below. It is a 'great crowd', Grapheus says, a show to remind people how much money matters to the city. But when the coins come raining down, the crowd stretch and knock shoulders and snatch money out of each others' hands, they catch coins with their teeth, bonnets, hands, they stamp on each other's feet, they punch, pull hair, curse and swear. They are shouting, crying, bellowing. The shower of coins is meant to be a guild advertising its craft. In this world of metaphor, nobody thinks that people might need the money.

At the end of the evening, after the feasting, the dancing in the manner of the court, there is another show, 'a marvellous night-time spectacle'. On the Grote Markt square there is a tree, cleverly made, moderately tall with branches full of fruit and leaves, and two naked statues, Adam and Eve. A huge and alarming snake hangs from the tree. It is Eden, stuffed with gunpowder. A little flame starts around Eve's bare feet and rushes up to her belly, which explodes in a hundred other flames, which catch Adam and then the snake and then the tree in tiny flames which sound like a thousand arquebus shots. According to Grapheus the noise is terrible, extraordinary and curious. The statues are burned down to ash.

The grandees know what is happening. The people are sure they are hearing an attack. They see fire, their worst fear in narrow, often wooden streets. The suddenness of the flames, their scale and the sounds like thunder throw the spectators down on the ground, shouting and screaming, or struggling to get away any way they can.

The gentlemen of the city are proud that they paid for the whole show. They consider it what Grapheus calls a 'voluntary show of love'.[6]

12

The Meat Stall

Seventeen square feet of trotters and sausages, lights and lungs, bowls of set blood along with the flayed head of a great ox and the head of a pig ready to make brawn and a whole pig split open and a brace of fowl. In 1551 Pieter Aertsen painted a true original, a landscape of butchers' flesh.

It is not the prettier kind of market that Aertsen painted later, grapes that might as well be varnished, traders like minor goddesses, orderly things set out for sale on wide pewter trays. Then he was generalizing. Here on this meat stall he is specific. There is plenty, but laid out roughly and nobody is selling. Only one figure wears the red butcher's apron; he is off to the side with a bucket, a pot and a fire. The building is ruinous, fallen open front and back and with an indulgent chaos of oyster shells on the floor.

Aertsen was famous for holy pictures that went well on altars and in old people's homes.[1] He was a self-effacing man and very tall, which was the one thing he couldn't hide. He was said to let his pictures go sometimes for wretched prices, but he did well enough to own two houses and run his own workshop.[2] In a time before authorship was everything, when copying in an artist's workshop made it hard to be precise about what an 'original' meant, his name had value enough for a Spanish merchant in 1542 to feel the need to check that the painting he was buying was really from the hand of Pieter Aertsen.[3]

He could see live meat most days from his houses on the Ossenmarkt, where cattle were traded, but his new picture was a strange thing. It was not yet usual to make pictures of lifeless things for their own sake; there had to be a story to tell, a human portrait to show.

The Church thought so. The humanists reading Latin texts, friends of Aertsen such as the doctor and scholar Hadrianus Junius, knew how much the Romans valued pictures about stories. But they also knew of ancient Greek painters like Peiraikos who meticulously painted small things, and the Greek notion of rhopography or painting the ordinary. It was a classical licence to give things pride of place in a picture instead of relegating them to decoration or side details.[4] Then the things themselves could teach lessons.

There are fish on the side in Aertsen's picture, and some pretzels, all food good for Lent in contrast to all the other fleshy offerings, so perhaps he meant some moral point about not choosing self-indulgence. It doesn't seem likely. Fifteen years later his nephew Joachim Beuckelaer painted a butcher's shop with the same flayed ox head and a glory of meat, but with a man checking a tankard and a couple cuddling by a fireplace in the background, a sociable view of the same sort of image with no suggestion of moderation. Aertsen's version is more vivid, and very different because it is political.

Time and place are specified, the date on a bright white sign attached to the roof of the barn: '1551 10 martius', 10 March 1551, which means late in 1551 since the year began on Good Friday. In the top left-hand corner there are the prints of two hands, the severed hands from the Antwerp coat of arms, a mark more usually on the back of paintings. The hallmark on the plate beneath two fish is the rose and crown of Antwerp silversmiths. Through a gap in the wall we see the kind of holy scene that Aertsen put behind his markets and kitchens to draw attention to the spirit as well as the belly: a moment in the Gospel story of the Flight into Egypt. The Virgin is on her donkey turning to give bread or cash to a boy. This scene is not in the Bible, and the line of walkers behind the Virgin is nothing like the usual images of a desperate escape, but the scene does turn up in a couple of other Antwerp paintings around the same time and nowhere else.[5] There were regular processions through the city streets dedicated to showing the Seven Sorrows of Our Lady, of which the flight into Egypt is one: the crowd, the Virgin's attention to someone in the crowd, and the act of charity belong in one of those processions.

So the true subject of this odd picture is Antwerp in 1551.

Aertsen is showing the city's old ways and how they were being pushed aside, which is why he shows meat. The city's butchers were used to a comfortable monopoly, a guild of only sixty-two members which could pass its privilege to sons and grandsons. They were angry at the taxes on slaughtering beasts which they had had to pay since work had started on the city walls; they were trying to recover from floods which had ruined the pasture land where they fattened the thin cattle they bought in Denmark or Friesland or Holland; but worst of all, there were out-of-town butchers selling on the streets.

Rivals were not allowed. Butchers had the grandest, most assured of guilds with the grandest of all the guildhalls, the Vleeshuis, a seven-storey brick and stone monument in the Brabant style, built at the start of the 1500s by the same architects as the cathedral tower, with turrets just like the houses of princes and a meeting room of gilded leather which looked out and down on the city. The building was a more convincing town hall than the old town hall itself.[6] And yet their rivals, ignoring the law and customs, were disrespectful enough to bring in joints and chops and sell them openly on the streets.[7]

The law helped less than expected. The Antwerp butchers won the first round when the city confirmed their privileges, but the out-of-towners appealed; and instead of doing what he was supposed to do, which was to agree with the city, the Emperor seemed to think the question needed a proper official inquiry. The system was coming apart just like Aertsen's meat stall, which is a jumble of stuff standing in a broken house, open to the winds.

We know Aertsen's picture found an audience, because four copies survive. Most likely the buyers were from Antwerp, because Aertsen, like other Antwerp painters with a good living, such as Frans Floris or Pieter Bruegel, stayed away from the public and international markets, the *panden*. Clients came to his workshop.[8] Still, we don't know exactly who chose to live with this landscape of blood and sinew, or exactly why. One Antwerp merchant, Jacques Walraven, was close enough to Aertsen to pay for his funeral and ring the church bells in his honour when he died;[9] he took an Aertsen with him when he went away to Amsterdam in 1591, but it was not this picture. The widow of the merchant and tax farmer Frans Schot had one of his pictures in her estate when she died in 1602, but it was a picture of fruit.[10]

On the sign with the date, Aertsen has written: 'Behind here are 154 rods of land for sale immediately, either by the rod or all at once, according to your convenience.' It hardly fits a butcher's stall, but it could be a reminder of the boiling market in space and ground inside the city; the Ossenmarkt where Aertsen worked was assembled over five years, with many different builders working independently, not even consulting except to divide up the land. They built what they wanted as they wanted, and sold it on.[11]

But Aertsen had one acre of land in mind, and one man in particular: the man who turned the city into his own estate, cut it up and reshaped it, gave it a new set of monuments and even a whole new district with a grid of canals that inspired the shape of Amsterdam. He was the victim of Gaspar Ducci's men on the steps of the Bourse: Gilbert van Schoonbeke.

Gilbert started as an outsider, as his father did; the van Schoonbekes were from Liège. He had his father's name, his father's contacts, but not a penny of his father's money, and he was not quite family; he was the child of the unmarried Beatrix van der Veken. When papers finally came from Brussels in June 1544 to make him officially his father's son he was already twenty-five and his father had been dead four years.[12]

Like his father, he bought and sold land – he even worked on sites his father had once owned – but he was much more than a dealer. Land for the older Gilbert was a sideline, one more commodity to buy low and sell high like fish or gold or bales of wool. His son was also after profit but he did not mind sharing some of it with the people who bought his plots of land, so they would be involved in his longer view, which was nothing less than the very shape of the city. He bribed and shared, and kept the city's grandees happy, because his deals were the politics that the city could not manage for itself with its thin credit and its huge debts.

It was a quite short brilliance. His rise began in 1542 and fourteen years later he was dead.

He began by cutting up the land around Koningstraat, a street his father had opened. His main resource was friends: his aunt by marriage Anna Stegemans, wife of Ducci, sold him an impressive site and allowed him four years to pay for it. By the time he had to produce cash, he'd already disposed of the land and the houses on the site and he was on to the next deal with the money. He'd also involved important friends 'for mutual profit, damage and loss': the city secretary Willem van der Ryt and the city *stadsrentmeester* Michiel van der Heyden with his notorious taste for presents and percentages. Van Schoonbeke decided, but everybody shared.

He bought land from the monks of Baudeloo, this time in partnership with the lawyer Hubrecht de But, and did a deal to open a street called Jodenstraat across the grounds of the Carmelite church. The name is curious for a city which officially had no heretic Jews. The council paid for the new street while van Schoonbeke sold off parcels of land for prices that kept rising because they were close to one of the most important city streets, the Huidevetterstraat, the tanners' street. As usual, he didn't do construction; he wasn't one of the masons, carpenters and builders who tried to shape their scraps of the city. He made other people build. The new owners on Jodenstraat had to construct at least one house straight away, so the street was full by 1552 and with all the right people: Cornelius Grapheus himself lived there.

Van Schoonbeke picked up a house and garden that had belonged to a Florentine merchant who couldn't pay his mortgage, and he did the deal with two partners, who reassigned their shares to him on the day of the sale. It was the last deal in which he felt the need for cover. He bought a city block on what is now Borzestraat, cut a large house called the Dragon into two houses and made apartments out of the largest rooms. He bought an estate called The Three Moons from the children of Lombard merchants who had moved on from their 'grounds and houses'; he split the big house, sold the other houses, and the Lombardstraat opened. He made a public deal with Michiel van der Heyden, now mayor, by buying a large house from him on the corner of the modern Lange Noordstraat. When he didn't have cash he paid in *renten*, the promise to make payments at regular intervals like an annuity. He raised money on his property when he needed it, enough to keep the machine moving.

He had rules: move fast, have friends and take all the chances you can make. He interrogated the shape of the city for all the blank spaces, whatever they might have been: a garden, a courtyard, convent grounds or archery courts, a place for spreading out bleached linen or the unbuilt gap between streets. He thought about what the city might need: a new weigh house, a new market for the old-clothes dealers, a hall to show off tapestries and sell them, new wharves to end the six-week queues on the river and the long waits at the docks. He found a way to control the land where those things would happen, so he was there waiting when people and businesses started to move. On his own, again and again, he was making the kind of change Antwerp made when the new Beurs opened, pulling the city towards a new distract, unbalancing it brilliantly.

He did inherit one other thing from his father: a job. Like van Schoonbeke senior, he was weighmaster, running the old weigh house down by the river, a wreck of a building with too many uses which might have been designed for fraud. It was cramped, crowded, ramshackle, with no room for storage so goods had to wait outside for days and then to hurry things along only 100 items were checked out of each load. The law said all goods coming into Antwerp had to be weighed so tax could be collected, but between the muddle and the sampling they never were. It could be dangerous to mention this. It was the reason Gaspar Ducci's men went after van Schoonbeke on the steps of the Beurs.

The magistrates thought of repairing the weigh house, maybe expanding it, but there was no room down on the wharf by the Scheldt and the land around was too expensive. The weigh house had to be quite literally re-placed. Van Schoonbeke saw his chance. In a city which nobody planned, whose finances were always fragile, necessary change depended on men like him, and there were very few such men. He produced an ambitious, detailed scheme, not just for a new building but for a new city district. He knew where to look. The city had its artillery warehouse and its civic warehouse, the 'Houten Eeckhof', on land close to the Horsemarket and nowhere would be 'more appropriate, useful and fitting,' so van Schoonbeke said.

It was also hugely profitable for anyone who controlled the land in the new district. The city council accepted von Schoonbeke's proposal on 14 March 1547. Officially he bought the necessary land from the city only on 6 May 1547, but those seven weeks were no kind of risk; nobody could buy the land out from under him, because he'd found a front man to hold the land until a couple of mayors, Michiel van der Heyden and Lancelot van Ursel, could fully appreciate how kindly he meant to treat them. The city's old guard did like a little encashable respect. In return the city did much more than say 'yes'. They sweetened van Schoonbeke's deal: gave him twenty-five shiploads of brick and twenty-five of lime, gave him two years to pay for the Houte Eeckhof and the land around it, and threw in whatever they earned selling off the old weigh house on its costly site in the docks.

The city was getting what it needed. What it couldn't do as a political entity – taxing, borrowing, planning, making rules – it managed through friends, corruption, deals and private interests. In some ways it did rather well. Van Schoonbeke was used to thinking beyond immediate needs. He built not just a weigh house but a new kind of weigh house that was quickly imitated. He created a new city district to a new plan. The city accepted his ideas because nobody had an alternative to offer, but they were often very good ideas.

He did not plan to build one more trade hall with all kinds of uses, like the old one. He meant to build simply a weigh house, with reinforced ceilings to carry a store of grain if necessary. The city powers agreed. They had his plans for a rectangle of good brick and white stone. They fussed over the right materials and acknowledged in the end that 'the masonry is even better than the design details'.

The first plans involved weighing beams that were fixed inside the building, which was the usual layout, even though the need to bring goods indoors to weigh them caused most of the problems at the old weigh house. But on van Schoonbeke's second thoughts, the fixed beams became beams that could move along an iron bar in the ceiling, so the merchants' carts could stay outside under a canopy, the scales could roll out, the official weight in one balance and the goods in the other, with the weighmaster staying inside. Within six years Amsterdam built itself a weigh house on exactly the same principles.

Such a building needed open space on every side for the carts and porters and goods, and that created a new square. Its plan was nothing like the usual coming together of existing streets at a gap in the city. Indeed, there is no obvious precedent; there is a similar square in Palmanova not far from Venice, but that's in a star-shaped fort that was planned from the start, not cut into the middle of an intricate city.

At the middle of each of the four sides, straight streets struck out, named for the points of the compass; there was a dead-end street heading south but going nowhere to complete the pattern. The magistrates had all the streets open and paved within a year.

Resistance was not encouraged. The merchant and dyer Christoffel Quinget owned land where the West Street was going to run; if he refused to sell, the fixed geometry of the plan would be spoiled. He didn't see it that way. He reckoned his land would be worth much more when the weigh house was built and operational and he wanted to wait to do a deal. The city did not give him the chance. The Emperor sent an official who ruled that city and ruler were well within their rights to confiscate his property 'for the sake and profit of the community'. There was, of course, absolutely no need to improve the price.[13]

The land around the new square was van Schoonbeke's land, and he sold it quickly, four-fifths of it within eighteen months, for prices between two and four times what he had paid. Square and streets filled up, and a new quarter opened. The packers were the first to come and live there since it was close to their business, then people in the construction business, then the confectioners, the sugar-bakers who made the city air sweet at times, then wool traders, then the Hanseatic traders, the South Germans and the Italians. Van Schoonbeke sold his new quarter to the established families of the city, to the new rich, to merchants from across Europe.

One handsome building opened a new district. Van Schoonbeke both bypassed the city's money machinery, and also used its powers to buy when people were reluctant to sell, so he could plan streets and squares to his own ideas. He took a profit, of course.

Nobody else would or could make the plan, raise the money, find the bricks, clear the ground. Within a few years he had taken over the public works of the city. Between that and the farming of taxes, he controlled three-quarters of Antwerp's revenue. He had a large share of the profit in opening new zones from suburban avenues to new wharves. He stole the beer business and had to give it back, causing riots along the way. He also invented a ghostly forebear of the vertical firm which controlled anything a city needed to build from clay for bricks, peat to fire the clay, waterways to ship the clay and peat, the bought-and-paid-for politicians who could help make the plans and laws that made it possible to build and then the land itself. He was not a commander who wanted the city to be a defensive machine, not a duke who wanted the city to look imposing in order to keep the peace, and certainly not some royal who fancied grand display. He rebuilt a city with no purpose beyond the satisfaction of rebuilding, and money.

He did read Antwerp well. He knew the buyers of old clothes, the *oudkleerkopers*, because they were the ones who auctioned the property as well as the goods of the newly dead. For years they had been shunted from one market square to another. He offered them a new and settled home, the Vrijdagmarkt, to be the heart of a new district. He bought a garden and an estate in 1547 on Heilige Geeststraat, large enough for him to think in grand terms. He persuaded the city to pave the market square and the streets around and add a couple of useful bridges 'so wide that two carts could safely avoid each other'. Once the square was laid out it was simple to sell off the land around. The wealthiest *oudkleerkopers* moved there to live because at last they had the storage they needed both under the streets and overhanging them. After a while it was easy to tell how well a man was doing by how close to the market he could afford to live.

He understood the city's claustrophobia, and he made money out of offering relief. He had been buying courtyards, the open spaces where people could retreat. With that kind of competition very few people could afford the luxury of a proper yard of their own or a garden inside the city, so van Schoonbeke provided it just outside: a *hovenkwartier*, a district of courtyards, a suburb laid out with room for the rich to let their fantasy roam over the idea of a pleasure house and a house for the summer. It was only a half hour from the city, so there was no question of being isolated in the countryside. The city was booming, and so was the racket and confusion inside its walls, and so was the price of property; van Schoonbeke's rise depended on all the prosperity of the 1540s.

The man was brilliantly convenient. The Governor of the Hapsburg Netherlands, Mary of Hungary, 'took great delight in this same Ghillenberde', just as she did in Gaspar Ducci: one man she could ask to solve problems, who could put the magistracy and the city in their place. The city and the magistracy were not quite so sure. When business began to slow down around 1550, van Schoonbeke was not such an asset. When there was the prospect of war between the Hapsburgs and the French, the unfinished state of the city walls began to matter. He had taken over the city works, leaving nothing much to share; now times were harder and he was undercutting the other builders, so he was short of friends.

Jacob Maes was the city pensionary, paid to give legal advice to the city and make it work. He said Antwerp must have sunk very low if its future depended on a man like van Schoonbeke.

There was yet another project: cutting up the archery courts for a whole new district built around a hall where the tapestry-makers could show their work. Tapestry was art as fine as painting, full of intricate patterns and complicated storytelling, glinting with gold and silver thread. The designs of an Antwerp artist such as Pieter Coecke van Aelst were in the collections of François I of France, Henry VIII of England, Cosimo de' Medici and Philip II of Spain among many others, and it was only the Islamic disapproval of showing the human figure which spoiled his plan to show the Ottomans how the Turks lived.[14] It's true that Brussels was more famous for tapestry and Antwerp for paintings, but both were known in both trades. The Andalusian Pero Tafur had found paintings of all kinds in Antwerp a century earlier, but also tapestry in the Carmelite Church of St John. The Medicis sent a man from Bruges in 1448 to buy such woven art.[15]

In 1550 the tapestry-makers were still showing in the same church or else in the Vleeshuis because the butchers' hall had high rooms above the main floor with no direct sunlight to spoil the colours. Those rooms had elaborately carved fireplaces and fine leather-covered walls, and the tapestries lent a richness to the walk from stairs to meeting rooms. But a new hall for tapestries was a public good which could open up the south-eastern quarter of the city and make it as commercial as van Schoonbeke's zone around the new weigh house. There was a perfect site close to the Meir, but it just happened to be occupied already by the archery guilds. They practised, they drank, they caroused there. The guilds would move only if they could have a house for each one, four in all, in the same part of town.

The only obvious site for that was impossible because it belonged to the hostel and hospital run by a cloister of nuns, the St Elizabeth Gasthuis. Their prioress turned the city's offer down. She said she needed the land for pasture. She said it was intolerable to have a house of prayer next door to drinking clubs where men would make a fearful racket with their drums and pipes. She also pointed out that the city's offer was much too low; when the tapestry house was built, the land would be worth twice as much.

She knew what was involved in dealing with the city. In 1547, van Schoonbeke bought himself 270 rods (*roeden*) of land from a man called Jacob Wolffaert, who had bought it from the Gasthuis. To get the deal he needed the approval of Michiel van der Heyden and for his services van der Heyden required a gilded silver bowl decorated with 50 gold crowns, 100 Philippus guilders, a gold chain and a bowl worth roughly another 24 guilders. Then he went to the convent and worked his persuasive magic. Since Willem van der Ryt, the city secretary, had helped the process along, van Schoonbeke gave him a pair of silk sheets and a cup. Naturally both gentlemen ended up with some of the Gasthuis land.[16]

Nothing much, not even God, could stop the city when someone had made its decisions for it. The authorities would not consider raising the price they offered, and would not even think of finding some other site; so after lengthy, empty talks, the land was simply confiscated. The city did agree to build a wall between the nuns and the archers.

It still had more land than it could use. A quarter of the rest was sold off at a very modest price to van Schoonbeke: 154 and a half roods. Aertsen can be forgiven for missing out the half rood. The deal was done on 23 October 1551, which sounds as though it is after the picture was made, but the old calendar is misleading; Aertsen had five months to think about the deal.

Aertsen's friends and his customers knew Latin. If Antwerp was somehow the new Rome, as the new Beurs said in stone, they knew there were a thousand ways to imagine what was being reborn.

It had no army, no empire, and an imperial overlord of its own, so Caesar and Suetonius and Tacitus were not much help. But it was rich, vulnerable, corrupt and full of energy, just like the Rome that

Juvenal describes in his *Satires*, which were widely and often published in Antwerp. Between 1529 when Merten de Keyser's first edition neatly reprinted a version from Paris, and 1552 when van Aertsen's picture was on sale, there were at least nine editions from six different printers. In 1552 there were two from different presses. Most were neat octavos for reading, not show, but there was one in the smaller sextodecimo format: a pocket book of sorts. All this was close to Aertsen's circle – his friend Hadrianus Junius was one editor of the *Satires*.

Juvenal shows how vulnerable a great city can be, an example to be considered when war was imminent between the French and the Hapsburgs, when the fat years of the forties were followed by a downturn in business. The greatest fear for merchants and the new rich of Antwerp was the sheer fragility of their wealth. War could shut down the constant movement of ships and goods on which they depended. Their violently crowded city was full of sickness, which meant it needed a constant flow of new arrivals, and the streets were not safe. It was growing harder to ignore all that. The magistrates and mayor pursued their own interests, which were not always the merchants' interests, and their power came in part from a tight net of buddies and uncles and associates; corruption as a family value. Merchants were obliged to keep up the show, to keep the credit without which they could not function.

'The fanciest eaters,' Juvenal wrote, 'are the ones closest to ruin, with the light shining through the cracks in what is left of their lives.'[17] And here is Aertsen painting plenty, a fancy display for a dinner and a polished brass pot and a bundle of sticks to make fire, in a tumbledown building where the light shines through the walls. A city that read Juvenal would see the point at once. The *Satires* show Rome as a fretful, commercial city, a place where appearance is credit when it's not deception, where extravagance is a habit, where new men are trying to establish themselves at any cost and where any plan could come to ruin, given time. Juvenal says a rich man's spending is what gives him a worthy and creditable name and glory to go with it.[18] He says there's no shame in going bankrupt,[19] and some Antwerp merchants came to agree. His city, like their city, is constantly being rebuilt; '*aedificator erat Caetronius*', which means not just that a man called

Caetronius built things but that he lived to build, that he wanted to outdo mere temples.[20] And if the city seemed too packed, too airless, there was always the countryside all around it. 'You get another villa, sure one country place is never enough, then you expand . . .'[21]

The claim to be Rome was now more equivocal, not a simple claim on glory. Both cities were alive with gossip. Both were dependent on people going away to sea to make money; 'most men are now out voyaging', Juvenal writes.[22] They'll deal in anything, perfumes or stinking hides, because '*lucri bonus est odor*', profit always smells good.[23] Both cities were full of people operating on the edge of the law, because 'what respect for the law, what shame or fear can you expect from a greedy man in a hurry?' 'What causes crime, what leads people to mix up poisons or thrash about with steel blades is this one failing of the human mind: the mindless passion for unconscionable wealth.'[24] 'Nobody thinks it's enough to behave just as badly as the law allows; everybody wants to go even further.'[25]

Van Schoonbeke had a talent for making enemies of his friends. He fell out with his associate Jacob van Hencxthoven over the right to build brickworks on the clayfields of Hemiksem, and the price for a ship full of bricks. Van Schoonbeke planned to build four times as many brick factories on the same land, and to cut the price by a guilder a ship. Van Hencxthoven kept pointing out that this should not be happening, that he had signed the first contract before van Schoonbeke came along. Van Schoonbeke bought him off with a third of his own brick business, enough to stop the legal action van Hencxthoven was threatening. He did not get his approval. Van Hencxthoven said his conscience hurt him because he'd helped cheat so many citizens on behalf of van Schoonbeke, who didn't have 'a single hair on his body that he hadn't acquired by theft'.[26]

The city was as open as the meat stall, its walls still unfinished. The Emperor had approved new plans in 1540 for fine white stone walls to an Italian design to replace the old tumbledown defences, two years before Maarten van Rossum came on behalf of the French to threaten the city. Those would have been less than useful even if they had been entire, because they did not match the new habits of war. They were tall, designed to block stone cannon balls, and not thick to protect against the more destructive metal ones, and they had towers where the new styles of fighting required bastions. They would need to be replaced even if they had been entire.

In 1542 the French king had been assured that 'with the weakness of the walls and the want of order for defence' Antwerp 'may be easily forced, and cannot be succoured'.[27] The same foreign merchants who defended their city made it very clear afterwards that they would be leaving unless it was properly walled and defended. The city fathers could either demand much more tax to build formidably expensive walls or else lose the engine of the city's wealth.

Taxes were duly levied, on the butchers but also on bakers and brewers; in the end, everyone had to pay, however poor. The cash was found intermittently. The city borrowed and had to borrow again, with debts close to 1 million guilders and its future income mortgaged. Even so, seven and a half years after the new walls were begun, they were less than half completed: bastions missing, bridges not yet built, curtain walls between the bastions still just an idea; and the moat had not been dug. When as late as 1555 surveyors came to check the construction they found some of the new curtain walls were still so *caduyck* or rotten that they had to be pulled down and built again.[28] Workers weren't always paid. There was no process for masons to bid for work, and a remarkable number of those who got contracts were relatives of the city architect Peter Frans or else understood Michiel van der Heyden's taste for the finer things in life and hated to see him disappointed. Imperial inspectors also noticed work which did not seem absolutely necessary. Van der Heyden, in charge of security, had his own pleasure house built from the materials for the wall. He also connived in the theft of at least 57,546 guilders.

The scale of the city's debt was a secret the grandees in the magistracy kept even from the Brede Raad, the general council. The guilds, the merchants, the tradesmen on the council were not supposed to notice. That could not last. In 1548 the city was obliged to propose heavy new taxes and the tradespeople simply refused to pay. Mary of Hungary came to Antwerp to examine the accounts, the contracts for rebuilding the walls, any plans that anyone might have. She took a particular interest in what Gilbert van Schoonbeke had to say.

The new walls were bringing new space into the city, enclosing a zone to the north away from the mediaeval centre: the new town, the Nieuwstad. Van Schoonbeke had plans for the almost blank space. He wanted to make canals inside the walls so that ships no longer had to wait out in the river for as much as six weeks before they could unload. One canal would be for small ships coming down the coast from Zeeland which could anchor in a version of the old city moat, another for French and Spanish ships bringing oil and sugar and the all-important wine since nobody had much patience with the local stuff, a third for all the basic goods from the Baltic, England, Scotland and Amsterdam such as grain and fish and wool, and a fourth which would handle timber and in time be the base for a whole new set of breweries.

He had strategies to pay for all this, too. He would buy land at the price it would have fetched before the new district was planned so there was no need to borrow, and he would sell it on for its new and dizzy price. He would start sixteen factories to bring down the impossible price of bricks while the walls were still being built. The city would need to provide more cranes, at least small ones, and hire at least a hundred labourers to move goods by barge or cart from the new quays to the old city, but van Schoonbeke would add all sorts of 'assets' to make trade flow more smoothly.

He answered impossible questions with ease, but the plan did not all go well. Within a year the four planned canals had been reduced to three. Van Schoonbeke's bricks were indeed cheap, since they were 'nothing but earth'. The city printed hundreds of bills to send round the country to persuade masons to come from outside Antwerp, which they did, undercutting the city craftsmen. Still the work stalled. Mary of Hungary told them to get on with it, but the masters of the fortifications pointed out that their income from taxes and excises was more or less theoretical. However much the citizens paid, and hated paying, the cash did not go where it was needed. Papers were missing, money was scarce, van Schoonbeke was not doing his job of selling off city land even though it was the only practical way to raise enough to pay down the monumental debt, which had grown by more than 50 per cent since 1542 and by May 1551 reached 1,168,313 guilders. They complained about 'bad governance', about Gilbert van Schoonbeke and others who 'only want to spoil this good city, and make themselves rich and important'.

Not everything was van Schoonbeke's fault. He more or less finished two canals within six months of signing the contract but he could do no more until stubborn landowners were sued and bullied into selling. He had made a handsome building for the tapestry-makers, plain brick and bluestone, but it was finished almost too quickly; the tapestry-makers refused to move until they were promised no unfair competition from their grander colleagues who already had shops in the town. Bridges were still made under his regime, canals vaulted over, streets laid out.

The city was seeing its contradictions. The streets were a parade ground for strikers, for protest, for riot. In 1553 the dyers went on strike, held secret meetings, then marched to the sound of flutes and drums, then attacked some houses owned by Spaniards. Then the masons working on the city walls went on strike. In 1554 some members of the shooting guilds who were supposed to maintain public order, and some ward-masters, who were the local face of city government, joined the riots. They protested against the endemic corruption of a settled, closed class of rentiers who ran the city, and whose officer, the pensionary Jacob Maes, did not hide his contempt for the poor. They also objected to the gathering of 'eligibles' to fight in the Emperor's campaign against France.

When the city returned to calm, the Emperor was determined to investigate. When he found the leaders of the riots, they were whipped, banished or beheaded, and the shooting guilds were forcibly reformed: the city's order had been seen to crack, which must never happen again.

There was an even weightier issue: the business of beer. Beer was sometimes thin stuff brewed from grain already used, weak and cheap but cleaner than water, and it was also grand stuff sold in great variety: grey beer, sharp beer, double beer, local beers from Leuven and Hoegaarden but also from Brunswick and Danzig and Hamburg, from Gouda in the north and Rouen in the south. The best-seller of all was English ale. In a city famous for drinking, and for being drunk, beer was how all kinds of people quenched their thirst and washed away the world around them. An Antwerp translator, working in

1550 on a story in which fine Spanish ladies are courted with fine wines, felt obliged to add fine beers.

There were at least 376 pubs mentioned in the city records. In 1580 somebody produced a pamphlet called *Het mandement van Bacchus* in which the god of wine organizes a pub crawl round ninety-two named bars, with a full account of what you could drink there – wine, gin and beer. The night ends by the door of the hospital church, because all that careless pleasure can leave a man needing God and medicine.

By 1558 Antwerp was brewing 25 million litres of beer a year, and a year later it was selling 3 million litres outside the city. Antwerp beer was drunk even in Amsterdam. But before that could happen, there had to be basic changes – the quality of the water for a start, notoriously poor in Antwerp – and there had to be big breweries making the finer beers in place of the smaller neighbourhood kettles making small beer. In need of a plan and a change, the city again chose the man most available to be chosen: Gilbert van Schoonbeke.[29]

He couldn't sell the city land in the Nieuwstad to anyone else, so he might as well buy it cheap himself; and since there had always been a plan to build breweries he would be the one to build them. The Antwerp brewers faced fierce competition from the brewers of other towns because of their lower taxes, but that could be arranged. For a start, the Emperor rigged the beer market by ordering that anyone drinking 'foreign' beer within a radius of roughly three and a half miles of the city walls would first lose their 'upper garment', then on a second offence lose their citizenship and if they insisted on a third glass they would be perpetually banished. It was basic protectionism.

Antwerp beer had a doubtful reputation because of bad water, so van Schoonbeke opened the city wall for a lead pipe to bring it in clean from the River Schijn. The water went to the waterhouse he had built, was carried up by a horse-powered machine and delivered to the breweries, with a tap on the street for those who dared drink water plain. The brewers needed fuel, and wood was too expensive, but van Schoonbeke naturally had peat for sale. They needed somewhere to grind barley and he built watermills. He owned the storage spaces, controlled the transport of beer, he was even responsible for collecting the excise to be paid. When he was given an official monopoly, nothing changed.

The other brewers resented all this. They were forced to move from their various sites round the city where their customers were local and subject to pressure if a payment was late. They were now subject to van Schoonbeke, which was annoying in itself. Worse, there were rumours about the quality of the water in the new breweries, helpful drinkers putting out jugs of spoiled beer and claiming it was brewed in the Nieuwstad. 'It was,' some said, 'a shame that the city ordered people to drink such beer.' Since beer was basic to diet it was very easy to make an issue of the costs, the profits and the trustworthiness. The middle class, including the landowners in the Nieuwstad whose hope of a good profit on their land was blowing away, members of the guilds and ward-masters (*wijkmeesters*) in charge of keeping order, and the officers of the archery guilds all had a simple way to stir the city against van Schoonbeke.

On the evening of 11 July 1554 some three thousand people crammed into the Grote Markt to make their point. The crowd kept growing. The magistrates sent the archery guilds to clear the square but that only shifted the anger across the city. The authorities began to panic. The next day the city took away von Schoonbeke's privileges and sacked him and his two fellow tax collectors. It was all they could do. Imperial forces were otherwise engaged, as usual, and it was more than six months before a roughhouse of German infantry arrived to put down the riots once and for all.

Van Schoonbeke said he had done what he contracted to do, that he had actually broken up existing monopolies, but his rivals said he should surrender some of his profits to 'put an end to all the chatter about such profits and business finding its way into the hands of a private person with no benefit to either the prince or the city'. He did so, grudgingly. He moved on to his next business of supplying the imperial armies, which mostly meant paying them in kind. This time he was careful to have a seat on the board which watched his deals and checked his books. He had flown free too long to accept anyone else as inspector.

Aertsen was not pillorying van Schoonbeke alone. His friends and clients included two of van Schoonbeke's associates, after all: Walraven had been up to his neck in all the developments around the weigh house, and Frans Schot was van Schoonbeke's partner in his last career, provisioning the Hapsburg army that fought the French. Aertsen's subject is the state of the city.

Antwerp was full of riches, but had no money. There was no polity which had an idea of what the city should be; anyone determined enough and shameless enough and ingenious enough could control what was built, without saying what the point was. Antwerp had started to see what a city might be if it ran on its own interests, nobody else's, but it did not yet have the politics to resist an operator like van Schoonbeke.

Aertsen, as it happens, was an Amsterdam man by birth. Five years after making his picture of the meat stall he went back to his first home for good.

13
The Career

Getting out was the plan on many people's minds. Antwerp never had perfect order; it was an affront to imperial powers, a playground and a market for different nations who did not always even pretend to respect the city authorities. It was rich and broke all at once. Some people found it hard to work and sell in such a place. Others thrived in the disorder and came to depend on its way of protecting the unorthodox and the troublesome. An industrial machine for printing up knowledge could broadcast it anywhere. The looser the controls, the more usual the kind of contacts that were unlikely anywhere else.

Aertsen was leaving just as it seemed Antwerp might not be able to afford what made it so exceptional. The lack of order on the streets offended Spain's authority. Casual tolerance of religion was menaced by both Catholic and Calvinist forms of armed self-righteousness. There were supple minds, opportunistic in their way, who still knew how to use the city day by day, moment by moment, but now they also found themselves constrained and limited. They were always thinking again.

Consider the printer Christophe Plantin. He became the lodestar of the Northern Renaissance, but his survival depended on knowing what risks a man might survive and when he ought to run.

He was publisher of the new things to be known, his name on 2,450 books from his first rather limp titles in 1555 to his death in 1589. The list between is prodigious: all kinds of subjects from theology to anatomy to botany to travels in the Americas, from history to telling the future, printed in all kinds of languages. He printed long friezes which showed official events, funerals or royal visits, and glorified them. He produced a Bible in all its original tongues, an aspirational book that was scholarly, rather lovely but also a risk since different Churches took such different views of how to read Scripture, and how to eliminate anyone who was reading wrongly. He made books of emblems, pictures with captions to make a moral point, and works of devotion for prayer and thought at home. He was flexible enough to finance Calvinist presses out of town without being a Calvinist, and later his workshop was busier than ever with the new Catholic missals and breviaries to be sold through the Spanish shops of the Jeronymite friars. He even produced Richard Verstegan's notorious book of horrors, the *Theatrum Crudelitatum haereticorum nostri temporis*, to denounce the cruelty of the heretics he once financed.[1] Plantin chose the city and he used it.

He could have settled in Paris – he kept a shop on rue Saint-Jacques as business and refuge and he had family connections there; he could have accepted Frankfurt's persistent invitation after years of running his networks through the Frankfurt Fairs; but he never abandoned Antwerp, even after the city was burned and broken. It made sense to stay away at times, be in Paris on business rather than answer questions about religion, be in Leiden later when it was better to be a university printer than trapped in Antwerp under siege, but he always came back to the city which had made possible his business as publisher, printer and also humanist. The same factors that made the city unstable and defiant, the clandestine flow of information, the reluctance to impose uncomfortable imperial laws, the weakness of local guilds, the availability of money and the influence of foreign merchants in an empire which otherwise put a high value on every kind of orthodoxy, all this allowed Plantin his career. He fitted the Antwerp community of merchant humanists for whom knowledge was an ambition, not just one more ornamental habit.

Most importantly he was a foreigner, a Frenchman with a sad start in life: a mother who died very young of the plague and a wandering father who left him in Paris and never came back. He had some Latin and he had curiosity but he was exactly what he said – '*plebeus homo*', a commoner, a nobody in particular who had to invent himself. His family later insisted he was minor nobility who changed his name when he went into trade to avoid embarrassment, a legend proper for a great man, but his father knew grand houses only as a footman.

What his father did give Christophe was the habit of changing towns. He made his way to Caen in Normandy and apprenticed as a book-binder in a bookshop. He married Jeanne Rivière and they had their first child before they headed north.

They chose Antwerp, he explained in a 1574 letter to Pope Gregory XIII, because of all the foreigners just like him, 'the various nations congregating in the marketplace'. Since he was a man of doubtful orthodoxy writing to a holy person, he added praise for 'a King who is Catholic in word and deed'. When he came to write a preface to Ortelius' *Theatrum Orbis Terrarum*, he said how much he admired the brilliance and energy of the foreigners, and how it was they that made Antwerp into a true horn of plenty.

He arrived in 1548 or 1549, aged about thirty, one more skilled leather-worker and bookbinder looking for a living. He worked for an established market in expensive, lovely, portable and unnecessary things. He had a sideline in showy boxes gilded and inlaid with col-oured leathers that appealed to a merchant class with money to spend and papers to protect. He had a stock of engravings in his shop, he made cases for combs and mirrors, he dealt in lace, which was his young wife's business. But he was a very political craftsman who under-stood the uses of connections. The merchants knew his work and so they knew the man. He bound the city registers of Antwerp, which gave him official friends, and he made the books of grandees look good.

And then, in 1550, the leather-worker registered himself as a printer, long before he had a press or a book to print on it. There is a legend, quite plausible, that he'd been robbed in the streets while delivering a box which was to be used to deliver a jewel to the Queen in Madrid, and he was stabbed so deeply that he had to give up the sheer labour of heaving hides about and stooping to work on them. He did go on binding books if the clients had big enough names and deep enough purses, but not often, and he may have wanted an easier business. Per-haps the thugs who attacked him had money, and guiltily paid off a man who was already well known and might even be in danger of losing his livelihood. But more likely Plantin was glad of an excuse to imagine a place in the book world.

He told the Pope later why Antwerp was so good for a man who wanted to be a printer. There were all the materials he could buy,

13 & 14. The city in 1572 (*above*) resisted the Hapsburgs and needed a great citadel to keep it calm. The city in 1596 (*below*) was defeated and held fast by the Empire, a third of its population gone: peaceful but empty.

15. The first atlas of the world …

16. … made by Abraham Ortelius.

17. Christophe Plantin, his publisher …

18. … and the book that made his name.

19. The powers of Antwerp: aldermen feast in the van Lieren house.

20. Gaspar Ducci, who made the city all about money.

21. Gilbert van Schoonbeke, who shaped the city.

hier achter sĳ erue
te coope terstõt mett
roeyẽ elck syn ger
oft teenemale 154

22. Pieter Aertsen's *Meat Stall*: a vision of ramshackle Antwerp with a scandalous deal. On the small white sign to the right: 'Behind here are 154 rods of land for immediate sale, either by the rod or all at once, whatever suits you'.

23. The women of Antwerp: Catherina von Hemessen paints one of the first self-portraits of an artist at work, at a time when only men could join the painters' guild.

24. Dona Gracia, who ran the largest merchant banking house in Europe and saved her fellow Jews from the Inquisition.

25. Mary of Hungary: governor of the Spanish Netherlands 1531–55.

26. Margaret of Parma: governor of the Spanish Netherlands 1559–67 and 1578–82.

27. The Spanish Fury and the ruin of the town: 4 November 1576.

mostly the paper which came from around Troyes in France and which reached all the presses of the Netherlands through the docks at Antwerp. He was glad of the workers who 'can be taught in a short time' and who were used to workshops. He found that a foreigner could set up as a printer without much interference from the local guilds; only in 1558 did printers even have to join the guild of St Luke alongside painters. They came from France, Guelders, the Rhineland, publishing in ancient languages and modern ones from Danish to Italian and selling across Europe, often by way of the Frankfurt Fair: a true foreigners' business. More, in Paris publishers were hardly ever printers, but in Antwerp the same man both ran the machines and decided what they would print. There was a solid industrial base that smelled of heat and lead, machines that could always be rented out to do other people's work, to support personal choices and ideas.

Plantin had no fixed agenda for what he printed, but it is possible he tangled himself with the mystic Hendrik Niclaes, one of his friends. Niclaes was the kind of rich man who is sure God is talking to him but never quite explains what He is saying. He was determined to correct all the mistakes of Christianity, he said, and he had a brilliant strategy for coming through the turbulence of the Reformation: do as you're told so nobody suspects you, think as you want, and don't choose sides, because they will all be irrelevant in the blinding light of revelation. It was a sympathetic message, since Antwerp printers usually produced religious texts for the potential sales and not so much out of personal conviction.

Niclaes did have a great work to publish, *Den spegel der Gherechticheit*. He meant to correct the curious reputation of his Family of Love, based on his earlier book, which had argued for common ownership, clothes, 'that one may beholde the inward Members of their Body naked and bare', and people who 'do not vow or bind themselves in the Matrymony of Men'. He also had a habit of subsidizing printers. There is a single 'Chronicle of the Family of Love' which says Plantin meant to print for Niclaes, and raised the money for presses from their mutual friends in Paris; it also says Plantin stole from Niclaes, so it is not a friendly source. The problem is that nobody can find a copy of the great work printed in the right place at the right time, nor any evidence of where Plantin might have had his press.[2]

The record shows that it was 1555 before Plantin had his first permissions – his privileges – to print books. He probably still did not have a press of his own; printers took in each other's work and the name on the title page was often an afterthought. He rented workspace to produce three titles: Seneca in Spanish, one more in the long line of Antwerp editions of Ariosto's *Orlando Furioso* and a minor work by an Italian trader and humanist, Giovanni Michele Bruto, who happened to be in Antwerp at the time. For a novice like Plantin this was a local work by a local author, but in Italian. *La Institutione di una fanciulla nata nobilmente* is a manual on how to keep a well-born Italian girl marriageable. Plantin used this unpromising material to make more friends. He printed a special dedication to the town tax collector, Gérard Grammay, saying he was like a gardener offering his lord the first flowers of the garden: 'I present you this first shoot from the garden of my Press.'

His name was better known in 1558 when he printed the words to go with the ten-metre frieze that Hieronymus Cock produced of the 'magnificent and sumptuous, splendid and costly funeral for Charles V in Brussels'. Cock printed the gorgeously detailed copper engravings, but since Plantin produced the few words, his name was on the title page. His circle grew again. The book was paid for by Philip II's herald at arms, Pierre Vernois, who in turn had royal money to produce it. Plantin got to know the Spanish officials who came through Antwerp and kept in careful touch.

His printing was clean and elegant, often using typefaces designed by Garamond and Granjon which now look modern alongside their more Gothic rivals; the French influence included Guillaume Le Bé, from a family of paper merchants in Troyes, who made him steel punches to make moulds out of copper to make type. Plantin used copperplate engraving for his illustrations in place of blocky woodcuts, so he had the subtler perspective of crosshatching – pictures rather than posters. With that technique he later produced his own friezes to be stretched out like some early diorama, a report on who walked where and wearing what in a funeral procession or a royal visit, and he also fitted images into text so that the details made sense. His books used style to add to information.

There were always imperfections and botched sheets in the storerooms, but he made books well. An illustrated text had to go through the presses four times or more, the sheets liable to shift out of order, especially where they were left to dry. Late and early printings had to be married to make a book, sometimes, as with Montano's *Humanae salutis monumenta*, using pages printed ten years apart and illustrations from a quite different book, the *Horae* that Plantin produced a year earlier. Illustrations had to be printed onto previously printed text, a job done by specialists like Mynken Liefrinck, unusual as a woman among the presses; that was one more chance to stack them out of order. Sometimes the best evidence for Plantin's reputation is when things go wrong, as when Henricus Coracopetra complained to a friend that his Hebrew Bible was incomplete 'and it surprises me that Plantin, who is so careful in virtually everything, did not pay more attention to the collation of the sheets of the books he printed'.[3]

Books had to find buyers all over Europe and beyond. Plantin kept a shop in Antwerp, selling his books and other people's books, sometimes paid for and sometimes exchanged. He offered clergy thirteen missals for the price of twelve. He sold retail to other shops and the number in Antwerp itself was constantly growing – twenty-seven in the 1570s – but he was careful never to let debts run for too long; he bought quick payment with discounts. At the core of his organization was the Frankfurt Fair. He kept so much stock there that he needed a strongbox for books all year round. He bought and sold finished books of course, but he also did deals for type, paper, woodcuts. He met scholars with proposals for books. He met rich patrons who might subsidize scholars. He did publicity, making announcements and showing off proofs for an expensive and complex work such as the Polyglot Bible that would need supporters. He made sure of the bills of exchange that would keep the business rolling. And always he listened to news, watched for obstacles that might block sales routes or stop payments, and for books selling in other places. Late in his life, in 1586, he noticed Antonio Possevino's *Moscovia*, a wonderfully circumstantial Jesuit account of the court of the Russian Tsar Ivan the Terrible which had just appeared far over the Baltic in Vilnius. Within a year Plantin had his own edition out in Antwerp.

He put out the anatomy of Vesalius and carefully revised herbals, books on the drugs that doctors could use. He published geography, including Ortelius' book of maps of the world, the *Theatrum Orbis*

Terrarum, and astronomy, and half the scientific books made in the southern Netherlands, and two-thirds of those published in Antwerp in his time.[4] He made books in Hebrew, using the same type that had made Daniel Bomberg the most famous of Hebrew printers in Venice; Plantin was partners for a while with Bomberg's nephew. His French Bible was rather too close to the Calvinist Geneva version; its priestly translator René Benoist argued that 'since the spiritual war is open between us and the heretics, why shouldn't we plunder them?'[5] Plantin's excuse was to show another, French version which was even more 'corrupt', and a *nihil obstat* certificate from a cathedral canon. He had a best-seller.

Plantin produced editions of Greek and Latin authors and works on Roman forts and history and amphitheatres; works of devotion; and emblem books which are full of lessons told through nice illustrations and moral captions. We owe to him Guicciardini's description of the Low Countries, with all its exact pictures of institutions like the Antwerp Beurs and the people using them, and accounts of the time Philip II came to Antwerp and later when the Duke of Anjou made his formal entry into the town.

Bookbinders now depended on the one-time bookbinder, and almost every woodcutter and copperplate engraver was working for him; he dominated the print trade in the Netherlands. Philip II gave him the grandest of invented titles '*prototypographus*', the first printer, and set him to keep control of a singularly unbiddable trade whose profits often lay in defying authority. Plantin was supposed to have all kinds of honours and rights and liberties, not to mention freedom from beer and wine taxes, but the privileges were never delivered. He kept saying he couldn't even do the job, because his Dutch was not good enough to do all the examinations.

All this authority and skill was a fragile thing, vulnerable to any upset. Plantin ran out of paper in 1568 to print the Polyglot Bible and the project stalled. He urgently needed the subsidies that the scholar Arias Montanus was bringing from Spain. Montanus took far too long. His ship ran aground on the west coast of Ireland and he had to make his way overland to Antwerp across all Ireland and England. Plantin waited weeks, but then decided it was time to visit his shop in

Paris, where at least people were buying books. He had to learn how long it took money to get away from Madrid.

Even more pressing were the tides of religious enthusiasm. Plantin was away in Paris in 1562 settling a lawsuit, but his presses did not stop; three of his journeymen ran off 1,500 copies of a Calvinist work called *Briefve instruction pour prier*. They were denounced by, among others, a Spanish proofreader; proofreaders must have had a sense of superiority, because workshop rules had to tell them not to laugh at the pressmen. Since there was no point in alerting the indifferent Antwerp authorities, the proofreader went directly to Brussels. Margaret of Parma, who had been governor since 1559, wanted printers questioned to see if they could identify the type, but of course they could not, because some fonts were in use everywhere. Even so the journeymen were named, found and sentenced to service on the galleys. Antwerp refused on principle to feed prisoners once they were convicted by the Spanish, and in the confusion they managed to slip away.

Brussels had doubts about Plantin's true faith, and in any case he was the master, responsible for what his workers did. His presses shut down. His creditors, led by Cornelis van Bomberghen, insisted on selling off his goods on the Vrijdagmarkt, making an account of his books in store in Frankfurt and the paper that was a tenth of his assets. The sale only looked ruinous. If Plantin had been convicted of heresy, his goods would have been forfeit, but after this sale everything was in the hands of friends. When the official questions died down Plantin could set up a new company in 1563 with his seemingly vengeful creditor van Bomberghen as his main backer and bookkeeper, joined by three other members of his family. The only name on the title pages was Plantin, unless they were printed in Hebrew with the type van Bomberghen inherited from Venice; all the rest needed Plantin's investment, which was not money but the matrices and punches for making type. The partners now had a press and a publishing house for 'books in Latin, Greek, Hebrew, French, Italian . . . and anything they judge to be to the profit of the said company'. By 1566 there were seven presses rolling.

Around the same time Plantin started to write letters to the authorities announcing his perfect Catholic orthodoxy. He made sure of his Spanish connections in the Netherlands. He started to stock his shop in Paris, in case he needed ready money. He was still Hendrik Niclaes' man, though, not inclined to take sides too exactly between Catholic and Calvinist. One of his journeymen printers was going off to Vianen, in Protestant territory close to Utrecht, to set up a press. Plantin provided materials; there would be editions of Niclaes' work, but also some anti-Spanish and Calvinistic pamphlets. It was the old Antwerp tradition of printing anything, but not always admitting it, and no doubt the partners approved; but it was the wrong time. Spanish forces were pushing Protestants out of their territory and they reached Vianen.

Plantin insisted his journeyman write to apologize for daring to go against his orders. He did more to save himself. His good friends and new partners in his workshop were Calvinists. He waited to pay them off until hopes of a religious compromise were ruined by the arrival of the Duke of Alba as governor. Then he broke with them because, he said, they were not perfectly orthodox. He stayed and wooed Philip II's secretary Gabriel de Çayas as a new patron. His career became brilliant again.

14

Antwerp Is Lost

There were a few boys making trouble in the cathedral, so Abraham Ortelius told his friend Emanuel van Meteren. They jeered at the woman who always sat by the Lady Chapel asking for alms. She was infuriated, she threw water at them, they mobbed her, and all the holy stillness became riot. It was August 1566, only a few weeks since the statue of the Virgin Mary had been jeered on the streets; the cathedral priests decided it would be wise to get away from the church.

The city heard that they had been driven out. The Margrave arrived with magistrates to clear the building and shut the doors but some people took to singing psalms in Dutch in the choir, in front of the pulpit, which was like flying a Calvinist banner in a Roman church. An hour or so later, some of them went further: they started to attack the images.

Within an hour every church and convent in town was under attack. Little groups of men roamed the streets, maybe only six or eight of them, but people ran away even though there were lights outside buildings and the onlookers had weapons. The city seemed surprised that it didn't defend itself. Before one in the morning, the sculptures, the ornaments in the churches were smashed and gone, and the saintly figures above the gates of great houses and on the corners of streets had been ruined either by the image-breakers or by the owners, who did not want them climbing their property. As Ortelius wrote: 'The churches looked as though the devil had been at work there for one hundred years.'[1]

On all sides Antwerp knew this was much more than another disturbance. Canon Castillo wrote at once to Cardinal Granvelle, now counsellor to Philip II as he had been to Charles V. He told about murderous battles among the friars, two or three dead, and a consoling anecdote about a curé who put on the cloak and hat of a Calvinist to listen to a preacher, heard him to the end and then took his place on the stump to correct all his errors. But his conclusion was brutal: '*Anvers est tout à fait perdue*,' he wrote; 'Antwerp is completely lost.'[2]

Protestants who watched the more radical Calvinists demand their place in the city were not much happier. In September one of his correspondents warned the preacher Heinrich Bullinger in Zurich: 'No godly person can now remain at Antwerp in security and free from danger.'[3]

For what died that night was the city's secular advantage, which was not compromise but something more remarkable: a practical ability to include beliefs that were going to war in other places. The city did not have to approve of heretics, let alone honour them as it did the Sacraments and Our Lady; it only had to give them air.

The Joyous Entry, the great show at Antwerp in 1549, the fireworks and canvas monuments and allegorical girls, was meant to prove that power in the Netherlands was going to pass across easily from the unloved Charles to his even less loved son Philip. Antwerp would always keep its value: money, information, guns, books, ideas and connections. And yet the succession was never quite happening and the certainties faded. The city waited nervously for Philip, knowing his religious enthusiasms but vague about the temper of the man; he was hard for Netherlanders to read since he spoke no Dutch and no French.

Antwerp had reasons to be alarmed. Charles published the 'eternal edict against heresy' in 1550, the 'bloody edict' which required proofs of orthodoxy from anyone wanting to settle there. It was close to a declaration of the religious war that Charles wrote and preached about, but the city magistrates were still sure their old machinery of talk could work against it. After all, a warlike Empire needed the city's money; of the 1 per cent tax on exports in the mid 1540s, Antwerp accounted for 75 per cent of the whole take from the Netherlands, and Amsterdam only five. The magistrates knew they could still send to the governor Mary and expect to plead Antwerp's case.

It helped that heresy in Antwerp was still quite discreet. Most of the

Calvinist ministers stayed only a year or less. Most people who were drawn to Protestant ideas still went to Mass after reading the Bible. There was no true Protestant congregation until well into 1555, no anti-Church. The Calvinist elders fretted over the *salonpredikaties*, informal services for the grander and richer, which might draw attention to their private change of mind. Official gatherings were announced carefully, door-to-door by messengers, *weetdoeners*, who told only the faithful where to be and when.

Christophe Plantin had always been discreet, but now his beliefs and thinking were often coded. The notorious Guilherme Postel, a man who claimed to be the Pope of angels, used to be respected as a great teacher of oriental languages in Paris. Now the very presence of his students working on Plantin's Polyglot Bible was enough to make the texts and translations suspect to some in Rome. Arias Montanus had to insist he needed learning and competence, not perfect orthodoxy.[4]

Postel wrote to Ortelius to get him to give Plantin a message; he did not write directly to the printer, because everything was now indirect. He wanted to say that 'the high alumni of the school of charity' were 'not unknown' to him. He wasn't part of any sect or school, so he wrote, and he was horrified by some of the bloodthirsty prophets around, but he inclined to the Society of Charity which was also known as the Family of Love.[5] Plantin was disturbed even by such oblique acknowledgement of the very careful sect, but eager for a distinguished convert who'd made it known that he didn't much care for any other body of reformers. He was also puzzled. 'I don't know what you mean,' he wrote. 'I beg you, sir, to interpret this passage for me.' He then found the nerve – his phrase – not just to ask for an explanation but to launch a small sermon on how to approach 'the glorious facts of the eternal' by way of Jesus Christ.[6]

Postel wrote back with a phrase associated with the Family of Love: 'as God is my father, so Nature is my mother.' He said: 'I have written again to Ortelius but I don't know how much he understands. Talk to him in the language he knows.'[7] From all this Plantin made up his mind to tell Postel he was ready to 'rejoice hugely that you are heading in the direction of the path of charity'. He proposed that Postel go forward in the fear of the Lord, tame the sins of the flesh and then 'at his glorious resurrection, [the Lord] leads his people out of the shadows.'[8]

The central advice of the Family of Love was respect for outward forms, for regular orthodox worship. That done, your mind and your heart were your own.

That kind of moderation was going past its time. Calvinism was orderly and organized, thinking its own theology and forms of worship out from scratch and often flourishing where people were used to the discipline of working in industries; it was a formidable opponent to the order, power and hierarchical certainty of the Roman Church. With such a clear distinction, there had to be a choice.

Antwerp had no bishop, after all, and not much Church machinery to look for wrong ideas. The bishop designate, Filips Nigri, much opposed by the canons of what was going to be his own cathedral, died in 1563 without managing to be enthroned, and nothing more could happen until the determined Duke of Alba took charge.[9] The city admired the processions, the music, the splendour of the Church, but not the clergy. Half the canons lived outside the city. Through the 1540s when the walls needed to be rebuilt the clergy refused all invitations to pay taxes; they were denounced as a 'bunch of fellows who live by the begging bowl and don't pay excise or tribute'. Even during the iconoclasm, when the streets were full of Calvinist propaganda, there was remarkably little Catholic resistance. In France good Catholics sometimes beat the theology out of their neighbours.

The nobility of Brabant might want to reset their relationship with the King of Spain, but not all of them wanted to end that relationship and fight the King. They were not quite at the point where they had to choose between Protestant rebellion and submission to Church and Spain.

For the moment Antwerp was still useful, always the way-station if not the final destination, a space quite close to being safe in Hapsburg territory. The Protestant matron Anne Hooper had to get out of England 'by my husband's bidding and the advice of my friends', and the Lord, she said, conducted her safely to Antwerp. She didn't mean to stay there but she knew she could find 'a party every way suitable' to take her on to her relatives at Frankfurt. William Salkyns reassured

Heinrich Bullinger, anxious in Zurich for his friends and flock in England, that his delayed letters were on their way to Antwerp and they 'shall be conveniently and safely forwarded'. Even when communication with the Protestants in England had virtually collapsed, Antwerp still seemed the solution. 'I do not know how you can address any letters thither [to England],' Peter Martyr told Heinrich Bullinger: 'I am myself in the same predicament, and there is only, I think, one way left, namely, to send them to Antwerp; for if you have any friends there, they will be able to forward your letters, whithersoever you wish, without much trouble.'[10]

It couldn't last. The reliable city was already full of riots that drew imperial attention. Antwerp had to ask for help to maintain order and since some of the local ward-masters had also been rioters the help had to come from outside. In 1555 Charles began to lose patience. He ordered the reorganization of the police to control the streets. Even when Philip was proclaimed King of Spain and the Americas in 1556, and even though he was already married to Mary Tudor of England, he stayed put in the Netherlands. He had his priorities, which other people got wrong. Thomas Sampson told Bullinger that 'our languishing Penelope' (Mary Tudor) 'is waiting the return of her Ulysses' (Philip II), 'who is celebrating bacchanalian orgies at Antwerp ... most disgusting accounts are given of their dancing, nightly buffooneries, and ravishing of virgins'. Sampson, writing from Strasbourg, made assumptions.

Nobody could think any more that Antwerp was safe. Sir John Cheke, once Regius Professor of Greek in Cambridge and then Secretary of State to the very Protestant King Edward VI, was 'in the country where he thought himself secure' with a safe conduct and a satchelful of astrological readings to reassure himself his papers would protect him. He dared to spend time in Brussels with the ambassador of the Catholic Mary Tudor, and then set out for Antwerp and the boat that would take him to England. It was 15 May 1556. 'Even there he was caught in the High Way,' as his biographer John Strype writes. He was 'unhorsed, blindfolded, bound and thrown into a wagon', 'legs, arms and body tied to it'. He was shipped to England and the calm of the Tower of London to reconsider all his errors, quickly.[11]

*

Philip needed the Netherlands and Antwerp for the usual reason, which was money. There was no silver left to pay for his war with France.

He demanded money from the States General, the assembly of the Netherlands. The Netherlanders paid him back in grievances; he wasn't fighting wars for them, they said, but for Spain and Italy, who were paying much less. They took two years to agree any money and then they gave it only on their own tight terms. When in 1559 Philip finally defeated the French and went back to Spain, his northern lands were still not settled. He was very aware that religion was unsettling the whole territory.

The habit of casual tolerance was challenged. Giovanni Zoncha had found a kind of freedom in Antwerp for a while, not just the girls and guns and food in Lent. He liked the doctrines going discreetly about town, and felt entitled to a certain liberty of thinking. He had to ask friends for books in Italian, since Antwerp was no longer the main centre for printed heresy in all languages. He especially wanted the works of the most unorthodox Peter Martyr Vermigli and his account of shunning superstition. Vermigli defended the Reformers' idea of the Eucharist to which both Lutherans and Catholics fiercely objected, the one which denied the bodily presence of Christ. And yet, exiled from Italy, he had made a distinguished life for himself in the north, in Oxford, Strasbourg, Zurich; he was a challenge but maybe also an example.

Zoncha asked for Vermigli's books but in the next paragraph he was worrying that the Spanish would impose the Inquisition on Antwerp, that his idea of liberty might not be secure. He says there's no need for any Inquisition to make sure God is praised, which is something his Lutheran friends did not need to be told. He really hopes that all will go well.[12]

The court and the orthodox also worried. Every Sunday Maximilien Morillon wrote from Brussels to his protector Cardinal Granvelle. Morillon was entirely orthodox and grandly connected, since his father had been secretary to Charles V. He wrote down the anxieties of the Hapsburg world. He complained that heretics, even Anabaptists, were escaping justice and the authorities seemed to do nothing effective to stop them. He reported posters being nailed up around

Antwerp urging bloodshed and the taking of property. There were rumours of merchants ruined and bankrupt because there was no ready money to be had. The villagers were refusing to pay their taxes, which was ordinary enough, but there was a new development: villagers were refusing on principle, not because of a bad harvest and on the strength of their local privileges. They claimed to have their own rights.[13]

Throughout 1566 preachers came into the countryside teaching Calvin's ideas. These 'hedge preachers' were in Antwerp by June and a Frans Hogenberg print shows the crowds that came out to pack together up against a palisade, behind a coppice, on the edge of a hamlet; they were both discreet and unmissable. Prominent and distinguished persons went out to hear the new Word. Lutheran ideas were already common enough in the merchant world and were said to be changing the minds of the city's literary guilds, the Chambers of Rhetoric. Philip was advised to drop his strong rules against heresy, but he refused just as issues of the spirit eclipsed even hostility to foreign rulers. The iconoclasm in Antwerp, that night in August 1566 when so few people did such damage to the images of holiness, was directed at churches and sometimes saints on gateways; there were no looters, except of church silver, no attacks on imperial officials or the town hall. God, and how to think about Him, was now an issue.

Morillon told Granvelle there were crowds in town in early September a month after the iconoclasm, more than he'd seen for a long time, coming back for the new 'liberty of religion'. People were talking about the Inquisition again. Catholic churches were full for Mass, although the matins service, vespers and the singing of 'Salve' after vespers were all 'sleeping'.[14]

Everything was unsettled. Antwerp was reminded that it had rivals. The English Merchant Adventurers flitted to Emden and to Hamburg after Philip lost his temper over the English seizing ships carrying silver to Antwerp. Then the city had to subsidize the German Hanseatics, building them a palace on the scale of their Venetian palace, but since they didn't need this one grand gift the city could offer, only a few stayed in residence.[15]

Castillo found Hieronymus del Rio, one of the big players on the

Beurs, sending what he could back to Genoa or to Spain, saying that if he could find a buyer for his splendid ships and warehouses he'd sell so he could go back to Spain. There was talk that he'd do no more deals in Antwerp, where the market produced only damage and scandal. Since the city lived from seaborne trade, this was an alarming prospect.[16] There was also a priest chased in the street by children. There was alarm about the Portuguese 'infected' by Calvinism, but then they were mostly Jews sent to encourage dissension, Morillon told Granvelle.[17]

William of Orange, called 'the Silent' because he never quite said what he was thinking, was now the visible leader of the nobles against Philip. He was not yet a rebel; he tried compromise, with a deal to share out the Antwerp churches. Even Lutherans would have their places of worship, although they offended Calvinists with their semi-Catholic ways almost as much as they infuriated Catholics. It might have worked. But volunteer armies fighting on the rebel side against the Spanish lost battles in March 1567 and William of Orange decided to leave the city. Antwerp's compromise, assigning some churches to Catholics, some to Calvinists and some to Lutherans, was not going to last. Armed rebellion against the Crown was disintegrating, Protestant worship was becoming ever more discreet and Philip and Charles had every reason to think they were winning.

They were wrong. The problem was philosophical and therefore profound. Their insistence on authority, holy and political, was now being seen as a violation of the privileges and even the 'freedom' the Netherlands had known. Jacob van Wesenbeeke said so, and he was the one-time pensionary of Antwerp who had helped broker the deal over churches. He preached in print about 'natural ingrained freedom, which man above all esteems and will not allow to be taken away'.[18]

The seeming blasphemy and desecration of the iconoclasm, the *beeldenstorm*, was lese-majesty to the powers in Madrid, the political act of rebels as well as thieves and heretics. Allow anything like it, and the monarchy itself was at risk. Margaret of Parma took up the governorship of the Netherlands in 1559 and reckoned Protestant preaching in any form was a cause of 'scandal'. Philip was urged to come back to the Netherlands, which is what a good mediaeval monarch would do to put down rebellion, using himself as a godly symbol as well as guns, but he was busy with Ottoman attacks and preoccupied about being a widower without an heir. The unorthodox would have to be put down some other way.[19]

He decided on the brute kind of action. Margaret of Parma had never seemed a very plausible governor, but now she felt obliged to resign and go into temporary exile in Italy. In place of her attempts to manage the situation, the new governor was the gouty, calculating, foul-tempered Duke of Alba. Troops came with him, as did some of the machinery of the Inquisition. It was just as people had feared, although it was not quite the Holy Office as in the south; 'inquisition' was becoming the word for any official inquiry where a man might be expected to tell the truth. When the Council on Finance heard evidence under oath in Antwerp in 1565, that was 'a form and kind of inquisition', and the magistrates protested.[20] But in the years until the Spanish lost control of Antwerp, some 525 persons from Antwerp were condemned for treason or heresy. From the spring of 1567 there was a steady procession of Protestants and others heading north from the city; an 'exodus' some called it.

And yet Antwerp's burgomaster, Nicolaas van der Laan, who had authorized the handing of churches to Protestants, was left in peace. When in 1572 William of Orange was driving the cause of open rebellion, Antwerp was quiet, no spontaneous uprisings.

The calm convinced nobody.

The mapmaker Ortelius had a life that depended on the city. He lived with his sister, had no obvious entanglements, never married, and made his nephew his heir, but his world was not narrow; he was friends with his neighbour Plantin the printer, and Bruegel the painter, dozens more. He seemed to know everyone and corresponded with those he didn't know.

At twelve, the age when merchants' sons often began their apprenticeships in dealing, he was left to support a mother and two young sisters. He was not left destitute. His grandfather was an apothecary out of Augsburg with a mansion on the Kipdorp in Antwerp, and money and holiness just enough to create a fine stone Calvary out by the execution grounds in Berchem. His father was an antiquary who tried to teach Ortelius Latin, and failed to give him Greek, but who did leave a network of buyers and sellers when he died.

Ortelius started by buying the best maps he could get, his friend Johannes Radermacher remembered, had his two sisters mount them on linen and then he coloured them. He wasn't spoiling the maps or making them vulgarly pretty; he used colour to make the information more clear, the shape of the landscape and the politics of frontiers. Some he sold locally, some he managed to sell in Italy, where maps were a most commercial local art, and some he took to the Frankfurt Fairs to buy and sell. He made a point at the fairs of listening to scholars who were there to get books, letting their talk teach him; he met the geographer Mercator. He had a boyhood enthusiasm for mathematics, but he never went near the university schools that already existed at Ingolstadt and Leuven. He learned by looking, collecting and dealing, which was exactly how merchants expected their sons to learn.

It helped that the city wanted new trades and he provided one. His *Theatrum Orbis Mundi*, a book of maps of the world, was the most successful and the most expensive best-seller in the whole century, a wonder of the Antwerp book trade. It was an atlas before Mercator invented the term. It was a claim on a privileged kind of information, not exactly secret but proprietary and handled with discretion, the kind that the Emperor Charles liked to give as gifts and also needed in order to administer the Netherlands: he mapped the dykes in 1533, the polders in 1534, and as Count of Holland he mapped to find out what he was meant to control.[21] It was the most official art. With Ortelius, maps reached the booksellers and the public, laying out what was becoming known about the world.

He needed to travel, for learning as much as business. 'In the thirtieth year of his age', which was 1557, 'having many great matters in his head . . . [he] began to entertain a conceit of travelling into diverse and sundry foreign parts and countries of the world,' so his friend Francis Sweerts wrote.[22] But Ortelius could travel only when wars and magistrates allowed.

He was in England, he carved his name with the artist Joris Hoefnagel on some large and flat druidic stone in Poitiers, he went to Italy once with Pieter Bruegel and twice with Hoefnagel. He knew the humanistic

circuit. In 1575 he set off on a grand tour through bits of France and
Belgium, mostly close to the Rhine, with the Calvinist city chaplain
Vivianus, a painter called Jan van Schille who did guided tours and a
22-year-old called Jérome 'to take notes' ('*describebat ex autographo*').
They saw Roman roads and aqueducts and the site of Roman mints, a
monastery library, iron-ore workshops, and places that had once been
under water. They also chased the shadow of that old fraud Sir John
Mandeville, the 'noble knight who, having gone around almost the
whole globe, died in Liège'; but whose travels were a gaudy fiction.
Ortelius and the others were fascinated by him; he filled the gaps in the
world they knew, perhaps a touch too conveniently for truth. They
were shown 'his sword, saddle and spurs which he is said to have used
while roaming through the total world, something much clearer proved
by his itinerary, printed and available everywhere . . .'[23]

It was a process of finding out, but an odd one. Travel was on the
borderline of the real, since so much of the information that came
back from new-found lands was bizarre and impossible to test. Ortelius created his book of maps and, as Alexander Grapheus wrote in
Ortelius' *Album Amicorum*, he 'opened with this brief work the easy
way to distant places so a man can sit safe at home, away from danger
or nuisance, and go anywhere he wants on the face of the globe from
one pole to the other'.[24]

Anything could swim or dance in the mind. All round the maps in
Ortelius' *Theatrum* there are fantastic creatures: feathered whales off
Brazil, prophets in trees in Kazakhstan, a snake dolphin with two great
water spouts off the coast of Wales and another in the Adriatic, mer-
maids like islands in the Bay of Bengal. There is a sphinx with a fish's
tail writhing on Arabia Felix alongside Persian birds which are slaughtering snakes, there are elephants in India but also hairy elephants on
the African Equator, just west of Prester John. In the fine confusion,
where the Western Ocean starts, there's a sea serpent with a beak at
one end and a bird's claws at the other tangled up with a man playing
a lute.[25] All this has the charm of decoration, but in a careful work
that was valued for plain information it suggests the wonder, the fantasy and the uncertainty of travel.

Ortelius' itinerary ended at the great Frankfurt Fair. He had been
going for years, buying and selling maps and books, but even these

essential journeys were now conditional. He had to go up before the magistrates in Antwerp to swear oaths that he was absolutely compelled to go to Cologne and then to Frankfurt for his business, and he was definitely not travelling just to disobey His Majesty's ban on going abroad from the Low Countries. He was made to declare that he had no intention of changing his residence or his domicile, that he was not deserting. He said he would return to Antwerp the moment his business was done, 'with no fraud and no trickery'.[26]

Movement was everything to a trading centre, but now it was blocked by war and travellers' nerves. Later, when Antwerp was entirely in Spanish hands, the deliberate closing of the Scheldt made things worse, but already Justus Laureins told Ortelius he wouldn't be coming to Antwerp in 1567, because his neighbours in Cassel were very nervous 'about the change of religion'. Johannes Thorius wrote, rather redundantly, from London to say he heard every day 'the saddest news of the state of our country; but it is not just our country, the whole of Christendom is shaking and breaking apart and threatens utter ruin'.[27]

The ordinary machinery of life and contact was rusting. Nobody was very keen on the imperial postal system, run by the Tassis tribe, which was hereditary, political because it did what emperors wanted, and slow because it ran along fixed routes. Giovanni Battista de Tassis, the Antwerp postmaster, was very aware of this when he tried grovelling to Sir Philip Sidney, who was an assiduous writer of letters to Antwerp merchants and Flemish savants, to the botanist Clusius and the Romanist Justus Lipsius. Tassis grovelled by post, of course, in 1575, kissing hands 'a thousand times' and promising to be 'a servant always most prompt to obey you'. A few days later one of Sidney's regular correspondents, the law teacher Jean Lobbet from Strasbourg, was writing: 'I do not like to use the services of Tassis, the distinguished Master of Posts at Antwerp. Let's not complicate what can be done simply.' Lobbet was in the business of sending out newsletters which gave him trouble with the authorities, so he proposed getting to know a London merchant who did business with Antwerp, then getting him to hand letters over to some known German merchant who could get them to Brussels, all of which seemed simpler than using the imperial machine.[28]

This personal post depended on persons being available, reliable and having good luck. Ortelius was always corresponding as he put together his books of maps, always waiting for information or exchanging it. He knew very well that the ship that was meant to carry letters might leave port earlier than expected; or copies could be stolen, or perhaps lost by negligence like the pages of Herodotus that Andreas Schottus sent to the publisher Plantin from Toledo; or the carrier might have fallen into the hands of pirates 'and reached you having been stripped of everything'. Letters were often opened on the way. Sometimes the trusted agent upped and moved town and the route was broken; or nobody wanted to do the job any more for the money. Johannes Sambucus, the Hungarian scholar, couldn't send books from Ghent to Augsburg even for ten gold florins or more, and to send them with the Fuggers by way of Venice was likely to take three months.[29]

It was difficult even in the best years. In the 1560s people started to tell each other it was the wrong time to send letters away or risk travelling yourself. Information had a circulatory system and it was clogging up. Ortelius himself complained of 'disordered times ...' with all the various denominations of pestilence – the Catholic Evil, the Gueux Fever, the Huguenot Runs, not to mention plagues of black horsemen and soldiers. 'I expect,' he wrote to Emanuel van Meteren in 1567, 'that everyone, after having done all he can in the way of robbing and murdering, will be so tired as to wish for the peace which he once had but did not value.'[30]

Publishing did not mean only type, presses, paper. For Ortelius it meant having a collection to share and discuss, keeping his library open to interested readers, being available in Antwerp as well as putting what he knew in books. He had to be known and seen.

His 'familiar and loving friend' Francis Sweerts remembered that 'he had at home in his house images, statues, coins of gold, silver and copper of the Greeks, Romans and others. Shells brought from India and our antipodes. There was marble of all colours. Also tortoise shells, some so marvellously large that ten men, sitting around them, might at once eat. Others again were so small they were hardly as large as a pin's head.' Some came from distant trading, some from the docks. He had sundials, globes and astrolabes, he had precious stones and plants and insects and pictures of insects, information and also ways to get information.

He had manuscripts, at least a hundred, of works like Paul the Deacon's *History of the Lombards* and Magnus Gruberus on the origins of the Rhine. Naturally he had maps, and he was always meticulous about acknowledging his sources so we can identify many of them, but he also had the raw materials for making and understanding them: the 'printed books, manuscripts, geographical charts, old marble inscriptions, coins and ancient maps on copper' that he cites on the title page of the *Thesaurus Geographicus* published by Plantin in 1596.

As for taste, he owned Bruegel's extraordinary image of the death of the Virgin Mary: a grey room full of figures and dim light which seems like the very colour of sorrow. Ortelius wrote that Bruegel painted what nobody could paint, and he meant the loss, the grief, the pain around this bed.[31] He collected the works of Albrecht Dürer, who once had high standing in Antwerp, but was sidelined because of the greater grace, people said, of Italian artists. He organized his collection by author, not subject, which was a radical idea; he cared about a particular eye and mind. Two great volumes, gilt-edged and leather-bound, held Dürer's woodcuts and engravings, mostly collected when someone as connected as Plantin complained how hard and costly it was to find anything by Dürer in the Antwerp print shops.[32] Ortelius even gave the Dürers away, too generously at times ('you rewarded him too much with those beautiful pieces of Albrecht Dürer', he was told by the archaeologist and engraver Goltzius, who was himself a dealer on the side).[33] When there was any question of some rare piece by Dürer turning up, people sometimes asked if it might be one that had been stolen from Ortelius.[34]

'His house might truly be called a shop of all manners of learning to which men flocked from everywhere as they did in former times to Plato's Academy or to Aristotle's Lyceum.' Minor royals came visiting after battles; 'other princes and men of all sorts came into his house in large groups to see and behold all there was to be seen.'[35] People assumed his library was open if they asked politely. The lawyer and Catholic pamphleteer Louis d'Orleans wrote to say he'd mentioned the name of Ortelius to a friend from an old noble family, who now wanted to meet the great geographer. 'I couldn't refuse such a great man,' d'Orleans wrote, presumptuously, adding that if Ortelius' various occupations allowed it, maybe he could just tell them what time after dinner they could come to contemplate the library.[36]

It mattered very much that other people appreciated his collections. 'If I were closer to you,' Justus Lipsius wrote from Leiden when he was working on his great work on what ancient writers made of ancient history and ancient things, 'I know I could get help from you and from your library.'[37] Lipsius needed Ortelius' formidable collection of coins and medals to see the heavy weapons on Trajan's column in Rome, the different kinds of crosses used for crucifixions, the layout of amphitheatres.[38] Ortelius in turn wanted the learned world to know what he had, which was the point of publishing his book on the incised heads of goddesses and gods on all the coins and medals he owned, and then giving copies away across Europe.[39] 'I reckon I can rival anyone in these parts for the number and the quality of my coins,' he boasted to his nephew in London. 'On books and coins, I believe I have spent more than two thousand crowns.'[40]

He had to be open like a library, like a shop, just like the humanist merchant class of Antwerp that Ascham so much admired. Among all the elegant work the self-conscious world of books, the Republic of Letters, left behind, all the stately collections of letters, the mutual compliments that soar far over any visible top – the *Theatrum*, according to Guilherme Postel was 'after Holy Scripture, the greatest work of the world'[41] – there was furious calculation. The Republic had to go on making a living. Before the Spanish took back control in 1585 Ortelius was the man to contact in Antwerp. Daniel Printz wrote from Cologne to say that their friend Crato wanted maps, 'four or five, about an ell high and about four to five ells long', and 'if they're not too dear, buy eight for another friend of mine.'[42] Nicolaus Rhedinger wrote from Breslau to ask about books in Spanish and French that might be for sale. He wanted to make a list, then Ortelius would find and buy the right titles, and the man who carried his letter would settle the bill.[43]

THE TWO ANTWERPS

You could buy the maps loose, pick just your home town or your chosen place of business, or else buy the books that held them all, which were what the trade liked best; the bookshops of Cologne, so the atlas-maker Mercator wrote to Ortelius, were 'preoccupied with their books and not at all interested in maps'.[44] The *Civitates Orbis Terrarum* meant to glorify the city as the new power in the world by collecting city maps from Moscow to Mombasa to Mexico City. Anyone could send in images of their own town if it had been left out.

The collection was issued first in 1572, a kind of appendix to the *Theatrum Orbis Terrarum*. It went into six volumes over the years, selling and selling. Copper engraving made possible its bird's-eye views instead of the old flat woodcut plans. One of its creators, Georg Braun, promised readers that it would be as though 'one does not see the pictures of the cities, but the cities themselves'.[45]

It had a moral, almost a political point. Man had been 'born wild in woods and caves and groves,' Braun wrote in the preface to the *Civitates*, had to run from fire and be buffeted by the winds that rocked the trees, needed architecture for the sake of roofs that would withstand those winds and keep human beings sheltered. 'It was so much easier to live together, and surrounded by walls, than to be alone,' he wrote.[46] Cities stood for ideals, for reason, for tolerance and a kind of civic virtue. Gentleman humanists approved of the cosmopolitan mix of people.[47] 'The subject is a popular one,' as Braun told Ortelius.

The *Civitates* and its authors were products of Antwerp. Braun had been tutor to a rich merchant's son in the city in the 1560s, which gave him a network of traders with facts about the world. He was a cleric, a theologian, a minor ecclesiastical civil servant working for the Curia in Rome, and he found morality in his maps. Joris Hoefnagel was the son of a merchant who was had been successful there. Joris added the images of costume and daily life to the maps, a new kind of information filed by place, but also, he said, pictures of human beings so the Muslim Turks had to ban the book 'however useful it might be to them'.

The cities were defined by their walls, except for Moscow, which didn't even have 'a proper end', and sometimes walls so high that it is hard to see at Constantinople how any ship could dock. Sometimes the walls make a screen for the city: Leipzig is reduced to a few horsemen parading, Hamburg to a few ships and Vienna to the background for a single covered carriage. The walls take in countryside, as at Nîmes, and sometimes, as at Rome, the walls swallow the hills and the groves, which are speckled with monuments and temples.[48]

Then there's Antwerp, both of the Antwerps.

The first version of Antwerp was published in 1572 while the Duke of Alba was working on the city. He imposed a bishop, and staged raids for forbidden books. The second Antwerp is in the fifth volume, which appeared sometime before 1598, when Antwerp had played its part in the Dutch revolt against Spain, lived out the brief independence of its Calvinist years, been broken under siege, lost half its population to the North and was recovering once again under Spanish rule. The later one has all the conventions of a city pacified: a view from the east looking out over the walls and moats of the city to the busy river, crowds in the streets and markets, even a parade.

The early one is quite different. The view is from the south, looking the long way downriver so all the houses, town hall, cathedral are reduced in scale. The one detail that dominates, in the foreground because of the viewpoint, is the great citadel that hangs on the city like a wax seal, newly finished when the first edition of the *Civitates* appeared. This city was to be seen through the eyes in the fort.

Cosimo de' Medici in Florence was told there were plans to build a castle in Antwerp, 'although it seems some citizens grumbled'. The citizens had been told that Philip's mind was made up about the plan, they were warned that soldiers would be billeted in their houses and the city walls broken and the moats and ditches filled if there was no citadel; so they agreed. Cosimo was told the city was calm, but the great Corpus Christi procession had armed soldiers all along the streets and marching as an escort around the Holy Sacrament. His Paris correspondent told him, helpfully: 'After the troubles in Antwerp tapestries are to be had at the very best prices.'[49]

For years this citadel had been something to discuss, not build. It might spoil the look of an ideal fortified city. It would mean even higher taxes. It raised questions from the fashionable Italian books. Alberti in his *De re aedificatoria* had said that good rulers build their palaces in the middle of the city, but only tyrants build fortresses across the city walls; so the position of the citadel was all-important. Anyone with Greek knew that Sparta needed no walls, because the city had trusted warriors, that a city with walls was a city of women, that Plato disapproved of the walls that Aristotle defended. Fortifications were not just an expensive strategy. They could never not have meaning.[50]

More than anything, as Machiavelli pointed out, a citadel might be needed to control the locals, to serve as 'bridle and bit', but that would be a second choice. Indeed, 'the prince who is more afraid of his people than of foreigners should build fortresses, but one who is more afraid of foreigners than of his people should do without them.' 'The best fortress that exists is not to be hated by the people.'[51]

Chiappino Vitelli, once the strategist of the Medici defence against the Barbary pirates, came up from Florence to join the Duke of Alba. He was asked to choose the site for the new fortress, and promised he would soon send the plans that were being made to Cosimo. Sharing plans between proper Italian noblemen was not treason at all. Vitelli brought with him Francesco Paciotto, a man who made everyone's skin crawl because he didn't bother to defer to the grand and powerful, which horribly embarrassed the men who did. Paciotto was a mathematician of skill who had built the first of the new pentagon forts in Turin, a city whose duke wanted simply to intimidate. The fort was unusual and considered perfect in its way, much studied by military architects from across Europe who knew how tricky it could be to build what seemed such a simple plan. Paciotto used much the same design in Antwerp and the same secrets, and not being properly noble, he was accused of treason.

In Turin the fort was practical, capable of defending the city. In Antwerp the citadel stood upriver from the city, which meant any enemy fleet could sail past all Antwerp before its forces ran into defensive fire. The citizens begged that the city walls should not be torn down until the castle was finished, and they told Alba fiercely that merchants had a habit of running away from territory where they did not feel free and safe. They did agree to pay a special tax on meat, capons and rent 'and other similar things' to raise money for the new fort.[52]

Paciotto's first failure of tact was to break down a section of the walls the city had been building laboriously for a decade. He rushed to finish only two of the five bastions on his fort, not the ones facing outwards in the city's interests but those that trained cannon directly on the city streets. Buonaiuto Lorini from Florence was serving in Flanders while all this was being built and he described how gun positions were built with timber taken from houses that had been dismantled. He saw the way the high water table was used to deepen the moat and how the piazzas with no place for guns allowed more flooding if need be, all to protect the citadel from the city, and 'not by chance'.[53]

At someone else's suggestion, probably the scholar Montanus, who designed the thing, a monstrous bronze effigy of Alba was made from the melted remains of enemy guns. Alba was going to be present and inescapable. He towered over a two-headed figure on the floor whose arms carried a tangle of symbols for everything he thought he had defeated: a hammer for iconoclasm, a document for attempts to soften religious policies, a mask for the enemy's hypocrisy. The statue was on public show for only three years, but it made its point.[54]

For Alba had his own campaign against the city's past, its particular identity. He was not only battling heresy, and the prospect that citizens might not think and do as their imperial masters required; he was determined on making Antwerp conform to his view of how the world worked, by weapons and not by cargo. He was 'making ... townes of warre of towns of merchandise'.

DEALING WITH MADRID

For years Rome had been debating how to respond to all the Protestant changes in worship. In 1568 the Curia settled on a new and rather conservative breviary. It had to be used everywhere and every priest would have to buy a copy; it was a prodigious print run with almost no apparent risk. Naturally the first licence went to Paulus Manutius, the papal house printer, who was required to split his profits with the

Vatican, but from the start he was allowed to bring other printers onto the job.

The scheming began at once. Plantin wanted the right to print for the Netherlands, and he needed help in the Curia.[55] He was lucky: the statesman Cardinal Granvelle, an old customer of Plantin's from his Antwerp days, was in Rome. He had once even suggested what titles Plantin should print. Now Granvelle talked out a deal with Manutius, beating down the printer's price from 500 écus to 300. Plantin could then demand a 'privilege' for 'all the Germanies' and the right to pay by instalments or else with a tenth of all the books he printed. He settled for 'Flanders' on the contract and he did not rush the payments. Only 232 écus ever reached Manutius through the thickets of Zurich bills of exchange payable in Rome on Flemish merchants.

Plantin had to brush aside Emmanuel Filips, who claimed a royal privilege in the Netherlands for breviaries, and then he could start widening his plans. The books he had to sell were a standard text in an international language, so they were welcome outside his legal territories. He started to sell in Portugal and Spain. After a while he asked for the right to sell there, pulling in Gabriel de Çayas from Philip's court to help him and using his friendship with Benito Arias Montanus, who was working in Antwerp on the Polyglot Bible. Philip II was persuaded to order in large quantities but he did something even more helpful: he persuaded the Pope that he should be allowed to tweak the breviary text to match his own ideas. Plantin would be printing a new, or at least revised, book, which was not the one Manutius was producing. He could set aside the deals he made in Rome.

The King's official order meant more presses, sixteen of them, along with more workers, fifty-six at times, and more room for them to sleep; the workshop boomed. It was not comfortable, though, to have Philip as such a dominant customer. The 'Sea Beggars', Protestant rebels under sail, were blockading the Scheldt and making the city sclerotic. The promised subsidies did not arrive from Madrid and Plantin had to go borrowing from his Spanish patrons for the wages of his discontented workers. He told Madrid that he was late delivering books because his workers had threatened to go on strike for higher pay now he had a solid order; he said he'd had to threaten to shut down the workshop to persuade them to go back. In fact, he had been paying off his pressmen, and the threat was directed at Madrid: pay up or there will be no more books. He also had family anxieties, with a daughter and a business in Paris at the time of the St Bartholomew's Day massacre of Protestants. He came to a wretched view of his craft. He called printing 'a pit or a chasm that has to be fed ... or else it will swallow and devour its master and everyone else involved'.[56]

Philip's punctilious editing had made Plantin's edition possible in the first place, but it was now flustering the workshop. The King fussed over fonts and paper and the colour of rubrics. The proofs came back with the text changed in his own writing. He had to be discouraged from ordering books on expensive parchment and reminded how easy it was to sell a simple octavo. He also had to be persuaded to pay. Plantin, who ran an elaborate system of discounts to the book trade, sometimes going as high as 40 per cent, showed his irritation by never cutting his prices for the King. Madrid paid slightly more for tens of thousands of volumes than Plantin's bookseller customers, when the Treasury paid at all. Plantin was complaining in 1583 about 'the grievances I have suffered through fifteen years by obeying his Majesty's orders without payment or recompense'.[57]

He was not alone. Philip had been fighting local rebels and distant Turks simultaneously and by 1575 the money was gone. Banks in Genoa wanted at least their interest and it did not arrive. For a while the personal credit of the new governor, Luis de Requesens, was all that brought in money, mostly from Antwerp merchants. When Requesens died in March 1576, the money was finished.

Alba's soldiers were also unpaid and they were furious. The imperial authorities had no way to control the troops, Spanish and German, so the men used the city's own defences to wreck it. A mutinous mob piled into the citadel through the back entrance in November 1576 and rushed forward to fight the city on its own ramparts. Their grievance was with the Spanish and not the city, but the city was rich and they were hungry.

Geeraest Janssen told a London colleague that citizens fought very courageously with many killed on both sides, but eventually the Spanish infiltrated the city through any weak point they could find, the overlord's forces invading his own territory. Carolus, the great bell of the cathedral, sounded the alarm. The citizens put on armour and picked up their guns, if they had them, but the mutineers got to the Grote Markt square by the cathedral and drove the citizens along the narrow streets to the walls, where some of them were forced to jump to save themselves. Some were dredged from the canals or the moat and others drowned, and some boats sank under the weight of all the desperate passengers. Janssen says the streets were filled with the dead.

The soldiers had only just begun. Now they ran at the houses in town, broke down or shot through any door that did not open at once to them. They went after the master of each house, beating, stabbing, menacing and killing. They demanded all the money, then they demanded more, then they either pillaged the houses or tried to ransom them. Janssen crammed a lifetime's assets into a cellar for five long days, and waited to be found. When the soldiers came he was buried deep under a pile of peat and squatting on his money.

He was sure the city could never again be the same. As he said: 'there were many people in Antwerp who were rich and mighty but are now poor.'[58] Everything was expensive. Getting out was difficult and there was no obvious refuge. Worse, the balance that had made the city so exceptional had broken. Imperial powers now chased all heretics instead of leaving the merchant class alone. The Spanish troops spared only Spanish merchants and they spent five days trying to ruin the English, Germans, Italians, Portuguese and Hanseatics on whom the city also depended.

The mutineers set fires. They burned down whole streets, some 500 houses, 'besides which many persons who are still being found daily'. Houses burned on some of the bridges. The old art market, the *pand* by the Grote Markt, was ashes. Nobody was buying in any case, and the painter Jacob Gheens said when he moved out of town that he wasn't a heretic, he wasn't going because of debts or crimes but 'simply in order to earn a living for himself and his wife, seeing that his aforesaid craft and trade had largely come to a halt'.[59]

Plantin had to put out three fires threatening his presses and pay off the soldiery at least nine times to save his family and his property. The soldiers helped themselves to his cash before making their very high ransom demands, so he had quickly to find someone else to pay them.

Luis Pérez, a Spanish merchant, obliged and the debt was carefully acknowledged in the workshop accounts. Plantin was still made to keep thirty soldiers and sixteen horses in his house, and when they left, much of his furniture and goods went with them.

There was a sense of the city being cleared. Soldiers torched the new town hall, and the attic stores that held the city's records. They did Alba's work unintentionally, spoiling the paper trail back to the past. Alba did more; he 'pulled down the highest and strongest tower within the towne, called Croneburge ... the onlie monument of antiquity'. His campaign 'struck such a terror into everie man's heart that an infinit number of merchants and of the wealthiest citizens, departed foorth of Antwerp ... leaving their lands and inheritance to the wide world'.[60]

The Spanish mutineers had to be beaten back, and it took grand alliances – Brabant with Holland and Zeeland – to push them out. The city had its revenge a year later in 1577 when the Spanish were gone and the Calvinists were in control. Citizens invaded the citadel as the mutineers had invaded the city. They drained the moat to its marshy bottom, tore down the bastions facing the city and reduced them to heaps of earth, and pushed over the watchtowers. Brass Alba was melted down.

The citadel was brought back into the city with its rather splendid houses intact and its classical gateway and its useful, external walls. William of Orange had his official base there. A new map of 1581 shows a disorderly space between fort and city with the outlines of the old walls just visible, but it also shows new kinds of order. There was talk of planning straight streets for their beauty as well as their safety. The defences had become avenues. There were trees planted all along the walls which later in the century did so well the leaves and seeds spoiled the water of the moat for the city's breweries.[61]

The rules of the familiar world were all changed. Plantin had no more deals with Philip II to keep his presses busy, which at least spared him the endless task of dunning Philip for what he owed. He still managed to produce some of his most famous work, herbals from Dodoens, Clusius and Lobelius, editions of the *Theatrum Orbis* of Ortelius, the Guicciardini description of the Netherlands, a fair amount of music, a

French Bible in 1578 and a Latin one in 1583 from the now Calvinist republic of Antwerp. But he very rarely worked alone or on his own initiative. His books were often printed 'to order', subsidized by their authors or funded by publishers and printers in Cologne or Paris. He was appointed printer to the new University of Leiden and went away to make his life possible.

All around him was a quite new order of things. William of Orange was trying to bring southern territories into alliance with the northern rebels but he kept finding other divisions besides the religious. The cities had a fanciful notion to go back to being city states as in medi-aeval times, not uniting at all. In Ghent in 1578 there was one more rebellion, but this time artisans and workers against the nobles who were supposed to be leading the revolt against Spain. Unpaid soldiers mutinied against the States General. Orange proposed a religious peace which would have left everyone free to practise either Catholic or Protestant worship, but he never dared put down public agitation against the Catholic Church. Instead of the old simplicities – a distant Spanish ruler to resist – there was the kind of confusion that rules out compromise.

Catholic practices were banned in Antwerp from 1581 except for marriage and baptisms. Churches had been wrecked again, a city offi-cial leading the men with hammers and axes to smash the altar art that had been one of Antwerp's famous products. Convent grounds were remade into straight streets and new districts, converted to civic ideals. The city even proselytized. The renegade Abbot of St Bernard brought his wife along to use a few lewd words with recalcitrant nuns to persuade them 'it was not good to live so secluded a life.'

The worthy made a profit selling off the past. The Fuggers' news-letter reported that 'four ships lie here laden with sculptured and carved statues, bells, brass and stone effigies of saints, brass candle-sticks and other such like ornaments from the churches. All these are to be dispatched to Narva and Moscow. The consigners hope to do good business with them.'[62]

15

The City Chooses

The Spanish prowled and battled and took back towns like Leuven; they would soon have back a kind of control of the southern Netherlands. William of Orange came to believe that nothing would be resolved without French help, and he knew he needed help; England was a Protestant ally, but Elizabeth of England was not eager to conquer territory and have to rule it. The consequence was the Duke of Anjou.

Antwerp lined the streets to watch its new ruler arrive on 19 February 1582. The Duke rode under a baldachin, the canopy that usually covers a throne, an altar or a tomb, with footmen trotting along to carry the thin columns that supported it. He was asserting his power over the territory of Burgundy, a state that the Hapsburgs inherited and then abolished, but a memory just strong enough to be the basis for a claim on power.

This was the first joyous entry since 1549 when Antwerp was honouring Charles and Philip as inevitable rulers, and still trying politely to insist on its particular privileges. Now it was celebrating, as the 1582 official book explains, that 'the sovereignty of those Low Countries was taken from the King of Spain for his perjuries, tyranny and abominable extortions.'[1] It was also finding the limits of its autonomy. It had to accept Anjou as the rightful successor to the discarded Philip II despite his lack of any clear claim to rule in Burgundy, his unmissable Frenchness, his Catholic faith (not to mention, as people usually did, his excessively large nose). It did so to play along with the immediate politics that Antwerp had once been able to bypass: the English desire to smash the Spanish by proxy, the French perpetual war with Hapsburg Spain, and William of Orange's need for troops and subsidies. Stages around the city showed David beating up Goliath, since

Anjou was the French king's youngest son, and Discord, Violence and Tyranny running away at the very sight of him.

No merchant platoons from the various nations marched in showy clothes this time; only 'the German merchants ... well mounted and dressed in the German fashion' greeted the Duke, followed by 'the English merchants in fine order, all wearing riding jackets in black velvet'.[2] There was no time, so the official account says, and no money to match the show of 1549, and no foreign merchants eager to hire painters, builders, theatricals to make their own points. Instead, the city stores were raided for the floats and trucks that made up the two annual street processions, six out of the twenty-two in stock: the elephant bearing a war tower bristling with cannon, the prancing seahorse, the sea monster with Concord riding on its back, the giant Antigoon adjusted to drop the flag of Spain just as Anjou passed, the Mount Parnassus and the Cave of Discord which amounted to a confession of the vices which lived there, and the Maid of Antwerp trundling on a float more like a city square, surrounded by signs of Concord but wearing armour. The parade of wood and papier mâché and paint was familiar, a welcome show of continuity, but grand civic occasions were supposed to be a show of the new and the spectacular; in 1549 only the giant and the Maid's float had been wheeled out of store. This welcome came from a much reduced city, one not in any position to argue over its fate.

The official book, which Plantin produced two months later, had pictures of all this. It showed the sheer number of armed men along the streets, almost 20,000 of them, all disciplined and ready: a militia under the city's colonels. The views of the whole area are laid out from the south like the first Antwerp map in the *Civitates*, but to show how things have changed. The dark seal of the citadel is gone, some of its walls broken and remade into the walls of the city itself. The Spanish threat to the city is no longer inside the city, although the troops all around suggest the threat is still real.

Anjou never did have serious power, or serious money from the States General or his French and English friends. He talked about religious peace and about having Mass said in his residence, which infuriated the staunch reformers. When William of Orange was wounded in an attempt on his life, there were rumours that Anjou had inspired the attack. Less than a year after his entry into Antwerp, which was always much more the city's victory parade than any true welcome, the rather ineffectual Duke turned his troops on the city to try to impose himself at last. A thousand Antwerp militiamen died, but Anjou had to run away. He never did return.

The city seemed to have only bad choices, unlike the northern provinces who had William of Orange as ruler and the prospect of independence. It was tempted to write an alternative story. Antwerp had broken with the Hapsburgs, and other cities were thinking about what power they might have in their own right. Antwerp was already famous as a hub, and it had history. Its network of connections was not rigid like courts and powers; the city could improvise. All the links from Portugal and the *novos cristianos*, through London, then out to the Rhine and the Alps to Venice and the states of Italy, and especially to Salonika and Istanbul, had allowed Antwerp a kind of detachment for a while.

When people did choose for themselves, the choices could be heroic. Dona Gracia, widow of the trader and banker Francisco Mendes, left Portugal for Antwerp because the Inquisition was coming, and she knew the law would soon allow rumour as evidence enough to break people. She left Antwerp for Istanbul by way of Venice and Ferrara to be a Jew openly, to stop the Emperor marrying her daughter Ana to a decrepit grandee and dividing the House of Mendes' fortune. She did not choose her time to go, she left unfinished business to settle and she carried her contacts with her, the House of Mendes on the road; but she was sure of a direction, towards being who she was.

Her business was always crossing frontiers. This flexibility was enough to allow the Portuguese Ambassador to Istanbul to imagine she might be considering a return to Portugal, even that she was a Christian at heart,[3] although this was the Dona Gracia who 'helped the Jews when they did not have money to leave, comforted them in Flanders and in the bitter mountains of the Alps and Germany', as Samuel Usque wrote in his *Consolaçam*.[4]

Yet in Istanbul, Dona Gracia established herself in the European colony in Galata, not the settled Jewish quarter. She took Spanish ladies and maids in her entourage and dressed her male servants in the Venetian style, not the usual Turkish caps and hoods. She also collaborated with the Portuguese; she did not respect the great divide in the world. Her agents passed on information about Portuguese held captive close to Hormuz, and tried to rescue others imprisoned in Muscat.[5] Her connections were good for starting rumours because no outsider could be sure where she truly wanted to be.

The connection that continued between Antwerp and Istanbul was her nephew Joseph Naçi, the man who had negotiated the safe passage of the House of Mendes out of Antwerp. In the West he was known as the 'Great Jew', in the Ottoman court he was '*Frenk Bey oylou*', the European prince. He was valued as a European who chose to be at the court of the other Emperor.

He was so well connected that the Venetian ambassadors to Istanbul complained of always tripping over him. Luigi Bonrizzo, secretary to the Venetian Ambassador in the 1560s, noticed Naçi's close ties, 'both domestic and of service', to the unlovely but most important Selim, who was the son of Suleiman and his heir. This Selim was no friend to Venice, so the city's ambassadors happily sent home stories of his fatness, his florid face 'so red it seems enflamed', his untrustworthiness, how he was 'more like a monster than a man' with limbs out of proportion, and how he was going white despite dyeing his hair and painting his eyelids black. He was short, which was not uncommon among the Ottoman rulers, but he made the fact obvious by surrounding himself with dwarves.[6]

He might be 'greedy, dirty, incontinent and always sudden in everything he does', as Andrea Badoaro wrote in 1573, and 'inclined to leave all the weight of such a great government on the shoulders of the pasha, his first vizier', but he was still nominally the ruler of the Ottoman Empire after Suleiman's death. Naçi, the Venetians agreed, had found the perfect way to influence him. Selim was sometimes at table for three days and three nights, drank half a carafe of spirits every morning, and then he drank wine; 'his thoughts change as he drinks', Costantino Garzoni reported, unsurprisingly. Wine was not proper in a Muslim court, but Selim was not pious like his sons. He relied on Naçi, who had no reason not to deal in alcohol, to bring him 'special foods and all the most delicate drinks so [Naçi] has great power'. Selim did not even bother with the usual tests for poison.

He also listened to Naçi 'and that is the greatest damage to all Christians, because being head of the whole Jewish nation here and having intelligence from everywhere, he lets his Majesty know the many failings of princes which cause the gravest upsets in other lands'.[7]

When the Jesuit Famianus Strada came to write the history of the Dutch rebellion, he made Naçi a conniving, flattering operator, opposed to Catholics and Spain but not to heretics, constantly ambitious for himself and for his fellow Jews; who wanted an island, perhaps Cyprus, for a new Israel. He goes to Istanbul, in this version, because the Senate at Venice turns down with scorn his request for islands where Jewish refugees could settle. He also 'laid the plot for blowing up of the Arcenall at Venice' which would have destroyed the city had the authorities not already shipped most of the gunpowder out to Corfu.

Having married, Naçi moved to the court of Suleiman's son Selim, where he found the prince 'in a vacancie of affairs, or not disposed to serious businesse, being altogether inslaved to his pleasures'. Naçi 'excelled in the art of flatterie, or the artifice of pleasures' and soon he could advise the prince to ask Suleiman to grant a city and some territory to the Jews. Naçi heard that the Moors in Spain were asking for Turkish help in a rising against King Philip, but he helped turn court opinion to the idea of invading Cyprus instead, 'so great was his envie to the Venetians', who controlled the island at the time. He hoped to be king of Cyprus, Strada says, 'vainly grounding upon some words spoken by Selimus at his table'.[8] He wanted Cyprus to be Israel.

The Turks helped Antwerp unknowingly at first. Turkish manoeuvres kept Charles and then Philip from an all-out war on heresy. The Duke of Alba argued against any grand alliance to take out the Turks precisely because he wanted to concentrate on putting down rebels in the Netherlands. Cardinal de Granvelle groused that 'we're worse off than the French, because besides all their sects we have Lutherans, and all kinds of Anabaptists.' He heard from Wigle de Zuichem in Brussels, just before Christmas in 1565, that the King absolutely must come north just because of the story circulating that 'there's no chance of the King coming, because the Turk keeps him well in his cage.'

Granvelle's letters report rumours about Turkish manoeuvres mostly for what they say about Netherlandish politics. 'I don't know,' his side-kick Morillon told him about reports of a Turkish advance with a large force, 'if these rumours are spread here because some people want them to be true'. When things went better, he wrote from Brussels that 'the news from Hungary is better than some people would like.' When the Council of State discussed the Turkish campaigns in Malta, one of the company 'tugged his neighbour by the sleeve saying "Good news for us, the King cannot come"'.[9]

Helping Antwerp could undo Venice, the great rival who had sneered when Naçi asked for a new Israel. Helping Protestants in Antwerp and the Netherlands could unsettle the Hapsburgs, even defeat them, and it was the Hapsburgs who had tried to steal his family's business and marry its wealth to a ruinous old aristo. It was not hard for him to choose sides. He talked to Suleiman about opening a Turkish staple at Antwerp as early as 1564, which would have made the city the new centre of trade from the Levant and brought the Ottomans to the North Sea.

When Selim became Sultan in 1566 he was persuaded to send a letter 'to the Lutherans' in Antwerp with an offer of money, guns and men against the Spanish enemy. The same year, William of Orange on the Protestant side sent an envoy to Naçi in Istanbul. Nothing seemed to happen but Naçi went on pushing the Ottomans to support the nobles rebelling against Spain. His campaign collapsed after the sea battle at Lepanto in 1571 because the Ottoman defeat by the forces of Spain, Rome and Venice left them blocked out of the Mediterranean route to Antwerp. But by now the rebel Sea Beggars flew the red flag with a crescent on it in the interests of the Dutch Revolt, with the slogan 'Liever Turks dan Paaps', better Turks than Papists.[10]

The city came very close to making the same choice, to bringing the Ottomans on the North Sea and changing the shape of empires. In 1582 Anjou was persuaded to license 'Greek merchants' and those from Istanbul's quarter for foreigners to bring Ottoman wares to Antwerp 'by way of Poland or Moscow as well as by the straits of Heracles', which is Gibraltar, and to trade without barriers and buy for export to Turkey.[11] Venice was to lose the Ottoman staple, and Antwerp was to be the new heart of their western trade, a ceremonial as well as a practical change. Antwerp promised a proper mansion for the new nation, and a brilliant official welcome for the first ship to reach Antwerp from Ottoman territory.

The city of many nations was being opened one last time. The convention was ratified on 20 November 1583.[12]

ENDGAME

But what happened next was fighting. Alexander Farnese, son of Margaret of Parma, led Spanish forces back into the southern Netherlands. They tightened their hold on Antwerp in a siege that lasted fourteen months. The great Beurs, the Exchange that had been imitated across Northern Europe, and almost plagiarized in London, burned down quite accidentally along with various merchants' stock-in-trade; a brazier turned over and the coals worked too fast for the city's secular heart to be saved. The river which gave the city its port and its usefulness to the world was blocked deliberately by a floating wall of Spanish ships.

Plans to break the rafts in front of this floating wall of ships were 'held by many to be nothing but mockery and procrastination'. When the attempt was finally made, four ships laden with gunpowder, chains, gravestones and millstones sailed out. The first blew up too soon, the second beached and exploded on the sands, and the Spaniards simply opened their blockade when the third ship came into sight so she went up in flames well clear of them. The fourth and largest was the city's great hope, but it was manned by four sailors who decided they'd rather not be martyrs, so they cut down the sail, threw away their fuses, stole a hundred small kegs of gunpowder and became heroes for the other side.

The Scheldt was still sealed shut. The city was starving and it had to fall. When it did, there was no celebration, not even the public fuss that was usual for the reading of any important proclamation. The troops were exhausted and wanted to go home. The city could only wait quietly, hoping for the food and wine and beer that was promised from the Spanish camp.[13]

Alexander Farnese, the conqueror, had his own joyous entry into Antwerp in 1585. As was usual, the maid Antwerpia presented him ceremoniously with the keys to the city, but unusually he did not hand them back. He fixed the keys to the collar of the Order of the Golden Fleece which he was wearing, to bind the city to an old chivalric order of the Empire.

Farnese was not as brutal as Alba had been. The Calvinist preachers were taken off by ship to northern territories, and within four years half the city's population followed them, because Protestants were under orders to convert to Catholicism or go away.[14] The fabric of the city remained, but Calvin's republic metamorphosed into a capital of the Counter-Reformation and neither version of the city had the uses or the importance of the glory years in Antwerp.

If Protestants wanted to leave they could sell their property and take the proceeds, something imperial law denied to other heretics. Converting to Rome was an obligation for anyone who chose to stay, but it was delayed until the end of a time of reconciliation. Farnese offered Antwerp 'oubliance generalle et perpetuelle', he wanted an 'oubli du passé', meaning that the past had to be forgotten.[15]

Farnese was a gardener, as it happens, but the gardens of Antwerp proved as fragile as its glory. They had been spoiled by the siege and now their whole usefulness was lost while the city was unable to connect with the rest of the world. The great garden that Coudenberghe made, all its curiosities and recipes and knowledge, was dead. Even as calm returned Maria van der Laen, friend to Clusius, wrote in 1605 that 'the heritages of the gardens do not recover as they do in other cities and we do not have the pleasure of the garden.'[16]

The Spanish rebuilt the bastions, and made the fort once again 'stupendous' and 'matchlesse', as John Evelyn said in the next century, but also 'one of the Sweetest places in Europe'. Already in 1590 a map tries to suggest that civic calm is back. The moat has been flooded again, but it is dotted with large and placid swans.[17]

A whole other story was built over the past, so the city's present baroque glories may be the worst possible evidence for its most remarkable years. In Rubens' time, which is the seventeenth century, Antwerp was firmly under Spanish control and it had lost its ramshackle autonomy. Rubens worked within the imperial system as painter and as diplomat, and imperial diplomacy was never Antwerp's trade. In the 1610s he made paintings about the change in the city and about the Hapsburg claim on all its past, with the help of the great Bruegel's older son Jan.

The pictures don't quite own up to being propaganda.[18] They are called 'allegories' of the senses, of sight and smell, hearing, taste and touch. Each one is a gallery, almost a catalogue of things set in a garden or a grand room which usually has a view of a palace, and one has a portrait of the couple then in charge of the Spanish Netherlands, Albert and Isabella. The ruling Hapsburgs could feel a kind of security while there was a truce between the warring North and South of the Netherlands. Fighting did not break out again until Bruegel had finished all the details.

Taste is nibbling while the old satyr Silenus pours wine, Touch is holding a naked baby, Sight closely contemplating a painting, Smell sitting in a glorious wildness of roses, Hearing holding a kind of harp between a deer, a baby and a cockatoo. Some of the goods all around are obvious – walls of pots and paintings for sight, a cluster of musical instruments and a table of clocks for hearing, oysters and a boar's head for taste – but there are surprises: Touch has her baby, but she is surrounded by shining grey armour, by gauntlets, shields, a crossbow and a cannon – not comfortably tactile things. Antwerp had dealt in arms often enough, kitted out armies across Europe, so the English constantly fretted over their shopping lists of serpentine powder, sulphur and saltpetre, of copper bullets, of gunpowder, hand guns and pike heads, and when all this would have the right passport to pass Antwerp customs.[19]

There's something close to nostalgia in these pictures. The arms trade and also the trade in musical instruments were important earlier, like the sale of paintings and sculptures; and the wine trade went through Antwerp. This is the culture, the heritage of the city, now displayed as part of the Hapsburg possessions; we're meant to see its glories but not to ask how it came to be.

Around the same time, the Jesuit Carolus Scribanius produced a Latin pamphlet on Antwerp with boldface boasts that Antwerp was the jewel on the world's signet ring. The ring was Belgium or the Netherlands, or more exactly by 1610 the southern Netherlands. The city was also the pupil of the world's eye, the laurel in its sacred groves, the delight in Paradise and the sun in the sky; Scribanius was a shameless booster.[20] He produced the more historical *Origines Antverpiensium* in the same year, defining the place he was boosting. He was proud of a river where 'I've seen up to 2,500 ships waiting two or three weeks at anchor before reaching the quay to unload. There wasn't a day when five hundred didn't come and go.'[21] This was a distant memory since the Scheldt had been blockaded for years, by the Spanish and then the Dutch, but Scribanius wants to make the success of Antwerp, its riches and its reach across the globe a constant. He honours the crusader margraves for opposing Muslims, just as Charles V did, setting aside how close Antwerp came a few decades earlier to building the Turks a mansion of their own. Somehow he makes it seem part of crusader tradition to go after the other 'enemies of Christendom', Lutherans, Calvinists, Mennonites. He honours art in Antwerp but only the paintings of the Counter-Reformation. He leaves out the city's literary clubs, the Chambers of Rhetoric who made a show on stage out of moral arguments; they were suspected of Lutheran ideas. You would hardly guess that Antwerp had once been concerned to protect its heretics.

Scribanius and his students churchified the history of Antwerp for almost a century. This had advantages, since the Jesuit College in Antwerp was famous for careful scholarship when he led it, but the new baroque buildings, the artistic traditions around Rubens, were already making it hard to see the earlier city clearly. His student Papenbroch produced a remarkable manuscript: *Annales Antverpienses*, a calendar of events year by year and a book of source materials, which was not printed until the nineteenth century but kept as a reference for local historians in the College library, a guide to correctness. He tells the past through the interiors of churches, which are wonderful evidence; but the piety of the guilds and the loveliness of their chapels is nothing like the whole story of masters, apprentices, rules and crafts. Indeed, his insistence on the visible continuity of architects and developers emphasizes the physical city despite all the shifts in culture, faith and business. He also gives official persons with Hapsburg connections more than is their due. He says Gilbert van Schoonbeke built the new Beurs, but Gilbert was only twelve when it opened.[22]

The printers, booksellers, publishers had gone north. Amsterdam, it was said, was feeding off the corpse of Antwerp. Plantin and Moretus had business in Leiden; their press now tended to produce popular books about medicine instead of the scholarly theses of a few years earlier. But it was still old man Ortelius in Antwerp who gave advice on publishing to his rich cousin Emanuel van Meteren in London. He was the memory of the old capital of books.

Van Meteren wanted money – he's genteel; he asks for an honorarium – from the printer of his *History of the Netherlands*. Ortelius warned him printers hardly ever pay; they get the words for nothing and sometimes they get money from the author as well if the engravings are very expensive, or the prospects for sales do not seem good, and all they give back is a few free copies. They can do this, Ortelius reckons, because authors will go on writing of their own accord, 'for themselves or to gratify their inclination and that for various reasons, for the sake of honour, or to acquire friends, or to receive remuneration from their patrons or to earn a reputation (for which reason many fools write books nowadays').[23]

A city that had argued through every kind of heresy was now wretchedly quiet. Ortelius knew people on both sides of a divide which had become a war, South against North, Spanish against the Dutch with a taste for independence. He could never be exact about what he truly thought.

Perhaps what he believed was proper and legal, but the authorities had doubts. When the Duke of Alba rode in to clear out the Protestants, nobody touched Ortelius; so he cannot have been suspect then. By 1573 he had the most respectable title of Cosmographer to the King. When Alexander Farnese broke into Antwerp, everyone's orthodoxy had to be proved. In February 1588 the town clerk of Antwerp was asked to write two reports on Ortelius for the Privy Council, which was a kind of Ministry of Justice.

Almost half the city had been Protestants; there were Protestant armies in the North and if they fell on Antwerp there were not enough Spanish soldiers to hold it; so the Spaniards were going to need loyal Catholic citizens with guns. It would help if they were the only people with guns. The conscript citizen guard was checked, with a sign by each name to show if the man was Catholic, Lutheran, Calvinist or even Anabaptist. Ortelius was marked down as Catholic but his weapons were still taken away; some people knew how close he had been with Peeter Heyns, one of the Calvinists who had been ruling the republic. The arms were quickly returned, but the doubt lived on.[24]

Everything always had to be perfectly careful. A strategy of concealment runs all through the *Album Amicorum*, the book where his friends honour Ortelius, as it did through the life of the city. In Ortelius' circle it was at least still possible for opponents to talk. The Emperor's chaplain is a few pages from the Calvinist leader in Antwerp, Marnix van Sint Aldegonde with his bleak slogan '*Repos ailleurs*', 'rest is somewhere else'. A Calvinist diplomat, Jan van der Does, who had been one of the gentry opposed to the Inquisition and the imperial campaign against heresy, is close to Andre Dudith, who had been a counsellor to Maximilian II and a bishop in Dalmatia.

It's true Dudith became a scandal when he decided to marry and turn Protestant. He writes that a man 'who hides his life lives well'.

The city bustled in its glory days, its traffic was ferocious, almost every lane was some kind of market, legal or not; and merchants went to the Exchange with bands of musicians like a parade. When the diplomat Sir Dudley Carleton visited in 1616 he admired the look of the city, how it 'exceeds any I ever saw anywhere else for the beauty and uniformity of buildings, height and largeness of streets, and strength and fairness of the ramparts', 'the buildings are all kept in perfect reparation.' But he found it quiet even on workdays, grass growing in the streets, schoolboys and their Jesuit teachers filling the old English traders' house. The palatial Hansa headquarters was empty.

'In the whole time we spent there I could never set my eyes in the whole length of a street upon 40 persons at once; I never met coach nor saw man on horseback; none of our company . . . saw one pennyworth of ware either in shops or in streets bought or sold.' As for the great Beurs that had become the model for exchanges across Northern Europe, 'two walking peddlers and one ballad-seller will carry as much on their backs at once as was in that royal exchange . . .'[25]

The city had been the hub of the whole world that Europeans knew. What happened there helped change the world and how we think about it. But it was only a city, a site with walls that was liable to rise and fade with time. It could be hollowed out; and it was.

Acknowledgements

All books are the work of a community, and I have every possible reason to be grateful to mine. This book was planned, stalled, researched and stalled during the long illness of my beloved husband John Holm, interrupted by his death and finished in the confusions that followed. I needed the help of all my friends, and I'm left with a nagging sense that in the disorganization of grief and lawsuits and moving vans I may not have begun to thank all those who helped me along the way.

I can at least be sure of my debt to very patient publishers, Stuart Proffitt at Allen Lane, Haye Koningsveld at De Bezige Bij and Claiborne Hancock and Jessica Case at Pegasus, and to my wonderfully supportive and ruthless and judgemental agent David Godwin. Lisette Verhagen at DGA and then PFD kept the faith very kindly. Alice Skinner at Allen Lane tidied a book out of my various cybertraces and Jane Birdsell was the model of a fiercely attentive and tactful copy-editor. Cecilia Mackay helped find the pictures which also tell my story. Ian Moores made the maps. Mark Wells made the index.

I know how much I owe to the people who helped with research and translation. Mary Boyle guided me through the texts of Georg Wickram, Katie McKeogh helped me trawl the National Archives at Kew, Patricia Vieira Machado excavated books from the University of Coimbra library, which is no small achievement, and Gustav Zamore understood the untranslated letters of Erasmus. Daniel Naamani not only translated and annotated for me but also attempted the barely possible task of teaching me to speak Dutch properly. Maurizio Arfaioli at the Medici Archive Project explained the Medici holdings at the Archivio di Stato in Florence, where Francesco Martelli was very helpful. At the city archives of Antwerp, Stad Antwerpen FelixArchief,

Melinda Boutard and Marie-Juliette Marinus were generous with advice.

Libraries but also librarians made the book possible. I owe my usual debts to the Wellcome Library and the Warburg Institute in London, the library of the University of Amsterdam and especially the staff at Bijzondere Collecties and the PC Hoofthuis; and in Zurich to the wonderful deep basement of open stacks at the Zentralbibliothek, but also the Handschriften and Alte Drucke departments, who make it easy to work calmly and well. Qona Wright at the British Library helped me chase language books, as did Francesca Galligan at the Bodleian in Oxford. Peter Rogieste was very generous with time and ideas at the essential Erfgoedbibliotheek Hendrik Conscience in Antwerp, where readers can easily fill all the gaps they find in this book. At the Plantin-Moretus Museum in Antwerp I entered a treasure house of the ideas and attitudes of the sixteenth century as well as wonderful visual material: Marijke Hellemans and Dirk Imhof helped me find my way.

At MAS, the Museum aan de Stroom in Antwerp which manages what was once known as the Vleeshuis collection, I'm very grateful to Annemie de Vos. I saw my sixteenth-century Antwerp with the help of Eddy Kerssens, who found me all the towers I had missed, and Clement Caremans and Timothy De Paepe at the Vleeshuis, who showed me the reservoirs for making beer and the meeting rooms. Timothy De Paepe also helped me hear the music of Antwerp. For their guidance and their generous help with sometimes very odd questions, I thank: Wim Aalbers, Andrea Bardyn, Cordula Boecking, Chanelle Delameillieure, Bert de Munck, Claudia Goldstein, Elizabeth Alice Honig, Guido Marnef, Elke Oberthaler and Jonas Roelens. Zhanna Etsina at the Hermitage in St Petersburg and Anna Hamberg at the Gustavianum in Uppsala were very helpful. It also seems to me that we credit the books that helped and informed us, but not always the museum exhibitions: so I want to mention the show on François I and Dutch Art at the Louvre and especially the glorious Bruegel show at the Kunsthistorisches Museum in Vienna which gave a context to the KHM's own dazzling collection.

All this kindness would have been worthless without the support of friends like Adriana Bebiano, Rosemary and Nicholas Boyle, Nicholas

Faith, Celia Haddon, Emma, Peter and Alfred Letley, Jacinta Matos, Lynda Myles, Vania Pegas, Lidewijde Paris, Anna and Mario Pelli, Dean Roth, Dayle Schwarzler, Ernst van den Boogaart and Corinna van Schendel, and Wesley van den Bos.

It should go without saying that all the lapses and eccentricities of this book are entirely my responsibility. I can only plead that a subject as rich and various as Antwerp in the sixteenth century needs to be seen from a hundred angles, many of them oblique.

Notes

THE EXCEPTION

1 See V. Rossato, 'Anvers et ses libertés vues par Giovanni Zonca, hétéro-doxe vénitien (1562–1566)', *Revue d'Histoire Ecclésiastique* LXXXV:2 (1990) for transcriptions of Zoncha's letters from the dossier of his later trial for heresy in Venice: Lent (Zoncha to Giovanni Raxello, 20 February 1563), p. 306; weapons and girls (no date), p. 308; Inquisition, (Zoncha to Giovanni de Sere, 9 April 1565), p. 310.

2 Eugenio Albèri (ed.), *Relazioni degli Ambasciatori Veneti al Senato* (Florence, 1839–63), I:i, p. 6.

3 Albèri, *Relazioni*, I:ii: Bruges' loss, p. 22; ships, p. 23.

4 Wallop to the Council, 25 November 1543, *Letters and Papers, Foreign and Domestic, Henry VIII* (London, 1864–1908), vol. 18, pt. 2, pp. 226–7.

5 Albèri, *Relazioni*, I:i, p. 298 (despatch dated 1546).

6 Ibid., I:ii: likeness to Venice, p. 201; astonishment ('*mi son stupito*') and well of deals ('*fonte della contrattazione*'), p. 202; clothes and debts, p. 204.

7 Luigi Firpo (ed.), *Relazioni di Ambasciatori Veneti al Senato: III Germania* (Turin, 1968): Alba, p. 108; interest rates, p. 122; marketplace, pp. 120ff.

8 Albèri, *Relazioni*, I:v, p. 6.

9 Albrecht Dürer, *Records of Journeys to Venice and the Low Countries* ed. Roger Fry (Boston, 1913; online at ebooks.adelaide.edu.au).

10 Albèri, *Relazioni*, VIII, p. 291.

11 For a brief account of these imperial dreams, and others, see Arthur H. Williamson, 'An Empire to End Empire', *Huntington Library Quarterly* 68:1–2 (March 2005), pp. 227–31.

12 Henri Lefebvre, *La Production de l'espace* (Paris, 1974); tr. Donald Nicholson-Smith (Oxford 1991) p. 268.

13 For a discussion of the limits of the Golden Age, see An Maria Kint, 'The Community of Commerce: Social Relations in Sixteenth-Century Antwerp' (Columbia University PhD dissertation, 1996), pp. 3–8.

14 Ortelius, *Aurei saeculi imago* (Antwerp, 1596). For a discussion of this ethnography, see Ernst van den Boogaart, *Vreemde Verwanten* (Nijmegen, 2019), pp. 334–8.

15 Cardano, *De rerum varietate* (Avignon, 1558), book 17, ch. 96, p. 856.

16 *Novelle di Matteo Bandello* (Milan, 1814), 4:9, p. 14.

17 Hans-Gert Roloff (ed.), *Georg Wickram: Sämtliche Werke IV* (Berlin, 1969): schools, p. 104; '*einem herlichen und geschickten mann*', p. 106; warnings, pp. 112–13; buildings, p.141.

18 Martin S. Soria, 'Some Flemish Sources of Baroque Painting in Spain', *Art Bulletin* 30:4 (1948), p. 249.

19 Harold J. Cook, 'Trading in Medical Simples and Developing the New Science', in Palmira Fontes da Costa (ed.), *Medicine, Trade and Empire: Garcia de Orta's* Colloquies on the Simples and Drugs of India *(1563) in* Context (London, 2016), pp. 133–4.

20 The book was Guicciardini's *Descriptio Germaniae Inferioris, Dce's copy* now in the Royal College of Physicians' library, London (shelfmark 125/13, 17d).

21 R. W. Grey (ed.), *Bibliographical and Historical Miscellanies* (1854), I:12, pp. 6ff.

22 Inventory scattered through Vierschaar Inventarissen van nagelaten goederen 1525–1566, FelixArchief Antwerp, V 298; no folio numbers. The full inventory is included in Natasja Peeters and Maximiliaan P. J. Martens, 'Piety and Splendor: The Art Collection of Antwerp Burgomaster Adriaan Hertsen', in A. Golahny, M. M. Mochizuki and L. Vergara (eds.), *In His Milieu: Essays on Netherlandish Art in Memory of John Michael Montias* (Amsterdam, 2006).

23 Letter to Philip II, 29 February 1568, in Fernando Álvarez de Toledo, Duque de Alba, *Epistolario del III Duque de Alba* (Madrid, 1952), 2:34.

I 1507

1 Luc Rombouts, *Singing Bronze: A History of Carillon Music* (Leuven, 2014), pp. 59, 78. See also Fernand Donnet, *Les Cloches d'Anvers, les fondeurs anversois* (Antwerp, 1899), which gives a wonderfully circumstantial account of the making of Carolus. Donnet, as secretary and librarian of the Académie Royale d'Archéologie de Belgique, among many other roles, produced carefully documented studies of physical monuments.

2 Cornelius Grapheus, *Le Triomphe d'Anvers, faict en la susception du Prince Philips, Prince d'Espaigñe* (Antwerp, 1550) pp. Ciii verso, Ciiii [= iv].

3 Coen Maas, *Medievalism and Political Rhetoric in Humanist Historiography from the Low Countries (1515–1609)* (Turnhout, 2018), p. 269.

4 Lodovico Guicciardini, *Beschrijvinghe van alle de Nederlanden* (Amsterdam, 1612), translated in An Maria Kint, 'The Community of Commerce: Social Relations in Sixteenth Century Antwerp' (Columbia University PhD dissertation, 1996), p. 74.

5 Maas, *Medievalism and Political Rhetoric*, p. 280. The book was Jacobus Meyerus, *Compendium chronicorum Flandriae* (Antwerp, 1538).

6 J. R. Hale (ed.), *The Travel Journal of Antonio de Beatis* (London, 1979), pp. 50–51.

7 Rombouts, *Singing Bronze*; Donnet, *Les Cloches d'Anvers*.

8 The plague ordinances are collected in A.-F.-C. van Schevensteen, *Documents pour servir à l'étude des Maladies Pestilentielles dans le Marquisat d'Anvers* (Brussels, 1931). Pigs were banned (e.g. 3 September 1513, p. 14; 24 July 1518, p. 21); along with ducks and geese (again on 8 August 1534, p. 27; 16 September 1578, p. 151 and 9 May 1584, p. 200). Geese were banned again on 5 June 1546 (p. 35).

9 Christopher P. Heuer, *The City Rehearsed* (London, 2009), p. 232, n. 72; the original titles are '*moosmeiren*', '*gruismeesters*', '*pachters van de beerput*'.

10 Van Schevensteen, *Documents pour servir à l'étude des Maladies Pestilentielles*: filth ('*syn seer vervuylt*'), 22 Jan 1530 (p. 24); skins, 27 June 1557 (p. 43); barbers, 16 Sept. 1578 (p. 151); gutters, 8 April 1578 (p. 149); stinking animals, 27 June 1557 (p. 43).

11 See Clé Lesger and Jan Hein Furnée, 'Shopping Streets and Cultures from a Long-Term and Transnational Perspective', in Furnée and Lesger (eds.), *The Landscape of Consumption: Shopping Streets and Cultures in Western Europe 1600–1900* (Basingstoke, 2014), pp. 7–9.

12 Ilja Van Damme with Laura Van Aert, 'Antwerp goes Shopping! Continuity and Change in Retail Space and Shopping Interactions from the Sixteenth to the Nineteenth Century', in Furnée and Lesger (eds.), *Landscape of Consumption*.

13 Cited in Kint, 'The Community of Commerce', p. 142.

14 Augustin Thiys, 'Le Navigateur Dierick Paesschen en 1511', *Bulletin de la Société Royale de Géographie d'Anvers* IX:1 (Antwerp, 1884–5), pp. 355ff.; and Roger Degryse, 'De Palestinaschepen van Dierick van

Paesschen (1511–1521)', *Mededelingen (van de Marine Academie)*
XXIII (Antwerp, 1973–5), pp. 15ff.

15 For the annuity and mortgage, see Frederik Buylaert and Yves Huy-
brechts, 'Blue Blood in the Red? Nobles on the Antwerp Annuity Market
(1490–1493)', *Edad Media* 19 (2018), p. 191.

16 Cornelius Grapheus, *Memorabilis conflagratio templi Divae Mariae
Antverpien – heroico versu velut ob oculos posita* (Antwerp, 1534).

17 See Virgil, *Aeneid* III: 554–87 for description, VIII: 407–53 for the forges.

18 See Rutger Tijs, *Crowning the City* (Antwerp, 1993), p. 107, for a full
discussion.

19 For a discussion of *commoditas, ornamento, venustas* and *utilitas*, and
their relation to *commoditeit, sieraet en profijt*, see Jochen De Vylder,
'The Grid and the Existing City', in Piet Lombaerde and Charles van den
Heuvel (eds.), *Early Modern Urbanism and the Grid* (Turnhout, 2011),
pp. 86–7.

20 For a narrative of the 1542 siege, see Jervis Wegg, *Antwerp 1477–1559:
From the Battle of Nancy to the Treaty of Cateau Cambrésis* (London,
1916), pp. 220–25.

21 Lodovico Guicciardini, *The Description of the Low Countreys* (London,
1593): engines, p. 22r; defences, p. 27v; rents, p. 26v.

22 Tijs, *Crowning the City*, pp. 61, 62, 75.

2 THE CITY AS IDEA

1 Iain Buchanan, 'The Collection of Niclaes Jongelinck: I: "Bacchus and
the Planets" by Jacques Jongelinck', *Burlington Magazine* 132:1043
(February 1990), pp. 102–5; and 'II: "The Months" by Pieter Bruegel the
Elder', *Burlington Magazine* 132:1049 (August 1990), pp. 541–3.

2 See Michael Limberger: *Sixteenth-Century Antwerp and its Rural Sur-
roundings* (Turnhout, 2008).

3 Ortelius at the rural kermis is Lucas van Valckenborch, *Village Fair*, in
the State Hermitage Museum in St Petersburg; Ortelius at Tivoli is in a
Hoefnagel print of 1581 published in book III of Braun and Hogenberg,
Civitates orbis terrarum (Antwerp, 1581).

4 See Claudia Goldstein, *Pieter Bruegel and the Culture of the Early Modern Dinner Party* (Farnham, 2013), pp. 96–100 for the jugs; pp. 78–80 for
the plays.

5 Limberger, *Sixteenth-Century Antwerp*: gentry, p. 205; hinterland, p. 49;
boom, p. 84; Schoyte, p. 191; rent in kind, p. 111.

6 For general accounts, see Wim Blockmans and Walter Prevenier, *The Promised Lands: The Low Countries under Burgundian Rule 1369–1530* (Philadelphia, revised edition 1999): van der Beurse, p. 164; Bruges revolts, pp. 203–3; Antwerp growth, pp. 214–16; and Oscar Gelderblom, 'The Decline of Fairs and Merchant Guilds in the Low Countries 1250–1650' (published 2004 at researchgate.net/publication/253932534), *passim*.

7 J. de Sturler, *Les Relations politiques et les échanges commerciaux entre le duché de Brabant et l'Angleterre au Moyen Âge* (Paris, 1936): Ipswich convoy, pp. 402–3; first staple, p. 289; return trade, p. 301; galleys, p. 317.

8 Giovanna Petti Balbi, 'Bruges, port des italiens', in André Vendewalle (ed.), *Les Marchands de la Hanse et la banque des Médicis* (Oostkamp, 2002), p. 59.

9 See James M. Murray, 'Techniques commerciales et financières', in ibid., esp. p. 109.

10 Cornelius Scrib. Grapheus, *Spectaculorum in susceptione Philippi* (Antwerp, 1550), M3.

11 Georgius Schroegelius, *Elegia Enkomiastike in Clarissimam et Praestantissimam Belgarum urbem Handoverpiam* (Antwerp, 1565), p. A1v.

12 Danielis Rogerii, *De laudibus Antwerpiae, Oda Sapphica* (Antwerp, 1565): 'new Rome', p. B3r; 'whole world bustles', p. B4r; Beurs, p. B3v.

13 Maas, *Medievalism and Political Rhetoric*): history, p. 238; Barlandus, p. 395.

14 Ioan. Goropii Becani, *Origines Antwerpianae sive Cimmeriorum Becceselana* (Antwerp, 1569): Alps, p. 467; Vikings, p. 764; elephants, pp. 178–80; peoples of Europe, p. C1r.

15 Flavius Josephus, *Antiquities of the Jews*, book 1, chapter 4 at http://sacred-texts.com/jud/josephus/ant-1.htm

16 See Stephen H. Goddard, '*Probationes Pennae*: Some Sixteenth-Century Doodles on the Theme of Folly, Attributed to the Antwerp Humanist Pieter Gillis and his Colleagues', *Renaissance Quarterly* 41:2 (Summer 1988), pp. 242–67, with an invaluable catalogue of transcriptions on pp. 263–7. I have made my own translations and not relied on these attributions. Doodles are in Vierschaar Inventarissen van nagelaten goederen 1525–1566, FelixArchief Antwerp, V 298: 1233,1234,1235,1239,1244, 1245,1246.

17 See Herman Pleij (tr. Diane Webb), *Dreaming of Cockaigne: Medieval Fantasies of the Perfect Life* (New York, 2001), pp. 77–85 for a brilliant

discussion of the text in *Veelderhanden geneuchlycke dichten, tafelspelen ende refereynen* (Antwerp, 1600).

3 KNOWING THINGS

1 Edward Surtz, 'St Thomas More and his Utopian Embassy of 1515', *Catholic Historical Review* 39:3 (October 1953), pp. 272ff.

2 See Romuald I. Lakowski, *International Thomas More Bibliography*, online at www3.telus.net/lakowski/Utopbibo.html

3 See Peter R. Allen, '*Utopia* and European Humanism: The Function of the Prefatory Letters and Verses', *Studies in the Renaissance* 10 (1963), pp. 94–7. For Erasmus' preface see Thomas More, *Utopia*, edited by George M. Logan and translated by Robert M. Adams (Cambridge 1989), p. 110; for Budé, p. 111. For the burgomaster, see the edition by Edward Arber (London 1869), p. 7 (quoting Erasmus to More, 8 March 1517).

4 Lorne Campbell, Margaret Mann Phillips, Hubertus Schulte Herbrüggen and J. B. Trapp, 'Quentin Matsys, Desiderius Erasmus, Pieter Gillis and Thomas More', *Burlington Magazine* 120:908 (November 1978), pp. 716ff.

5 Rev. Dr (John Allen) Giles (ed.), *The Whole Works of Roger Ascham*, vol. I, part II (London, 1865), p. 217: letter to Sir John Cheke, 11 November 1550. 'Low' from *Germania inferior*; 'the pits' from *inferorum*.

6 Johannes Radermacher to Jacobus Colius, 7/17 January 1604, in Jan Hendrick Hessels (ed.), *Epistulae Ortelianae* (Cambridge, 1887; repr. 2009), II:334 (pp. 787–91).

7 Florence Edler, 'Winchcombe Kerseys in Antwerp (1538–44)', *Economic History Review* 7:1 (1936), pp. 57ff.

8 Thomas More, *Confutation of Tyndale's Answer*, part 1, in R. S. Sylvester (ed.), *The Complete Works of St Thomas More* (New Haven, 1973), vol. 8, p. 20.

9 John Strype, *Ecclesiastical Memorials* (Oxford, 1822): Bayfield, 1/i p. 255; Constantine, 1/i p. 256; Mr Fyshe, 1/ii p. 63.

10 See Frederick C. Avis, 'Book Smuggling into England during the Sixteenth Century', in Hans Widmann (ed.), *Gutenberg-Jahrbuch 1972* (Mainz, 1972), pp. 180ff.; and 'England's Use of Antwerp Printers', in *Gutenberg-Jahrbuch 1973* (Mainz, 1973), pp. 234ff.

11 David Daniell, *William Tyndale: A Biography* (New Haven, 1994), pp. 14–16.

12 John N. King (ed.), *Foxe's Book of Martyrs* (Oxford, 2009), pp. 19–20; Andrew Hope, 'The Printed Book Trade in Response to Luther', in Vincent Gillespie and Susan Powell (eds.), *A Companion to the Early Printed*

Book in Britain 1476–1558 (Cambridge, 2014), pp. 273–5 for the chronology; cf. M. E. Kronenberg, 'Notes on English Printing in the Low Countries (Early Sixteenth Century)', *The Library* 4th series, vol. IX (1929), pp. 139ff. for details on van Ruremund; and Victoria Christman, *Pragmatic Toleration: The Politics of Religious Heterodoxy in Early Reformation Antwerp, 1515–1555* (Rochester, NY, 2015) for book laws (p. 71) and his widow's part (pp. 83–4).

13 Henry Ellis *et al.* (eds.), *Hall's Chronicle, containing the History of England* (London, 1809), pp. 762–3.

14 Daniell, *William Tyndale*, pp. 283ff.

15 Henry Walter, 'Life of William Tyndale', in *Doctrinal Treatises ... by William Tyndale* (Cambridge, 1848), pp. xxli–xxlii.

16 Stephen Vaughan to Henry VIII, 18 April 1531, *LPFD Henry VIII*, vol. 5, letter 201, p. 95.

17 Brian Moynahan, *Book of Fire* (London, 2002), pp. 21ff. for the English House; Daniell, *William Tyndale*, pp. 335–8 for John Rogers.

18 Baron Joseph Kervyn de Lettenhove, *Commentaires de Charles-Quint* (Paris, 1862), pp. 24, 27, 30, for years before Tyndale's arrest.

19 Daniell, *William Tyndale*, esp. pp. 374ff.

20 Paget to Petre 30 March 1545, *LPFD Henry VIII*, vol. 20, pt. 1, pp. 201–2.

21 Lodovico Guicciardini, *Beschrijvinghe van alle de Nederlanden* (Amsterdam, 1612), tr. in An Maria Kint, 'The Community of Commerce: Social Relations in Sixteenth-Century Antwerp' (Columbia University PhD dessertation' 1996), p. 23

22 Vaughan to Cromwell, Antwerp, 21 February 1539, *LPFD Henry VIII* vol. 14, pt. 1, p. 132.

23 Cosimo de' Medici to Giovan Battista di Simone Ricasoli, 3 February 1545 Archivio di Stato, Florence, vol. 3, f. 663.

24 Reinhard Bodenmann, Alexandra Kess and Judith Steiniger (eds.), *Henrich Bullinger Briefwechsel*, vol. 19 (Zurich, 2019): Myconius to Bullinger, 21 March 1547, letter 2855, pp. 437ff.; Myconius to Bullinger, 24 March 1547, letter 2859, pp. 445ff.

25 Nikolaus Schobesberger, 'Mapping the *Fuggerzeitungen*: The Geographical Issues of an Information Network', in Joad Raymond and Noah Moxham (eds.), *News Networks in Early Modern Europe* (Leiden, 2016), pp. 216–40.

26 Wyllughby to the Lord Marshal, 23 August 1587, Lincolnshire Archives 8ANC 10/18.

27 Jerningham and the Council of Tournay to Henry VIII, 28 February 1518, *LPFD Henry VIII*, vol. 2, pp. 1235–6.

28 Richard Herman to Cromwell, 2 November 1535, *LPFD Henry VIII*, vol. 9, p. 254.

29 John Coke, clerk to the Merchant Adventurers at Antwerp, to Cromwell, 30 June 1533, *LPFD Henry VIII*, vol. 6, p. 322.

30 Wingfield and Spinelly to Wolsey, 22 June 1521, *LPFD Henry VIII*, vol. 3, pp. 544–5.

31 Carne and Vaughan to Henry VIII, 22 August 1541, *LPFD Henry VIII*, vol. 16, pp. 525–6.

32 Van der Delft to Mary of Hungary, 18 June 1545, *LPFD Henry VIII*, vol. 20, pt. 1, p. 472.

33 Original source: Pieter van der Molen Brievenkopij, 1538–44, Insolvente Boedelskamer no. 2898 (FelixArchief Antwerp); see John J. McCusker, 'The Demise of Distance: The Business Press and the Origins of the Information Revolution in the Early Modern Atlantic World', *American Historical Review* 110:2 (2005), esp. pp. 298–9.

34 Oscar Gelderblom, *Cities of Commerce* (Princeton, 2013), p. 31.

35 Donald J. Harreld, 'Trading Places: The Public and Private Spaces of Merchants in Sixteenth-Century Antwerp', *Journal of Urban History* 29: 6 (2003), pp. 657ff.

36 Donald J. Harreld, *High Germans in the Low Countries* (Leiden, 2004), pp. 116–19.

37 Vaughan to Henry VIII, 3 March 1546, *LPFD Henry VIII* vol. 21, pt. 1, p. 161.

38 From van Schoonbeke's denunciation of Ducci, printed by Pierre Génard in *Un Procès célèbre au XVIème siècle: Gilbert van Schoonbeke contre Gaspar Duzzi* (Brussels, 1888).

39 Vaughan to Paget and Petre, 15 July 1546, *LPFD Henry VIII*, vol. 21, pt. 1, p. 638.

40 See Jeffrey Chipps Smith, 'Albrecht Dürer as Collector', *Renaissance Quarterly* 64:1 (2011): Indians, p. 26; bought in Antwerp, p. 29; Matsys, p. 37.

41 Pieter Martens and Konrad Ottenheym, 'Fortifications and Waterworks: Engineers on the Road', in Konrad Ottenheym and Krista De Jonge (eds.), *The Low Countries at the Crossroads: Netherlandish Architecture as an Export Product in Early Modern Europe (1480–1680)* (Turnhout, 2013), p. 361 (quoting British Library Sloan Add Mss 5229 f. 28v).

42 I'm following Nicholas H. Clulee, *John Dee's Natural Philosophy* (Abingdon, 1988) on the division in Dee's career.

43 György E. Szőnyi, *John Dee's Occultism: Magic Exhalation through Powerful Signs* (Albany, 2004), p. 105.

44 See I. R. F. Calder, 'John Dee Studied as an English Neo-Platonist (PhD thesis, Warburg Institute, London, 1953), ch. 6, note 35, for an excellent summary of Trithemius' life and work.

45 R. W. Grey (ed.), Letter of Dr Dee to Sir W. Cecyl', 16 February 1562/3, in *Bibliographical and Historical Miscellanies* 1:12 (London, 1854), pp. 6ff.

46 Cf. Augustin Thys, *Historique des rues et places publiques de la ville d'Anvers* (Antwerp, 1873), p. 291.

47 See Colin Clair, 'Willem Silvius', *The Library* 5th series, vol. XIV:3 (1959), pp. 192ff.

48 For a discussion of the statistics, see Jan De Meester, 'Migrant Workers and Illicit Labour: Regulating the Immigration of Building Workers in Sixteenth-Century Antwerp' in Bert De Munck and Anne Winter (eds.), *Gated Communities? Regulating Migration in Early Modern Cities* (Farnham, 2012). On London, Amsterdam and other major cities, see Jelle van Lottum, *Across the North Sea: The Impact of the Dutch Republic on International Labour Migration c. 1550–1850* (Amsterdam, 2007), pp. 99ff.

49 A.-F.-C. van Schevensteen, *Les Traités de pestilence publiés à Anvers* (Antwerp, 1931), p. 6 (for copying).

50 Hugo Soly, 'Continuity and Change: Attitudes towards Poor Relief and Health Care in Early Modern Antwerp', in Ole Peter Grell and Andrew Cunningham (eds.), *Health Care and Poor Relief in Protestant Europe 1500–1700* (London, 1997), pp. 92–3.

4 THE GARDEN OF KNOWING

1 De Lobel, *Plantarum seu stirpium historia* (Antwerp, 1576), A2; Johannes Goropius Becanus, *Origines Antverpianae* (Antwerp, 1569): '*plantarum contemplatione percipiendu*', Db. For the context, see Charles van Hulthem, *Discours sur l'état ancien et moderne de l'agriculture et la botanique dans les Pays Bas* (Ghent, 1817), pp. 7–8, and Florike Egmond, *The World of Carolus Clusius: Natural History in the Making, 1550–1610* (Abingdon, 2010), ebook, pp. e12ff.

2 For Montanus, see Florike Egmond and Sven Dupré, 'Collecting and Circulating Exotic Naturalia in the Spanish Netherlands', in Sven Dupré et al. (eds.), *Embattled Territory: The Circulation of Knowledge in the Spanish Netherlands* (Ghent, 2015).

3 Donald F. Lach, *Asia in the Making of Europe*, vol. II, book 3, p. 422.

4 G. H. Tucker, 'To Louvain and Antwerp, and Beyond', in Luc Dequeker and Werner Verbeke (eds.), *The Expulsion of the Jews and their Emigration*

to the Southern Low Countries (15th–16th Centuries) (Leuven, 1998) and *Medicina na Beira Interior, Cadernos da Cultura* 23 (November 2009), esp. Antonio Manuel Lopes Andrade, 'As tribulações de Mestre João Rodrigues de Castelo Branco (Amato Lusitano) a chegada a Antuérpia em 1534 . . .'.

5 Daniel H. Garrison (ed. and tr.), *Andreas Vesalius: The China Root Epistle (1546)* (New York, 2015): imported, p. 22; everywhere, p. 44; first patient, p. 16.

6 Florike Egmond, 'Figuring Exotic Nature in Sixteenth-Century Europe', in Palmira Fontes da Costa (ed.), *Medicine, Trade and Empire: Garcia de Orta's* Colloquies on the Simples and Drugs of India *(1563)* (Farnham, 2015), pp. 181–4.

7 De Lobel, *Plantarum seu stirpium historia*, A2.

8 Lodovico Guicciardini, *Descrittione di tutti i Paesi Bassi* (Antwerp, 1581), p. 11.

9 Sachiko Kusukawa, *Picturing the Book of Nature* (Chicago, 2012), p. 156.

10 Édouard Morren, *Pierre Coudenberg, sa vie et ses oeuvres* (Ghent, 1866), pp. 10, 15; P.-A. Cap, 'Pierre Coudenberg: un apothicaire belge au XVIème siècle' in *Journal de pharmacie et de chimie* iii 40:2 (Paris, 1861), pp. 449, 451, 455.

11 *Val. Cordi Dispensatorium* (Leiden, 1571), p. 319.

5 THE LESSON

1 Ad Meskens, *Practical Mathematics in a Commercial Metropolis* (Dordrecht, 2013), p. 36.

2 Kristine Forney, '"Nymphes gayes en abry du Laurier": Music Instruction for the Bourgeois Woman', *Musica Disciplina* 49 (1995), p. 158.

3 Andrea Bardyn, 'Women in the [*sic*] Medieval Society', in, Véronique Lambert and Peter Stabel (eds.), *Golden Times: Wealth and Status in the Middle Ages in the Southern Low Countries* (Tielt, 2016), p. 291.

4 Kaat Cappelle, 'Law, Wives and the Marital Economy in Sixteenth-Century Antwerp', in Anna Bellavitis and Beatrice Zucca Micheletto (eds.), *Gender, Law and Economic Well-Being in Europe from the Fifteenth to the Nineteenth Century* (Abingdon, 2019), pp. 228–41. Laura Van Aert, 'The Legal Possibilities of Antwerp Widows in the Late Sixteenth Century', *History of the Family* 12:4 (2007), pp. 282ff. Laura Van Aert, 'Trade and Gender Emancipation: Retailing Women in Sixteenth-Century Antwerp', in Bruno Blondé, Peter Stabel, Jon Stobart and Ilja

NOTES

Van Damme (eds.), *Retail Circuits and Practices in Medieval and Early Modern Europe* (Turnhout, 2006).

5 Meskens, *Practical Mathematics*, p. 40, n. 29.

6 H. Meeus, 'Peeter Heyns, a "French Schoolmaster"' in, Jan de Clercq, Nico Lioce and Pierre Swiggers (eds.), *Grammaire et enseignement du français 1500–1700* (Leuven, 2000): schoolbooks, p. 309; plays, pp. 310ff.

7 Gabriel Meurier, *La Guirlande des jeunes filles en françois & flamen* (Antwerp, 1580). Earlier printings go back to 1564.

8 Claude Luython, *Dictionaire en franchois et flameng ou bas allemant tresutile pour apprendre les deux langages* (Antwerp, 1552) f. 39v–40r.

9 J. L. Vives, *De Institutione Feminae Christianae* I, ed. C. Matheeussen, ed. and tr. C. Fantazzi (Leiden, 1996; originally published Basel, 1538): attractive wife, pp. 40–41; Plutarch, pp. 38–9. The French translation was published as *L'institution de la femme chrestienne* (Antwerp, 1579).

10 Peeter Heyns, *Le Miroir des mesnagères* (Amsterdam, 1595), p. 2 recto and verso.

11 Anna Bijns, *Iste est ... pulcher et syncerus libellus* (Antwerp, 1529)

12 Cornelius Valerius, *Colloquia cum dictionariolo sex linguarum ... eas linguas discere volentibus utilissima* (Antwerp, 1579).

13 *Colloquia et Dictionariolum Septem Linguarum* (Antwerp, 1586), ch. 5 *passim*.

14 See Rocío G. Sumillera, 'Language Manuals and the Book Trade in England', in José María Pérez Fernández and Edward Wilson-Lee (eds.), *Translation and the Book Trade in Early Modern Europe* (New York, 2014), pp. 63ff.

15 Luython, *Dictionnaire en franchois et flameng*.

16 Gabriel Meurier, *Dialogue, contenant les coniugasions Flamen-Francois* (Antwerp, 1562), p. 31.

17 Luython, *Dictionaire en franchois et flameng*, f. 43r.

18 *Vocabulair pour aprēdre Latin, Romain & Flameng* (Antwerp, 1525), Dvii, Ii.

19 Gonzalo Suárez Gómez, *La Enseñanza del Francés en España hasta 1850* (Barcelona, 2008), pp. 48–9

20 Gabriel Meurier, *Vocabulaire François-Flameng mis en lumière* (Antwerp, 1562) p.2

21 Cf. Gómez, *La Enseñanza del Francés en España*, pp. 54–5.

22 Noël van Berlaimont, *Vocabulare van nieus geordineert ende wederom gecorrigeert* (Antwerp, 1536, following and revising a *Vocabulaire* first

233

issued in 1511), p. 12 for the menu; pp. 25–6 for Katerine's wares; p. 34 for dealing with a debtor face to face; p. 40 for asking money from your father; p. 42 for letters to your debtor.

6 THE CITY PUBLISHED

1 Cornelius Grapheus, *La Très admirable, très magnifique et triomphante entrée ... anno 1549* (Antwerp, 1550), p. Bii.
2 Mario Mazzolani, *Simone Turchi: storia di un delitto famoso e commento a una novella del Bandello* (Lucca, 1937); and in *Bolletino storico Lucchese* A – B (Lucca, 1936), Mazzolani checked Bandello's version against the archive material in Antwerp and found it remarkably accurate: p. 29, n. 3.
3 Cf. Adelin Charles Fiorato, *Bandello entre l'histoire et l'écriture* (Florence, 1979), pp. 506ff.
4 Ibid., p. 506.
5 *Novelle di Matteo Bandello* (Milan, 1814), 4:9, p. 11.
6 Fiorato, *Bandello entre l'histoire et l'écriture*, p. 567.
7 Ian Maclean, *Learning and the Market Place: Essays in the History of the Early Modern Book* (Leiden, 2009), p. 231, n. 15.
8 In Bandello's letter to his readers: *Novelle di Matteo Bandello* 4:9, p. 8.
9 Girolamo Cardano, *De rerum varietate* (Avignon, 1558), book 17, ch. 96, pp. 856–7 for Antwerp in general; book 9, ch. 53, pp. 334–5 for the murder and the chair.
10 See Giovanni M. Carsaniga, '"The Truth" in John Ford's *The Broken Heart*', *Comparative Literature* 10:4 (Autumn 1958), pp. 344ff.
11 Mazzolani, *Bolletino storico Lucchese*, p. 29.
12 Cardano, *De rerum varietate*, book 17, ch. 96, p. 856.
13 *Novelle di Matteo Bandello* 4:9, p. 14.
14 Ibid., novella VIII, pp. 187ff.
15 Mazzolani, *Bolletino storico Lucchese*, p. 13.
16 Ibid., p. 12.
17 Hans-Gert Roloff (ed.), *Georg Wickram: Sämtliche Werke*, vol. III (Berlin, 1968): sexual liaisons, p. 6; the bathhouses, p. 38; their time in Antwerp, pp. 39–40; their trick on the landlord, p. 40; the shoemaker's daughter and her custody of one boy's coat, pp. 48–9.
18 An Maria Kint, 'The Community of Commerce: Social Relations in Sixteenth-Century Antwerp' (Columbia University PhD dissertation, 1996), p. 344.

19 Alfons K. L. Thijs, *Van Geuzenstad tot katholiek bolwerk* (Turnhout, 1990), pp. 136–8; Maarten Bassens and Timothy De Paepe, *Hotel de Rosier: biografie van een Antwerpse patriciërswoning 1619–2017* (Antwerp, 2018).

20 Kint, 'The Community of Commerce', pp. 231, 235.

21 Bert De Munck and Anne Winter (eds.), *Gated Communities? Regulating Migration in Early Modern Cities* (Farnham, 2012), pp. 12–13.

22 Bert Verwerft, 'De beul in het Markizaat van Antwerpen . . .' '(University of Ghent thesis, 2007, online at https://biblio.ugent.be/publication/920637); Jonas Roelens, 'Fornicating Foreigners: Sodomy, Migration and Urban Society in the Southern Low Countries (1400–1700)', *Dutch Crossing* 41:3 (2017).

23 Hans-Gert Roloff (ed.), *Georg Wickram: Sämèliche Werke*, vol. IV (Berlin, 1969): the neighbour as *'zaenkischen, arglistigen . . .'*, p. 12; sword, p. 13; insults and disbelief, p. 14; bucket, back of the house, dishwater and garbage, pp. 14–15; the messenger and Robertus' response, pp. 25–6; party, p. 27.

24 Ibid., p. 104.

25 See reviews of W. E. D. Atkinson's edition of *Acolastus* in *Modern Philology* 64:4 (May 1967); *Journal of English and Germanic Philology* 66:3 (July 1967); *Bibliothèque d'Humanisme et Renaissance* 28:1 (1966).

26 Roloff (ed.), *Georg Wickram*, vol. IV: schools, p. 104; *'einem herlichen und geschickten mann'*, p. 106; warnings, pp. 112–13; buildings, p. 141; guided tour, p. 142; communal meal, p. 147; joy, p. 144.

27 On the *conversos* in Colmar, see Kaspar von Greyerz, 'Portuguese *Conversos* on the Upper Rhine and the *Converso* Community of Sixteenth-Century Europe', *Social History* 14:1 (1989). On Wickram's life and the issues raised in *Von guten und böesen Nachbarn*, see Jane Emberson, 'Of Good and Bad Neighbours: Middle-Class Life in the Work of Jörg Wickram', *Sixteenth Century Journal* 26:3 (1995). I seem to be the first to make a connection between the arrests and Wickram's text.

7 THE UNSETTLEMENT

1 A full transcript of his Inquisition testimony is in Guilherme Henriques, *Ineditos Goesianos*, vol. 2 (Lisbon, 1898): *'moçidade'* meaning childhood or kidhood, p. 61; *'sendo eu muito moço'*, p. 73.

2 See Elisabeth Feist Hirsch, 'The Friendship of Erasmus and Damião de Goes', *Proceedings of the American Philosophical Society* 95:5 (1951), pp. 556ff.

3 On de Goes' paintings, see Natasja Peeters, 'Art Fever: Art in Houses of Iberian Residents in Antwerp, a Study of Confiscation Inventories (1532–1567)', *Dutch Crossing* 32:1 (2008), pp. 75–6; on Bosch and ergotism, see Laurinda Dixon, *Bosch* (London, 2003); on ergotism in Portugal, see George Barger, *Ergot and Ergotism* (London, 1931), p. 57.

4 Henriques, *Ineditos Goesianos*, pp. 62, 73 (Lutheranism).

5 Albrecht Dürer, *Journal de voyage aux Pays-Bas* (Paris, 2009), pp. 27, 35.

6 J.-A. Goris, *Étude sur les colonies marchandes méridionales ... à Anvers de 1488 à 1567* (Leuven, 1925, repr. 1967), p. 26.

7 A. F. C. Ryder, 'An Early Portuguese Trading Voyage to the Forcados River', *Journal of the Historical Society of Nigeria* 1:4 (1959), esp. pp. 296, 299, 301, 302.

8 John Vogt, 'Notes on the Portuguese Cloth Trade in West Africa, 1480–1540', *International Journal of African Historical Studies* 8:4 (1975), pp. 623ff.

9 J. Denucé, *L'Afrique au XVIème siècle et le Commerce Anversois* (Antwerp, 1937), p. 48 for Rodrigues; cf. Allison Blakley, *Blacks in the Dutch World* (Bloomington, Indiana, 1993), p. 226. See also in T. F. Earle and K. J. P. Lowe (eds.), *Black Africans in Renaissance Europe* (Cambridge, 2005): Jorge Fonseca, 'Black Africans in Portugal during Cleynaert's visit (1533–1538)', pp. 113ff.; Kate Lowe, 'The Stereotyping of Black Africans in Renaissance Europe', pp. 44–7 (on Mostaert); Paul H. D. Kaplan, 'Isabella d'Este and Black African Women', pp. 153–4 (on Dürer).

10 A. R. Disney, *A History of Portugal and the Portuguese Empire*, 2 vols (New York, 2009), vol. 1, p. 147.

11 16 July 1544, Archives Générales du Royaume in Brussels: Office Fiscal du Conseil de Brabant 160/1233/3; printed in Aron di Leone Leoni, *The Hebrew Portuguese Nations in Antwerp and London at the Time of Charles V and Henry VIII* (Jersey City, 2005), p. 69. Di Leone Leoni searched archives across Europe for documents, and without his scholarship and energy this would be a thin story.

12 Kaya Şahin, *Empire and Power in the Reign of Süleyman* (Cambridge, 2013), pp. 67–8, 82, 102.

13 Gülru Necipoğlu, 'Süleyman the Magnificent and the Representation of Power in the Contest of Ottoman-Hapsburg-Papal Rivalry', *Art Bulletin* 71:3 (September 1989), pp. 401ff.

14 Alastair Hamilton, *Arab Culture and Ottoman Magnificence in Antwerp's Golden Age* (Oxford, 2001), p. 9.

15 François Soyer, *The Persecution of the Jews and Muslims of Portugal: King Manuel I and the End of Religious Tolerance (1496–7)* (Leiden, 2007), pp. 94, 182, 234, 285.

16 For the best recent account of the Portuguese context, see Disney, *A History of Portugal,* vol. 1, esp. pp. 154, 181ff.

17 Baron Joseph Kervyn de Lettenhove, *Commentaires de Charles-Quint* (Paris, 1862), e.g., p. 30.

18 Jeroen Puttevils, *Merchants and Trading in the Sixteenth Century* (London, 2015), p. 69.

19 Archives Générales du Royaume in Brussels: Office Fiscal du Conseil de Brabant B 1233 (160 [2]): interrogation of Andreas Balenus, 5 October 1540, printed in Herman Prins Salomon and Aron de Leone Leoni, 'Mendes, Benveniste, de Luna, Micas, Nasci: The State of the Art (1532–1558)', *Jewish Quarterly Review* 88:3–4 (1998), pp. 189–90: '*imprecationes contra cristianos et orationes ad deum ut quam primum mitteret messiam.*'

20 See ibid., p. 180, citing Archives Générales du Royaume in Brussels, Bx PEA 1504: 'Diogo Mendes', ff. 22–7 ('*les rois de Portugal et d'Angleterre ont escript en sa faveur . . .*').

21 Archivo General de Simancas, est. 369, doc. 112, cited and translated ibid., p. 140.

22 Torre de Tombo, Lisbon, CC:1 *maço* 49, doc. 87, cited and translated ibid., pp. 137–8.

23 J. D. M. Ford, *Letters of John III* (London, 1931), p. 96, cited ibid., pp. 147–8.

24 Translated and quoted in P. Grunebaum-Ballin, 'Joseph Naci, duc de Naxos', *Études Juives* XIII (1968), p. 34.

25 Di Leone Leoni, *The Hebrew Portuguese Nations in Antwerp and London*, pp. 70–71. Leoni's extraordinary collection of documents, and his most valuable interpretations, are the basis of this section.

26 G. H. Tucker, 'To Louvain and Antwerp, and Beyond', in Luc Dequeker and Werner Verbeke (eds.), *The Expulsion of the Jews and their Emigration to the Southern Low Countries (15th–16th Centuries)* (Leuven, 1998).

27 Andrée Aelion Brooks, *The Woman Who Defied Kings* (St Paul, 2002), pp. 118ff.

28 Ibid., p. 94.

29 David S. Katz, *The Jews in the History of England 1485–1850* (Oxford, 1994), pp. 3–6 (relying largely on the notes of Lucien Wolf – Wolf's papers

are so valuable it seems mean-spirited to point out that he was not a great man for footnotes).

30 Di Leone Leoni, *The Hebrew Portuguese Nations in Antwerp and London*, pp. 185–8, printing Archives Générales du Royaume in Brussels: Office Fiscal du Conseil de Brabant B 160/1233/2: Boisot's report, November 1540; see also pp. 28–31.

31 Giorgio Dati to Pier Francesco Riccio, 26 October 1545, Archivio di Stato, Florence, vol. 1170a, f. 171r: fresh matter '*cosa fresca*'; suspicious people '*gente sospettosa et massime hora temono scoprirsi*'; death-defying '*negocii quali son pericolosi et della vita*'.

32 Giorgio Dati to Pier Francesco Riccio, 28 March 1546, ibid., vol. 1172, f. 39.

33 Di Leone Leoni, *The Hebrew Portuguese Nations in Antwerp and London*, pp. 232–3, printing Archives Générales du Royaume in Brussels, Bx PEA 1177, f. 90r, July 1547.

8 MONEY

1 Schetz to Erasmus, Antwerp, 28 August 1531, in P. S. Allen *et al.* (eds.), *Opus Epistolarum Des. Erasmi Roterodami* (Oxford, 1938), p. 329. I am very grateful to Gustav Zamore for his help with the translation.

2 See Krista De Jonge, 'Bâtiments publics à fonction économique à Anvers au XVIème siècle: l'invention d'un type?', in Konrad Ottenheym, Monique Chatenet and Krista De Jonge (eds.), *Public Buildings in Early Modern Europe* (Turnhout, 2010), pp. 187–90, and Jochen De Vylder, 'The Grid and the Existing City', in Piet Lombaerde and Charles van den Heuvel (eds.), *Early Modern Urbanism and the Grid* (Turnhout, 2011), pp. 78–9.

3 Lodovico (Louis) Guicciardini, *Description de la Cité d'Anvers*, in de Belleforest's translation, from the 1582 Plantin edition (Antwerp, 1920), pp. 132–3.

4 Donald J. Harreld, *High Germans in the Low Countries* (Leiden, 2004), p. 663.

5 Jan Van der Stock, 'Hieronymus Cock and Volcxken Diericx, Print Publishers in Antwerp', in Joris Van Grieken, Ger Luijten and Jan Van der Stock, *Hieronymus Cock, the Renaissance in Print* (Brussels, 2013), p. 17.

6 Guicciardini, *Description de la Cité d'Anvers*, p. 39.

7 Hernando de Frias Cevallos to Simon Ruiz, 16 March 1564, in V. Vazquez de Prada, *Lettres Marchandes d'Anvers II* (Paris, 1960), pp. 11–12.

8 Guicciardini, *Description de la Cité d'Anvers*, p. 132.

9   See Pierre Génard, *Un Procès célèbre au XVIème siècle: Gilbert van Schoonbeke contre Gaspar Ducci* (Brussels, 1888), pp. 19ff for a transcript of the court proceedings on which this account is based.

10 See Hugo Soly, *Urbanisme en Kapitalisme te Antwerpen in de 16de eeuw: De stedebouwkundige en industriele ondernemingen van Gilbert van Schoonbeke* (Brussels, 1977), p. 133; and for property deals involving Ducci and van Schoonbeke, pp. 70, 139, 141, 155.

11 Génard, *Un Procès célèbre au XVIème siècle*, pp. 11–12.

12 Ibid., pp. 15, 17.

13 J.-A. Goris, *Étude sur les colonies marchandes méridionales . . . à Anvers de 1488 à 1567* (Leuven, 1925, repr. 1967), p. 378.

14 Archivio di Stato, Florence, Mediceo del Principato, vol. 13, f. 452, 11 March 1550.

15 Ibid., vol. 9, f. 10, 12 September 1547; vol. 1173, f. 329, 13 September 1547; vol. 12, f. 13, 10 October 1548.

16 Vaughan to Paget, 8 October 1545, *Letters and Papers, Foreign and Domestic, Henry VIII* (London, 1864–1908), vol. 20, pt. 2, p. 257.

17 Vaughan to Henry VIII, 7 June 1546, *LPFD Henry VIII*, vol. 21, pt. 1, p. 510.

18 Vaughan to Paget, 2 March 1546, ibid., p. 156.

19 Vaughan to Henry VIII, 26 May 1546, ibid., p. 456. Ducci was 'Jasper Dowche' to London.

20 Vaughan to Paget, 17 August 1545, *LPFD Henry VIII*, vol. 20, pt. 2, p. 66.

21 Vaughan to Paget, 2 March 1546, *LPFD Henry VIII*, vol. 21, pt. 1, p. 155; Vaughan to Henry VIII, 3 March 1546, ibid., p. 161.

22 Vaughan to Wriothesley, 8 October 1545, *LPFD Henry VIII*, vol. 20, pt. 2, p. 257.

23 Vaughan to Henry VIII, 9 September 1545, ibid., p. 148.

24 Vaughan to Paget, 11 June 1546, *LPFD Henry VIII*, vol. 21, pt. 1, p. 520.

25 Manuel Fernández Álvarez (ed.), *Corpus Documental de Carlos V*, vol. II (Salamanca, 1975), pp. 558–9.

26 See Daniel R. Doyle, 'The Sinews of Habsburg Governance in the Sixteenth Century: Mary of Hungary and Political Patronage', *Sixteenth Century Journal* 31:2 (2000), pp. 349–60.

27 Navagero to Charles V, 1546, in Eugenio Albèri (ed.), *Relazioni degli Ambasciatori Veneti al Senato* (Florence, 1839–63), I:i, p. 299.

28 Goris, *Étude sur les colonies marchandes méridionales*, p. 258.

29 See Enrico Stumpo, *Dizionario Biografico degli Italiani*, vol. 41 (1992; online at http://www.treccani.it/enciclopedia/gaspare-ducci_(Dizionario-Biografico)). Stumpo insists that Ducci did not come from Pistoia, but Crespole and Pescia are both in the province of Pistoia.

30 Vitorino Magalhães Godinho, *Os Descobrimentos e a Economia Mundial,* vol. II (Lisbon, 1982–3), pp. 9–11, 84, 110; Virgínia Rau, 'Feitores e feitorias "instrumentos" do comércio internacional português no século XVI', in José Manuel Garcia (ed.), *Estudos sobre História Económica e Social do Antigo Regime* (Lisbon, 1984), pp. 141–99.

31 See James D. Tracy, *Emperor Charles V, Impresario of War* (Cambridge, 2002), p. 267.

32 Goris, *Étude sur les colonies marchandes méridionales*, p. 377.

33 Vaughan and others to the Council with the King, 20 August 1544, *LPFD Henry VIII,* vol. 19, pt. 2, p. 54.

34 Vaughan to the Council, 9 December 1544, ibid., pp. 435–6.

35 Vaughan to the Council, 17 December 1544, ibid., p. 451.

36 Vaughan to Henry VIII, 12 June 1546, *LPFD Henry VIII,* vol. 21, pt. 1, p. 524.

37 Vaughan to Henry VIII, 9 February 1546, ibid., p. 91; Vaughan to Paget, 18 February 1546, p. 115; Vaughan to Henry VIII, 2 July 1546, pp. 592–3.

38 Gaspar Duchy to Paget, 11 June 1546, ibid., p. 521.

39 Vaughan to Henry VIII, 10 March 1546, ibid., p. 178.

40 Vaughan to Henry VIII, 22 June 1546, ibid., p. 549.

41 Vaughan to Henry VIII, 13 September 1545, *LPDF Henry VIII,* vol. 20, pt. 2, p. 162.

42 Vaughan to the Council, 4 July 1546, *LPFD Henry VIII,* vol. 21, pt. 1, p. 601.

43 Vaughan to Paget, 12 August 1545, *LPFD Henry VIII,* vol. 20, pt. 2, p. 51.

44 Vaughan to Paget, 25 August 1545, ibid., p. 95.

45 Vaughan to Henry VIII, 13 September 1545, ibid., p. 161.

46 Vaughan to Paget, 16 September 1545, ibid., p. 172.

47 Vaughan to the Council, 12 August 1546, *LPFD Henry VIII,* vol. 21, pt. 1, p. 726.

48 Guicciardini, *Description de la Cité d'Anvers*, p. 133.

49 Lodovico Guicciardini, *The Description of the Low Countreys* (London, 1593), 33r.

50 Thomas Wilson, *A Discourse upon Usury*, ed. R. H. Tawney (London 1925), p. 270.

51 Ibid., pp. 290, 299–300.

52 John S. Farmer (ed.), *Thomas, Lord Cromwell, 'written by W.S.'* (London, 1911: facsimile of 1602 edition): quotation, B3 verso.

NOTES

9 THE ART IN THE DEAL

1 Lodovico (Louis) Guicciardini, *Description de la Cité d'Anvers,* in de Belleforest's translation, from the 1582 Plantin edition (Antwerp, 1920), p. 39. See also Filip Vermeylen, *Painting for the Market: Commercialization of Art in Antwerp's Golden Age* (Turnhout, 2003), pp. 50–54.

2 Ibid., p. 62.

3 An Maria Kint, 'The Community of Commerce: Social Relations in Sixteenth-Century Antwerp' (Columbia University PhD dissertation, 1996), pp. 72–3, citing Gustaaf Asaert. A ship cost 5–25 Brabant pounds, a retable 5–115.

4 Michèle Bimbenet-Privat, 'Orfèvrerie et politique: le cas Vezeler', in Cécile Scailliérez (ed.), *François Ier et l'art des Pays-Bas* (Paris, 2017), pp. 299–306.

5 Martin S. Soria, 'Some Flemish Sources of Baroque Painting in Spain', *Art Bulletin* 30:4 (1948), p. 249.

6 Konrad Ottenheym and Krista De Jonge, 'The Architecture of the Low Countries and its International Reception, 1480–1680', in Konrad Ottenheym and Krista De Jonge (eds.), *The Low Countries at the Crossroads: Netherlandish Architecture as an Export Product in Early Modern Europe (1480–1680)* (Turnhout, 2013), pp. 22–36.

7 Hugo Johannsen, 'The Steenwinckels: The Success Story of a Netherlandish Immigrant Family in Denmark', in ibid., p. 129.

8 Pieter Martens and Konrad Ottenheym, 'Fortifications and Waterworks: Engineers on the Road', in ibid., p. 368.

9 See John Oliver Hand, *Joos van Cleve: The Complete Paintings* (New Haven, 2004) on composition for Germany, pp. 69–73; and Italy, pp. 51, 58–9. On the French portraits, see Cécile Scailliérez, 'Le Portrait "français" sous François Ier', in Scailliérez (eds.), *François Ier et L'art des Pays-Bas*, pp. 210ff.; and for landscape, pp. 57–8.

10 Carolus Scribanius, *Antverpia* (Antwerp, 1610), pp. 38–9.

11 Giorgio Vasari, *Lives of the Artists*, tr. George Bull (Harmondsworth, 1987), vol. I, p. 45.

12 For the text from *Accuratae effigies pontificum maximorum* (Strasbourg, 1573) in translation, see Josef Glowa, 'The Role of Art in the Cultural Competition between Germans and Italians in the Sixteenth Century', *Simiolus: Netherlands Quarterly for the History of Art* 37:3/4 (2013–14), pp. 187ff., esp. pp. 191, 197.

13 For a translation of the text from *De pictura antigua*, see Laura Camille Agoston, 'Male/Female, Italy/Flanders, Michelangelo/Vittoria Colonna',

Renaissance Quarterly 58:4 (2005), pp. 1175ff., esp. 1175 for the main quote. On Portuguese taste, see Colum P. Hourihane (ed.), *Grove Encyclopedia of Medieval Art and Architecture* (Oxford, 2012), pp. 28, 99. On Vasco Fernandes, see Lilian H. Zirpolo, *Historical Dictionary of Renaissance Art* (Lanham, 2016), p. 199, and Dalila Rodrigues, 'Vasco Fernandes ou a Contemporaneidade do Diverso', in Dalila Rodrigues (eds.), *Grão Vasco e a pintura europeia do Renascimento* (Lisbon, 1992).

14 For texts, see Alejandra Giménez-Berger, 'Ethics and Economics of Art in Renaissance Spain: Felipe de Guevara's *Comentario de la pintura y pintores antiguos*', *Renaissance Quarterly* 67:1 (2014), pp. 79ff., esp. pp. 80, 107–9.

15 Micha Leeflang, *Joos van Cleve: A Sixteenth-Century Antwerp Artist and his Workshop* (Turnhout, 2015), p. 21.

10 LISTEN TO THE CITY

1 Lodovico Guicciardini, *Descrittione di tutti I Paesi Bassi* (Antwerp, 1567), p. 69; Albrecht Dürer, *Records of Journeys to Venice and the Low Countries*, ed. Roger Fry (Boston, 1913), p. 43.

2 Mary Tiffany Ferer, 'Queen Juana, Empress Isabel, and Musicians at the Royal Courts of Spain (1505–1556)', *Tijdschrift van de Koninklijke Vereniging voor Nederlandse Muziekgeschiedenis* 65:1/2 (2015), pp. 15, 18, 22.

3 Date unsure but probably 21 September 1560, Archivio di Stato, Florence, vol. 4254, f. 61.

4 Léon de Burbure, *Deux virtuoses français à Anvers* (Brussels, 1880): archive documents at p. 21 (contract) and p. 37 (runaways).

5 Gabriel Meurier, *La Guirlande des jeunes filles en françois & flamen* (Antwerp, 1580), ch. XV, f. 53r &ff.

6 Erasmus, *Christiani matrimonii institutio* (Basel, 1526), translated by Michael Heath in Erika Rummel (ed.), *Erasmus on Women* (Toronto, 1996), p. 18.

7 Thomas Chesneau, *Traicté [sic] des danses* (Paris, 1564); [no author], *Apologie de la jeunesse sur le fait et honneste recreation des danses* (Antwerp, 1572), esp. b2v. Cf. Alessandro Arcangeli, 'Dance under Trial: The Moral Debate 1200–1600', *Dance Research* 12:2 (1994), p. 126.

8 Dürer, *Records of Journeys to Venice and the Low Countries*, p. 53.

9 Kristine K. Forney, 'New Documents on the Life of Tielman Susato, Sixteenth-Century Music Printer and Musician', *Revue belge de Musicologie / Belgisch Tijdschrift voor Muziekwetenschap* 36/38 (1982–4), pp. 18–52.

10 Dürer, *Records of Journeys to Venice and the Low Countries*, pp. 42–3.

11 Kristine K. Forney, 'Music, Ritual and Patronage at the Church of Our Lady, Antwerp', *Early Music History* 7 (1987),

12 See Eugeen Schreurs and Henri Vanhulst (eds.), *Music Printing in Antwerp and Europe in the 16th Century* (Almire Foundation Yearbook, Leuven, 1997) for Timothy McTaggart, 'Susato's *Musyck Boexken* I and II: Music for a Flemish Middle Class', p. 321; Stanley Boorman, 'The Music Publisher's View of his Public's Abilities and Taste', pp. 421, 425; and Robert Lee Weaver, 'Waelrant's Working Relationship with Jean de Laet, a as Given in the Prefaces to this Parbooks', pp. 247, 251, 255.

13 Maria Clelia Galassi, 'Il trittico dell'*Adorazione dei Magi* di Joos van Cleve per Stefano Raggio', in Gianluca Zanelli (eds.,), *Joos van Cleve, il trittico di San Donato* (Genoa, 2016), pp. 8ff.

14 Kristine K. Forney, 'Orlando di Lasso's "Opus 1": The Making and Marketing of a Renaissance Music Book', *Revue belge de Musicologie / Belgisch Tijdschrift voor Muziekwetenschap* 39/40 (1985/6), pp. 33–60.

15 For Rosenberger's claims about the negotiations, see Forney, 'New Documents on the Life of Tieinian Susato', p. 30. Cf Michael Roberts, *The Early Vasas: A History of Sweden 1523–1611* (Cambridge, 1968, 1986), p. 231, and Gary Dean Peterson, *Warrior Kings of Sweden: The Rise of an Empire in the Sixteenth and Seventeenth Centuries* (Jefferson, NC, 2007), p. 74.

11 1549

1 Lodovico Guicciardini, *Descrittione di tutti I Paesi Bassi* (Antwerp, 1567): privileges, p. 90; the most principal (*principalissima*), p. 84.

2 Stijn Bussels, *Spectacle, Rhetoric and Power: The Triumphal Entry of Prince Philip of Spain into Antwerp* (Amsterdam, 2012), p. 39.

3 Cornelius Grapheus, *La Très admirable, très magnifique et triomphante entrée . . . anno 1549* (Antwerp, 1550), p. Bii.

4 'Fiestas de Bins, hechas por la Serenissima Reyna Maria de Ungria', in Cristóbal Calvete de Estrella, *El Felicissimo viaje d'el muy alto . . . Don Phelippe* (Antwerp, 1552), pp. 182–205. See also Braden Frieder, *Chivalry and the Perfect Prince: Tournaments, Art and Armor at the Spanish Habsburg Court* (Kirksville, 2008), esp. pp. 135, 142ff., 154–6.

5 Stefano Ambrogio Schiappalaria, *Vita de Iulio Cesare* (Antwerp, 1578), pp. 461–2; translated and discussed in William Eisler, 'Celestial harmonies and Hapsburg Rule: Levels of Meaning in a Triumphal Arch for Philip II in Antwerp, 1549', in Barbara Wisch and Susan Scott Munshower (eds.),

'*All the World's a Stage . . .*' vol. 1: *Triumphal Celebrations and the Rituals of Statecraft* (University Park, 1990), pp. 374–5.

6 Cornelius Grapheus, *Le Triumphe d'Anvers, faict en la susception du Prince Philips, Prince d'Espaigne* (Antwerp, 1550) : rain, p. Aii; palace, pp. Lii–iii; money riot, M4; fireworks, pp. Oii–iii. This French edition explains what the Dutch edition can take for granted.

12 THE MEAT STALL

1 Keith P. F. Moxey, 'Reflections on Some Unusual Subjects in the Work of Pieter Aertsen', *Jahrbuch der Berliner Museen* 18 (1976), pp. 57ff.

2 Karel van Mander, *La Livre des peintres,* vol. I, ed. Véronique Gerard-Powell (Paris, 2002), p. 235.

3 Filip Vermeylen, *Painting for the Market: Commercialization of Art in Antwerp's Golden Age* (Turnhout, 2003), p. 158.

4 For a discussion of this development, see Charles Sterling, *La Nature morte de l'Antiquité jusqu'à nos jours* (Paris, 1952), pp. 37, 39, 42.

5 Charlotte Houghton, 'This Was Tomorrow: Pieter Aertsen's *Meat Stall* as Contemporary Art', *Art Bulletin* 86:2 (June 2004), p. 300, n. 135.

6 Konrad Ottenheym and Krista De Jonge, 'Civic Prestige: Building the City 1580–1700', in Krista De Jonge and Konrad Ottenheym (eds.), *Unity and Discontinuity: Architectural Relationships between the Southern and Northern Low Countries (1530–1700)* (Turnhout, 2007), pp. 236–7.

7 Ibid., p. 236.

8 Dan Ewing, 'Marketing Art in Antwerp, 1460–1560: Our Lady's *Pand*', *Art Bulletin* 72:4 (December 1990), p. 571.

9 Keith P. F. Moxey, *Pieter Aertsen, Joachim Beuckelaer and the Rise of Secular Painting in the Context of the Reformation* (New York, 1977), p. 115.

10 Houghton, 'This Was Tomorrow'. I have gone beyond her brilliant analysis of the content of *The Meat Stall*, but it is the essential starting point for my argument. See also Charlotte M. Houghton, 'A Topical Reference to Urban Controversy in Pieter Aertsen's *Meat Stall* ', *Burlington Magazine* 143:1176 (March 2001), pp. 158ff.

11 Hugo Soly, *Urbanisme en Kapitalisme te Antwerpen in de 16de eeuw: De stedebouwkundige en industriële ondernemingen van Gillbert van Schoonbeke* (Brussels, 1977), pp. 127–8.

12 See *De inventaris van het Sterfhuis van Gillbert van Schoonbeke*, printed in *Antwerpsch archievenblad* 17 (1880).

13 Jochen De Vylder, 'The Grid and the Existing City', in Piet Lombaerde and Charles van den Heuvel (eds.), *Early Modern Urbanism and the Grid*

(Turnhout, 2011), pp. 79–82, and Karl Kiem, 'The Weigh House: An Architectural Typology of the Dutch Golden Age', in Konrad Ottenheym, Monique Chatenet and Krista De Jonge (eds.), *Public Buildings in Early Modern Europe* (Turnhout, 2010), pp. 262–4.

14 Elizabeth Cleland *et al.* (eds.), *Grand Design: Pieter Coecke van Aelst and Renaissance Tapestry* (New York, 2014), pp. 18–19.

15 Ewing, 'Marketing Art in Antwerp', p. 560.

16 Soly, *Urbanisme en Kapitalisme te Antwerpen in de 16de eeuw*, p. 176 Soly's magisterial account of van Schoonbeke's career, with its meticulous attention to the surviving archival material, is the basis for my story here.

17 Juvenal, *Satire* 11, lines 12–13.

18 Ibid., lines 22–3.

19 Ibid., lines 50–51.

20 Juvenal, *Satire* 14, lines 86, 95.

21 Ibid., line 141.

22 Ibid., lines 276–7.

23 Ibid., lines 204–5.

24 Ibid., lines 177–8, 173–6.

25 Ibid., lines 233–4.

26 Soly, *Urbanisme en Kapitalisme te Antwerpen in de 16de eeuw*, p. 226.

27 Marillac to Francis I, 1 August 1542, *Letters and Papers, Foreign and Domestic, Henry VIII,* vol. 17, p. 323.

28 Soly, *Urbanisme en Kapitalisme te Antwerpen in de 16de eeuw*, p. 240.

29 Paul Verhuyck and Corine Kisling, *Het mandement van Bacchus: Antwerpse kroegentocht in 1580* (Antwerp, 1987) for the full text; see also Richard W. Unger, *Beer in the Middle Ages and the Renaissance* (Philadelphia, 2004), pp. 117, 192, 262. Unger builds on Hugo Soly's 'De brouwerijenonderneming van Gilbert van Schoonbeke (1552–1562)' *Revue belge de philologie et d'histoire / Belgisch Tijdschrift voor Bilologie en Geschiedenis* 46 (1968).

13 THE CAREER

1 Werner Waterschoot, 'Antwerp: Books, Publishing and Cultural Production before 1585', in Patrick O'Brien (ed.), *Urban Achievement in Early Modern Europe* (Cambridge, 2001), p. 242.

2 See Sandra Langereis, *De Woordenaar* (Amsterdam, 2014), esp. pp. 383–4, n. 21 discussing Leon Voet, *The Golden Compasses: The History of the House of Plantin-Moretus* (Amsterdam, 1969–72), pp. 22ff. On Niclaes and his thought, see Jean Dietz Moss, '"Godded with God": Hendrik

Niclaes and his Family of Love', *Transactions of the American Philosophical Society* 71:8 (1981); and compare Alastair Hamilton, *The Family of Love* (Cambridge, 1981).

3 Karen L. Bowen, 'Illustrating book with Engravings: Plantin's Working Practices Revealed', *Print Quarterly* 20:1 (March 2003), p. 21.

4 Werner Thomas and Johan Verberckmoes, 'The Southern Netherlands as a Centre of Global Knowledge . . .', in Sven Dupre *et al.* (eds.), *Embattled Territory: The Circulation of Knowledge in the Spanish Netherlands* (Ghent, 2015), p. 173.

5 Voet, *The Golden Compasses*, pp. 58ff.

14 ANTWERP IS LOST

1 Abraham Ortelius to Emanuel Demetrius, 27 August 1566, in Jan Hendrick Hessels (ed.), *Epistulae Ortelianae* (Cambridge, 1887, repr. 2009), I:17 (pp. 37–40); p. 39 for *'Des anderen dachs heeftet in alle kercken gesien ofter de duijvel sommyge hondert iaeren huijs gehouden hadde.'*

2 Castillo to Granvelle, 15 August 1566, in Edmond Poullet (ed.), *Correspondance de Cardinal de Granvelle, 1565–1586* vol. I (Brussels, 1877), CIII.

3 Thomas Sampson to Bullinger, n.d. (?June 1556), in Hastings Robinson (ed.), *Original Letters Relative to the English Reformation* (Cambridge, 1846), i:XCI; John Strype, *The Life of the Learned Sir John Cheke* (London, 1705), pp. 134, 136; Robert Horn and Richard Chambers to Bullinger, 19 September 1556, in Robinson (ed.), *Original Letters Relative to the English Reformation*, i:LXVI.

4 Giorgio Mangani, *Il 'mondo' di Abramo Ortelio* (Modena, 2006), p. 156.

5 Guilherme Postel to Abraham Ortelius, 24 April 1567, in Hessels (ed.), *Epistulae Ortelianae*, I:20 (pp. 46ff.).

6 Christophe Plantin to Guilherme Postel, 17 May 1567, in Max Rooses (ed.), *Correspondance de Christophe Plantin* (Antwerp/Ghent, 1883), I:30 (pp. 80–81).

7 Guilherme Postel to Christophe Plantin, 25 May 1567, ibid., I:31 (p. 84).

8 Christophe Plantin to Guilherme Postel, 7 June 1567, ibid., I:33 (pp. 86–7).

9 Guido Marnef, *Antwerp in the Age of Reformation* (Baltimore, 1996), p. 58.

10 Anne Hooper to Bullinger, 20 April 1554, in Robinson (ed.), *Original Letters Relative to the English Reformation*, i:LI; William Salkyns to Bullinger, 29 December 1554, ibid., i:CLXIX; Peter Martyr to Bullinger, 22 January 1554, ibid., ii:CCXXXIX.

11 Strype, *The Life of the Learned Sir John Cheke*, pp. 105–6.

12 See V. Rossato, 'Anvers et ses libertés vues par Giovanni Zonca, hétérodoxe vénitien (1562–1566)', *Revue d'Histoire Ecclésiastique* LXXXV:2 (1990) for transcriptions of Zoncha's letters from the dossier of his later trial for heresy in Venice: girls and weapons, p. 308 (no date); Lent, p. 306 (Zoncha to Giovanni Raxello, 20 February 1563). Inquisition, Peter Martyr, p. 310 (Zoncha to Giovanni de Sere, 9 April 1556).

13 Morillon to Granvelle, 27 January 1566, in Poullet (ed.), *Correspondance de Cardinal de Granvelle*, XXI; 2 May 1566, ibid., LXVI.

14 Morillon to Granvelle, 13 September 1566, ibid., CXIII.

15 Oscar Gelderblom, *Cities of Commerce* (Princeton, 2013), pp. 55–6 for merchants leaving town.

16 Castillo to Granvelle, 20 April 1567, ibid., LVI.

17 Morillon to Granvelle, 29 September 1566, ibid., CXX.

18 Quoted in Jonathan Israel, *The Dutch Republic: Its Rise, Greatness and Fall 1477–1806* (Oxford, 1995), p. 154. Israel's masterly work is the basis for this section.

19 See Violet Soen, 'The Beeldenstorm and the Spanish Habsburg Response (1566–1570)', *Low Countries Historical Review* 131:1 (2016), pp. 99ff.

20 Gert Gielis and Violet Soen, 'The Inquisitorial Office in the Sixteenth-Century Habsburg Low Countries', *Journal of Ecclesiastical History* 66:1 (2015), p. 49.

21 See David Buisseret, *The Mapmakers' Quest* (Oxford, 2003), pp. 55ff.; and Kees Zandvliet, *Mapping for Money* (Amsterdam, 1998), p. 31.

22 Abraham Ortelius, *The Theatre of the Whole World*, tr. ?William Bedwell (London 1606), unpaginated front matter.

23 Abraham Ortelius, *Itinerarium per Nonnullas Galliae Belgicae Partes* (Antwerp, 1584), pp. 15–16. See Klaus Schmidt-Ott's essay of the same name in Marcel van den Broecke, Peter van der Krogt and Peter Meurer (eds.), *Abraham Ortelius and the First Atlas* (Utrecht, 1998).

24 *Album Amicorum of Abraham Ortelius* in Pembroke College Library, Cambridge; facsimile tr. Jean Puraye (Amsterdam, 1967), p. 91v.

25 From the *Theatrum Orbis Terrarum* in Plantin's 1584 edition.

26 Document cited in P. Génard, *La Généalogie du géographe Abraham Ortelius* (Antwerp, 1881), p. 22.

27 Justus Laureins to Abraham Ortelius 25 February 1567, in Hessels (ed.), *Epistulae Ortelianae*, I:18 (p. 41); Johannes Thorius to Abraham Orteiius, 18 May 1567, in ibid., I:21 (p. 49).

28 Roger Kuin (ed.), *The Correspondence of Sir Philip Sidney*, vol. 1 (Oxford, 2012). Tassis wrote on 15 October 1575 (p. 541) and Lobbet on 22 November 1575 (p. 570); for Antwerp correspondents, see Sidney to Hubert Languet, 1 March 1578 (p. 818).

29 Fridericus Sylburgius to Abraham Ortelius, May 1592, in Hessels (ed.), *Epistulae Ortelianae*, I:213 (p. 510); Andreas Schottus to Abraham Ortelius, 11 February 1582, ibid., I:113 (p. 270); Johannes Sambucus to Abraham Ortelius, 22 September 1563, ibid., I:13 (p. 29).

30 Abraham Ortelius to Emanuel Demetrius, 13 December 1567, ibid., I:23 (p. 52).

31 *Album Amicorum of Abraham Ortelius*, 13v.

32 See Iain Buchanan, 'Dürer and Abraham Ortelius', *Burlington Magazine* 124:957 (December 1982), pp. 734ff.

33 Hubert Goltz to Abraham Ortelius, 21 February 1574, in Hessels (ed.), *Epistulae Ortelianae*, I:45 (p. 109); cf. Johannes Vincentius Porta to Abraham Ortelius, 10 October 1586, ibid., I:147 (p. 340).

34 Jacobus Colius to Abraham Ortelius, 25 January 1591, ibid., II:192 (p. 458).

35 Sweerts quoted from Ortelius, *The Theatre of the Whole World*. See Marcel van den Broecke, 'Abraham Ortelius's Library Reconstructed', *Imago Mundi* 66:1 (2014), pp. 25ff.

36 Ludovicus Dorleans to Abraham Ortelius, undated but probably 1594, in Hessels (ed.), *Epistulae Ortelianae*, II:260 (p. 612).

37 Justus Lipsius to Abraham Ortelius, 13 January 1591, ibid., I:189 (p. 454).

38 Jeanine de Landtsheer, 'Abraham Ortelius et Juste Lipse', in R. W. Karrow Jr *et al.* (eds.), *Abraham Ortelius (1527–1598): cartographe et humaniste* (Turnhout, 1998), pp. 144–6.

39 See Nils Büttner, 'Abraham Ortelius comme collectionneur', in ibid., pp. 170–71; and C. E. Dekesel, 'Abraham Ortelius: numismate', in ibid., p. 183.

40 Abraham Ortelius to Jacobus Colius Carbo, 19 January 1587, Hessels, *Epistulae Ortelianae*, I:149 (pp. 345–6).

41 Guilielmus Postelus to Abraham Ortelius, 1579, ibid., I:81 (p. 81).

42 Daniel Printz to Abraham Ortelius, 25 February 1579, ibid., I:82 (p. 193).

43 Nicolaus Rhedinger to Abraham Ortelius, 1 September 1581, ibid. I:110 (pp. 264–6).

44 Gerardus Mercator to Abraham Ortelius, 9 May 1572, ibid., I:38 (p. 88).

45 Johannes Keuning, 'The "Civitates" of Braun and Hogenberg', *Imago Mundi* 17 (1963), p. 42.

46 Georg Braun and Franz Hogenberg, *Civitates Orbis Terrarum*, facsimile of the Basel edition of 1618–23, ed. R. A. Skelton (Amsterdam, 1965).

47 Cf. Denis Cosgrove, 'Globalism and Tolerance in Early Modern Geography', *Annals of the Association of American Geographers* 93:4 (December 2003), esp. pp. 864–5.

48 The maps are most easily accessible in Georg Braun and Franz Hogenberg, *Cities of the World* (Cologne, 2008).

49 Archivio di Stato, Florence, Mediceo del Principato: 'grumbled' and 'shamefaced', vol. 4254, f. 256; tapestries 1177:245.

50 See J. R. Hale, 'To Fortify or not To Fortify?', in H. C. Davis *et al.* (eds.), *Essays in Honour of John Humphreys Whitfield* (London, 1975), pp. 99ff.

51 Niccolò Machiavelli, *The Prince,* tr. Peter Bondanella (Oxford, 2005), p. 75.

52 Archivio di Stato, Florence, Mediceo del Principato: sending plans, vol. 649, f. 76; piecework 649:80; learning lessons 649:97; merchants 4254:273; taxes 3080:216.

53 Buonaiuto Lorini, *Le Fortificationi* (Venice, 1609). The Antwerp reference is not in earlier editions.

54 Cf. Monica Stensland, *Habsburg Communication in the Dutch Revolt* (Amsterdam, 2012), pp. 44–6, 79.

55 Robert M. Kingdon, 'The Plantin Breviaries: A Case Study in the Sixteenth-Century Business Operations of a Publishing House', *Bibliothèque d'Humanisme et Renaissance* 22:1 (1960), pp. 133–50.

56 Leon Voet, *The Golden Compasses* (Amsterdam, 1969–72), p. 76.

57 Ibid., pp. 90–91.

58 Geeraert Janssen to Jacop Cool Sr, 14 November 1576, Hessels (ed.), *Epistulae Ortelianae,* I:64 (pp. 147–53).

59 Cited in Filip Vermeylen, 'Between Hope and Despair: The State of the Antwerpe Art Market 1566–1585', in Koenraad Jonckheere and Ruben Suykerbuyk (eds.), *Art after Iconoclasm* (Turnhout, 2012), p. 98.

60 [no author], *An Historicall Discourse, or rather a Tragicall Historie of the citie of Antwerp* (London, 1586; repr. in facsimile Amsterdam, 1979).

61 Piet Lombaerde, 'Antwerp in its Golden Age', in Patrick O'Brien *et al.* (eds.), *Urban Achievement in Early Modern Europe* (Cambridge, 2001), p. 110.

62 Victor von Klarwill (ed.), *The Fugger News-Letters* (London, 1924): 'lewd words', p. 52 (20 April 1581); 'fourships' 53 (6 May 1581).

15 THE CITY CHOOSES

1 Emily J. Peters, 'Printing Ritual: The Performance of Community in Christopher Plantin's "La Joyeuse . . ."', *Renaissance Quarterly* 61:2 (2008), p. 379. On the context and substance of the Entry, see also

Margit Thøfner, '"Willingly we Follow a Gentle Leader ...": Joyous Entries into Antwerp', in Jeroen Duindam and Sabine Dabringhaus (eds.), *The Dynastic Centre and the Provinces* (Leiden, 2014) and Anne-Laure Van Bruaene, 'Spectacle and Spin for a Spurned Prince' *Journal of Early Modern History* 11:4–5 (2007).

2 [no author], *La Joyeuse et magnifique entrée de Monseigneur Françoys, fils de France ... ensa tres-renommée ville d'Anvers* (Antwerp, 1582), p. 14.

3 José Alberto Rodrigues da Silva Tavim, 'Jews in the Diaspora with *Sepharad* in the Mirror', *Jewish History* 25:2 (2011), pp. 177–81.

4 Translated and quoted in P. Grunebaum-Ballin, 'Joseph Naci, duc de Naxos', *Études Juives* XIII (1968), p. 34.

5 Tavim, 'Jews in the Diaspora', pp. 178–9.

6 Eugenio Albèri (ed.), *Relazioni degli Ambasciatori Veneti al Senato* (Florence, 1839–63): Luigi Bonrizzo, 1565, 'close ties', III:ii, pp. 66–7; Marcantonio Barbaro, 1573, 'enflamed', III:i, p. 318; Andrea Badoaro, 1573, 'monster', III:i, p. 361; Costantino Garzoni, 1573, 'dwarves', 'eyelids', III:i, pp. 402–3.

7 Ibid., Andrea Badoaro, 1573, III:i, p. 361; Luigi Bonrizzo, 1565, 'damage', III:ii, p. 67.

8 Famianus Strada, *De Bello Belgico, the History of the Low-Countrey Warres,* tr. Sir Robert Stapylton (London, 1650), pp. 138–9 for these quotations; for the original Latin text, see *De Bello Belgico* (Antwerp, 1640), pp. 257–60.

9 Edmond Poullet (ed.), *Correspondance de Cardinal de Granvelle, 1565–1586* (vol. I, Brussels, 1877; vol. II, Brussels, 1880): Alba, II, p. 142 (note); 'worse off', I, p. 210; Viglius, I, p. 72; Orange, I, p. 65 (note); 'want them to be true', I, p. 251.

10 Mehmet Bulut, *Ottoman-Dutch Economic Relations in the Early Modern Period 1571–1699* (Hilversum, 2001), pp. 112–13.

11 Traian Stoianovich, 'The Conquering Balkan Orthodox Merchant', *Journal of Economic History* 20:2 (June 1960), p. 238.

12 J. Denucé, *L'Afrique au XVIème siècle et le commerce anversois* (Antwerp, 1937), p. 15.

13 Based on Victor von Klarwill (ed.), *The Fugger News-Letters* (London, 1924): burning of the Exchange, 26 February 1583, p. 74; 'mockery and procrastination', 15 March 1585, p. 79; gunpowder-laden ships, 6 June 1585, pp. 80–81; taking of Antwerp, 21 August 1585, p. 82.

14 See Jonathan Israel, *The Dutch Republic: Its Rise, Greatness and Fall 1477–1806* (Oxford, 1995), p. 219.

NOTES

15 See Violet Soen, 'Habsburg Political Culture and Antwerp Defiant: Pacification Strategies of Governors-General during the Dutch Revolt (1566–1586)', in Ethan Matt Kavaler and Anne-Laure Van Bruaene (eds.,) *Netherlandish Culture of the Sixteenth Century* (Turnhout, 2017).

16 Florike Egmond, *The World of Carolus Clusius: Natural History in the Making, 1550–1610* (Abingdon, 2010), ebook, p. e35.

17 Martha Pollak, *Cities at War in Early Modern Europe* (Cambridge, 2010), pp. 17–21.

18 Anne T. Woollett and Ariane van Suchtelen, *Rubens and Brueghel: A Working Friendship* (Zwolle, 2006), pp. 90–99.

19 For example, National Archives, London, SP 12/1/f100.

20 Carolus Scribanius, *Antverpia* (Antwerp, 1610), p. 136.

21 Carolus Scribanius, *Origines Antverpiensium* (Antwerp, 1610), pp. 74–5.

22 See Raingard Esser, 'The Diamond of the Netherlands: Histories of Antwerp in the Seventeenth Century', *Nederlands Kunsthistorisch Jaarboek* 64:1 (2014), pp. 348–69.

23 Abraham Ortelius to Emanuel Demetrius, 17 November 1586, in Jan Hendrick Hessels (ed.), *Epistulae Ortelianae* (Cambridge, 1887, repr. 2009), I:148 (pp. 341–2).

24 See René Boumans, 'The Religious Views of Abraham Ortelius', *Journal of the Warburg and Courtauld Institutes* 17:3/4 (1954), pp. 375–6.

25 Dudley Carleton to John Chamberlain, 5/15 September 1616, in Maurice Lee Jr (ed.), *Dudley Carleton to John Chamberlain 1603–1624: Jacobean Letters* (New Brunswick, 1972), pp. 212–13.

Index